what ~~economic, political~~ ... in ~~the Soviet Union~~ ... for women? Why ~~was~~ a coherent women's movement difficult to build? What did nationalism offer women in Ukraine? In this timely volume, leading Western specialists and their Soviet colleagues explore these issues which are of central concern to a society in transition.

The authors discuss the implications of reform for female labour in industry and in agriculture, the falling percentage of female deputies, new women's groups, the changing status of women's councils and the position of women in Ukraine. They also explore the controversial significance of glasnost for women. Glasnost has facilitated women's studies and helped to expose a range of social problems. Yet, as this volume demonstrates, it has also obscured the role of girls in youth culture, created images of irresponsible mothers, led to the spread of pornography and anti-abortion sentiments and given questionable space to women writers.

This book presents a thorough analysis of the impact perestroika, democratisation and glasnost had upon Soviet women as workers, consumers and political actors. It will be widely read by students and specialists of Soviet and women's studies as well as by journalists, civil servants and politicians.

Perestroika and Soviet women

PERESTROIKA AND SOVIET WOMEN

edited by

Mary Buckley

Department of Politics, University of Edinburgh

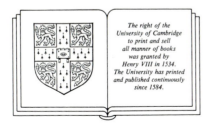

The right of the
University of Cambridge
to print and sell
all manner of books
was granted by
Henry VIII in 1534.
The University has printed
and published continuously
since 1584.

Cambridge University Press

Cambridge   New York   Port Chester
Melbourne   Sydney

Published by the Press Syndicate of the University of Cambridge
The Pitt Building, Trumpington Street, Cambridge CB2 1RP
40 West 20th Street, New York, NY 10011–4211, USA
10 Stamford Road, Oakleigh, Victoria 3166, Australia

First published 1992

Printed in Great Britain at the University Press, Cambridge

A catalogue record for this book is available from the British Library

Library of Congress cataloguing in publication data

Perestroika and Soviet women / edited by Mary Buckley.
   p. cm.
Includes index.
ISBN 0 521 41443 1 (hardback)   ISBN 0 521 42738 X (paperback)
1. Women – Soviet Union – Social conditions. 2. Feminism – Soviet
Union. 3. Soviet Union – Politics and government – 1985 –
4. Perestroïka. I. Buckley, Mary, 1951 –.
HQ1662.P39 1992
305.42′0947–dc20   91–31920   CIP

ISBN 0 521 41443 1 hardback
ISBN 0 521 427 38 X paperback

CE

Contents

Tables

Notes on contributors

Sue Bridger is Lecturer in Russian at the University of Bradford. She is author of *Women in the Soviet Countryside* (1987) and is currently working on a book on women's roles in agricultural reform in the USSR.

Genia Browning is Lecturer in Sociology at Woolwich College. She lived and worked in Moscow from 1967 to 1970. She is author of *Women and Politics in the USSR* (1987).

Mary Buckley is Senior Lecturer in Politics at the University of Edinburgh. She is author of *Women and Ideology in the Soviet Union* (1989), editor of *Soviet Social Scientists Talking* (1986) and co-editor of *Women, Equality and Europe* (1988). She is currently writing a book on new Soviet social and political agendas.

Barbara Heldt is Professor of Russian at the University of British Columbia. She is author of *Koz'ma Prutkov: the Art of Parody* (1972) and of *Terrible Perfection: Women and Russian Literature* (1987) and translator of Karolina Pavlov's *A Double Life* (1978). She is currently writing on Mariia Shkapskaia and on contemporary Russian writers.

Ol'ga Lipovskaia is editor of the journal *Zhenskoe Chtenie* published in Leningrad and author of numerous articles on women in the USSR. She is actively involved in trying to build a women's movement.

Solomea Pavlychko is a research scholar at the Institute of Literature of the Ukrainian Academy of Sciences in Kiev. She is author, in Ukrainian, of *Transcendental Poetry of American Romanticism* (1988) and of *Byron: his Life and Work* (1989). She has translated into Ukrainian *Lord of the Flies* by William Golding and *Lady Chatterley's Lover* by D. H. Lawrence. She is a member of Rukh and a founder member of the Women's Community of Rukh.

Hilary Pilkington is Lecturer in Soviet Society at the Centre for Russian and East European Studies of the University of Birmingham. She is currently writing a doctoral thesis on the social and cultural origins of non-formal youth groups in the USSR.

Natal'ia Rimashevskaia is Director of the Institute of Socio-Economic Problems of the Population of the USSR, Academy of Sciences, Moscow. She is co-author, in Russian, of *Family, Labour, Incomes and Consumption: the Taganrog Survey* (1977), and co-author of *People's Well-being: Trends and Prospects* (1990). She is co-author, in English, of *Women's Training and Employment: the Case of the USSR* (1989).

Judith Shapiro is Senior Lecturer in Economics at Goldsmiths' College, University of London. She is author of *Soviet Unemployment: NEP and its Labour Market* (forthcoming).

Elizabeth Waters teaches Russian and Soviet History at Australian National University, Canberra. She has written a number of articles on social issues in the 1920s and in the contemporary USSR, including prostitution, childcare and sexual equality. She has just completed a book on *Women in a Bolshevik World: Work and Family in Post-Revolutionary Russia* and is currently working on another on *Gender and Soviet Society*.

Preface

The chapters which follow were all written before the failed coup of August 1991. The processes of change which subsequently ensued were even faster than those witnessed from 1987 to 1991. This makes some of the issues discussed here more salient.

Bolder commitment to a transition to a market economy, for instance, is likely to quicken the pace of unemployment. Already, on 1 August 1991, the Soviet television news programme *Vremia*, had informed viewers that most of the workers recently laid off were women. The month before, the newspaper *Moskovskii Komsomolets* reported that unemployment had officially reached 8 million and might soon be 32 million. How women respond to unemployment, whether new unemployment benefits will be adequate, and how fast the economy can offer new opportunities in an expanded service sector, will be immediate issues. In this context, the notion of an 'adequate male wage' may become more popular. It already enjoys a resonance in some social groups.

In politics, immediate independence for the Baltic states, with other republics soon to follow suit, makes the relationship between feminism and nationalism more timely. And heightened discredit for the Communist Party creates more pressing questions about the character of the developing 'male democracy', as some Russian feminists dub it. The request that women withdraw from the Russian Parliament, during the coup, and leave its defence to men, is just one tiny aspect of a much broader and complex problem of woman's place in society.

The instabilities, tensions and disputes of economy, polity and society are unlikely to abate in the 1990s. Although, in many respects, women and men will experience common predicaments, problems and hopes, women will, nonetheless, endure many difficulties that are specific to them. Moreover, different categories of women, divided by nationality, education, occupation, political views, age, religion and geographic location across a huge land mass, will enjoy different advantages and suffer various constraints.

September 1991   Mary Buckley

Chapter 1

Introduction: women and perestroika

Mary Buckley

Moscow, 1990
Shopper: Give me 200 grammes of cheese, please
Shop assistant: You go and bring me some cheese, then I'll cut off 200 grammes

By 1990, an update of past research into the position of women in the USSR felt long overdue. The fate of perestroika carried serious implications for women's economic, political and social roles and the adoption of glasnost had already radically changed the nature of discussion about women's lives.

Economic reforms were bound to affect women because they made up 51 per cent of industrial labour and office workers and over 40 per cent of agricultural workers. Rationalisation of the labour force, greater mechanisation and efficiency, if successful, could result in higher rates of unemployment for women than men. Land reform would alter how women in the countryside worked. What the economy supplied, or failed to distribute, hit women as consumers, as did rationing from 1989 and sharp price increases in April 1991.

Political reform affected women as voters, as potential candidates in elections, as members of new informal political groups, as instigators of women-only groups, movements and parties and as activists in the more establishment zhensovety, or women's councils, and as employees in the Soviet Women's Committee. The policies of freshly elected soviets affected women as citizens. Nationalist developments and moves towards political decentralisation prompted questions about the relationship between nationalism and feminism and about what women's rights republic-level legislation might try to take away, such as abortion, or what fresh opportunities it might offer.

Changes in society, particularly the use of glasnost in the media, influenced discussions about a host of women's issues, such as prostitution, abortion, contraception and the self-immolation of Muslim women, topics which previously had been taboo. Articles exposed the existence of prostitution, deplored the horrific conditions of abortion clinics, lamented the lack of contraception and expressed shame at female suicides. In 1987 'moral panic' over new revelations gripped society. Regular media coverage of increases in crime, for instance, sometimes with lurid details of brutality, made women anxious, afraid and appalled. They felt vulnerable to mugging, theft and gang rape. In response, *Rabotnitsa* (Working Woman) in 1990 and in 1991 carried articles on self-defence for women.[1]

Due to glasnost, some democratisation and an end to the monopoly of the Communist Party of the Soviet Union (CPSU), a range of views about policy could be voiced. For example, opponents of abortion in 1991 tried, through the newspaper *Moskovskii Komsomolets*, to encourage readers to sign a petition to the European Parliament expressing the opinion that abortion was an 'act of violence and murder of a tiny being' and also 'violence against the body and against the dignity of woman'. Abortion was a 'crime against humanity' and a 'sin before God'.[2] Supporters of the right to choose, including members of the Radical Party, The Free Association of Feminist Organisations (SAFO), and the Anarchist-radical Union of Youth, demonstrated soon after outside the newspaper's editorial offices carrying placards which read 'No to sexism' and 'No to Vatican officialdom'.[3] The spread of pornography provoked similarly heated arguments about the difference between it and erotica and the popularity of beauty contests, supported by women's magazines, left puzzled opponents outnumbered.

This book sets out to assess the implications of the main aspects of perestroika and glasnost for women, whilst not duplicating the fresh literature that is already in print, or going to press, on prostitution, new women's issues and new women's groups.[4] It does not claim to be exhaustive, merely to evaluate key policy areas with a view to closing a gap which has developed in the literature. The contributors to this anthology do not necessarily share common views about the significance of reform in the Soviet transition period for state, citizen, economy, polity, nationality, gender, generation, society and literature. The aim here is not to present united interpretations, but to prompt debates across a range of issues.

The main findings of past research

Over the past two decades, a substantial literature on Soviet women's economic, political and social roles has been published in the USSR, USA and UK. Research has shown that in the workforce, female labour needs to be analysed as a distinct category, due to a segmentation according to gender. Women are concentrated in low-paid, low-skilled and often manual work and, on average, earn significantly less than men.[5] In politics, women are largely absent from top posts. For the entire history of the Soviet state there has been an inverse correlation between women and power. The weaker the political institution, the higher the percentage of women active in it.[6] And in home life, women continue to perform a huge share of domestic work – queuing for food, cooking, cleaning, washing clothes, caring for children and sewing.[7]

Since most women of working age are employed outside the home, or involved in full-time study, their stressful domestic shifts, not much eased by the spotty participation of Soviet men, mean that they suffer what Soviet social science dubs a 'double burden' or 'double shift'. Women sleep less than men due to the extent of their chores, relax less with friends, and visit the cinema, theatre and parks less frequently. Moreover, many still believe that this division of domestic labour according to gender is appropriate. Young Muscovite professional men in the early 1990s could still be heard claiming that '100 per cent men do not cook' and 'women are only half women if they do not have children'. Children's books socialise youngsters into traditional gender roles and pedagogical literature reinforces gender-role stereotypes.[8]

The nature of discussion about women's roles has varied according to historical context.[9] In the revolutionary situation of 1917 and after, debates took place around a host of issues, although lines stiffened after 1925. The meaning of socialism for women's liberation and what the latter meant for the former were among the topics discussed in the ebullient 1920s. Under Stalin, a rigid ideological straitjacket declared that the woman question was 'solved'. No more analysis was necessary since women were now emancipated and equal with men. During the relatively brief Khrushchev years, the silence began to thaw, befitting the policy of democratisation. But it was not until Brezhnev's claim that the USSR was in a state of 'developed socialism' characterised by many 'non-antagonistic contradictions' which still had to be solved down the long path to communism, that 'problems' in women's lives could be officially recognised. In a context of labour shortages and falling birthrates in the late 1960s and 1970s, economists, demographers and sociologists engaged in a lively debate about the significance of the female 'double burden'. But, although women's economic and social roles came onto the agenda, particularly their relevance to production and reproduction, many issues remained untouched. Not until the adoption of glasnost, particularly after 1987, did a range of 'new' issues enter the media and political debate.[10]

What is perestroika?

Perestroika – which translates as 'restructuring' or 'reconstruction' – began as a very general, if undefined, vision of change 'from above' in a highly authoritarian political system. Gorbachev was committed to developing an efficient economy within a 'socialist' system, as he understood the term, which could provide citizens with a much higher standard of living and an improved quality of consumer goods. How precisely to do this, was the problem. Back in 1985, Gorbachev clearly did not envisage that the process he was setting in motion would result in the loss of Eastern Europe, demands from Soviet republics for independence, the rise of new political parties, domestic political chaos and moves towards a free-market economy.

Gorbachev in 1986 described perestroika as a revolutionary process of interrelated changes in economy, politics and society. In the economy, he intended to transform the command administrative system of planning by drastically reducing the number of detailed commands sent down from above to factory managers and farm directors. He wished to give managers greater freedom in decision-making and space in which to take initiative. A policy of *khozraschet*, or cost-accounting, coupled with *samofinansirovanie*, or self-financing, were means to this end. A cooperative sector was also established, encouraging individual and entrepreneurial labour, but it was beset by bureaucratic problems concerning registration and taxes.[11] Land reform was referred to in 1986, but early opposition meant that it was something to be defined later. Taken together, the early economic reforms were intended to accelerate economic growth. By the early 1980s, it had already been acknowledged by economists that economic growth had drastically fallen (according to Abel Aganbegian to zero growth), that problems of supply and distribution were chronic, corruption was widespread and that radical change was therefore imperative.

One serious problem, however, was that the well-established structures and mechanisms of the planning system resisted change. Although, for instance, the Law on State Enterprise of 1987 encouraged ministries to interfere less in the way in which enterprises, or factories, were run, in practice little changed. Laws alone could not transform the system since, quite frequently, they were not implemented. Moreover, resistance to economic reform meant that its opponents would do all they could to counter it.

Thus political reform became pressing. Gorbachev may have had a hazy picture of what he meant by political reform in 1986 but, by 1988, he realised that critics of 'new thinking' had to be shaken out of their powerful positions. The fate of economic reform seemed to depend upon a renewal or revitalisation of political structures. If ministers could be made accountable to popularly elected people's deputies working in more powerful legislatures, then perhaps economic reform could move forward. The especially convened 19th Party Conference of June 1988 debated political reform and laid the groundwork for a new electoral system. The Supreme Soviet in December 1988 approved plans for that system and effectively voted itself, in its old form, out of existence. Henceforth, it would play a more active role in politics and be less of a rubber-stamp for decisions made elsewhere.

The process of *demokratizatsiia* went beyond electoral reform. Citizens were encouraged to elect their own factory directors and rectors of institutes. New emphasis was given to choice, and to reflection upon how best to choose. Gorbachev called upon citizens to develop a 'new psychology', 'new ways', 'new thinking' and to take initiative and responsibility. These characteristics were essential to successful economic reform. The people should no longer be passive cogs, recipients of decisions coming from elsewhere for which they would not take responsibility. New informal political groups were also encouraged to form, independent of the CPSU. Hesitant in 1987, and initially wary of interference from the KGB, in 1988 and 1989 they mushroomed in number and strengthened in confidence. Nationalist movements like Sajudis in Lithuania and Rukh in the Ukraine soon clashed with Moscow, demanding independence. In 1990, Article 6 of the 1977 Soviet Constitution was qualified, thereby ending the leading and guiding role of the CPSU and making way for new political parties. These parties lacked money, large memberships, experience, buildings and inter-republic networks, but political space for them now existed. Democrats, socialists, social-democrats, christian-democrats, protestants, monarchists, anarchists, anarcho-syndicalists, greens, workers, peasants, patriots, nationalists and fascists flourished in various groups, movements and parties, which formed, split and regrouped.

Before the 28th Party Congress convened in 1990, rumours of crisis in the CPSU, impending splits, and the need for new directions circulated. Resistance to the market and to the idea of private property brought those on the 'right' of the party together, as they called for 'more socialism'. Those on the 'left', such as Boris Yel'tsin, in favour of market solutions and more radical change, walked out of the CPSU, thereby earning popular support among the population. By 1991, striking miners saw 'the market' as the only way forward. Transition to a market economy, serious reductions in government subsidies and price increases became the issues of 1991. Looming on the horizon was the possible convertibility of the rouble, and a law permitting easier exit and entrance to the USSR. In the space of seven years, the undisputed control of the CPSU over economy, polity and society had been shattered. Its ideology was despised, and attacked, by millions. Yet it remained the strongest political party in membership, assets and experience. Its grip on power and policy was diluted, but remained, despite the election of democrats in Moscow, Leningrad and Sverdlovsk. Notwithstanding biting critics, communist values still appealed to many, for a range of ideological, moral, careerist and economic reasons. Moreover, the KGB remained a 'weapon' of the CPSU despite the development of various views within the secret service.[12]

Women's responses to perestroika

Soviet women have responded to perestroika in various ways. Some speeches delivered in January 1987 at the All-Union Conference of Women in Moscow linked women's futures to its fate. The general consensus seemed to be: 'who suffers most in society from the negative aspects of our life? Women. And because of this we shall indeed be the main strength of perestroika – we have a vital interest in it.'[13] But soon after, in 1988, journalist Larisa Kuznetsova caustically dismissed 'male perestroika eloquence', noting that 'Soviet women pinned great hopes on perestroika. But we still see the same queues in shops, the undeclared but disgraceful runaway prices, the terrible poverty of our ill-stocked chemists' shops and the spread of night shift work for women though it is forbidden by law'.[14] The initial hope that perestroika would ease women's lives was quickly met with scepticism. Although many women were pleased that glasnost meant that many problems which were previously ignored, such as the lack of contraception, were now discussed, all the talk had not improved their lives. As Larisa Vasil'eva put it in 1989:

Freed from many outdated ideas and inaccurate knowledge, glasnost blossomed. But daily life was subjected to new directions when sugar was rationed, and salt, matches, soap and washing powder were in short supply. Women

stood for longer in queues. At work there is the chaos of transition to
economic accountability. At home, a woman's husband – a worker or
employee – is annoyed about the success of cooperatives. Or if he is a cooperative worker, he is irritated by the tax system and by his precarious position.
But most worrying of all, school children, not believing what they hear, are
visibly sceptical.[15]

Talk of economic reform had given hope of improved life-styles. But,
by 1989, to many women daily life seemed harder than ever before.
Glasnost had exposed many problems in need of analysis, but it had
not improved the supply of contraceptives nor ended the horrific conditions of abortion clinics. It had revealed, condemned and deplored,
but it had not delivered. It had created 'moral panic' about crime,
homelessness and violence, but problems still existed. And crucial for
the future of the USSR, Soviet youth was alienated from the system
and from the reform process, reluctant to 'take initiative' in the ways
in which Gorbachev wanted. Support for perestroika seemed to come
from intellectuals over forty. At best, it was a revolution of the middle-
aged.

Many women, worn out by the pressures of daily life, remained
indifferent to new discussions of gender roles. Nevertheless, male
domination of society, politics and economics was finally aired by
glasnost, albeit in limited arenas, such as women's magazines, the
occasional article in academic journals, in the discussions of the Soviet
Women's Committee and in the meetings and conferences of new
women's groups. Women's studies, too, began to develop, albeit with
resistance from many Academicians. As an academic discipline, it was
alien to the USSR, notwithstanding the huge outpouring in the 1970s
of candidate degree dissertations on the position of women in the
USSR. The idea of 'women's studies' had always smacked of 'bourgeois feminism,' and had thus been ideologically unsound.

One of the most intractable and painful results of democratisation
for women was animosity among different nationalities. In the Caucasus, this took on violent and cruel forms. In despair, one woman wrote
to the Central Committee of the CPSU:

My mother is Russian, my father is Azerbaidzhani and my husband is Arme-
nian. Now my family is incensed. I must stay in Baku, but my husband and
two sons have been driven out of the house. Where they are now wandering, I
do not know. Of what are my children guilty? For what should I be blamed?
How should we live now? I am no longer young. I raised the children with
difficulty and thought that now we could just live. Who will answer for all of
this?[16]

Although many women in the Baltic States, in the Ukraine and in Georgia warmly welcomed national self-determination and looked forward to independence, in areas of violent confrontation, women in mixed marriages sometimes became refugees, fearing for their own lives, or for the lives of husbands and children. Painful separation, uprooting and death have been among the consequences.

Change in the USSR is currently rapid, turbulent, chaotic and unpredictable. By the time this manuscript is in print, many events will have taken place which are not mentioned here and new developments will have been set in motion. The issues raised, nevertheless, will be of relevance in new contexts. The aim of the chapters which follow is systematically to assess the significance of the years 1985 to mid-1991 for Soviet women across a range of economic, political, social and literary themes, thereby contributing to the history of the early years of the 'transition period', however long that may last.

Since perestroika was initially triggered by concern about the Soviet economy, the first two chapters explore the implications of reform in industry and agriculture for female labour. Judith Shapiro makes a strong case that the gradual decline in the proportion of female industrial workers is a part of a process which pre-dates perestroika. Economic reform, however, has already resulted in a limited restructuring of labour, which hit women with children first. Shapiro notes that the full impact of female unemployment among industrial workers is yet to come. She discusses various reactions to potential female unemployment and explores arguments for and against heavy manual work for women. Although many wish to see an end to it, some women may prefer to take on physically dangerous work rather than lighter jobs which pay significantly less.

One-third of the Soviet population still lives in the countryside. At a time of crisis in food distribution, Sue Bridger discusses the significance of female flight from poor rural conditions to slightly less miserable urban ones. Since 1986 a series of campaigns has tried to lure citizens back into the countryside, sometimes suggesting to women that they might find eligible husbands there. Women's work in the countryside remains unmechanised and time-consuming. Work on agricultural machinery is still closed to them but they are welcomed into dairying where they milk three times a day, rarely enjoying days off or holidays. Whenever dairying is mechanised, the jobs are given to men. Reform in agriculture after 1988 encouraged new family farms. Bridger illustrates how these have meant long working days, intensive labour due to the lack of mechanisation, and increased moral pressures within family units. Ultimately, she argues, the fate of life in the countryside is linked to the conditions in cities and how people react to unemployment, food shortages and inflation.

Political reforms followed early failed attempts to alter the running of the Soviet economy. Chapter 4 discusses the results of electoral reform for women's political representation, introduces fresh debates on the desirability of quotas for women deputies and highlights the heterogeneity of new women's groups. In chapter 5, Ol'ga Lipovskaia explores the goals and activities of a wide range of formal, informal and feminist groups and argues that a women's movement does not currently exist. She stresses that feminism in Russia, while sharing some concerns with Western feminism, has its own distinct character-istics. She notes that some Western feminists with a sudden interest in the USSR poorly understand it.

Feminism has become an element, sometimes an uneasy one, within nationalist movements. In chapter 6, Solomea Pavlychko describes the position of women in the Ukraine, traces how Rukh's women-only group developed and introduces the aims of other women-only groups in the republic. Both Lipovskaia and Pavlychko stress that new political parties and movements are run by men and generally neglect women's issues. They remain sceptical about the utility of the zhensovety, or women's councils, although Lipovskaia suggests that some zhensovety are being transformed into more 'informal' and energetic groups. Genia Browning's subsequent chapter contends that it is premature to dismiss the zhensovety out of hand. They appear to involve large numbers of women who reap some benefit from belonging to them. The zhensovety, however, retain a contradictory character. They often reinforce traditional gender roles, yet could challenge them if only the women active in them chose to do so. Hitherto, it seems, they have not.

Glasnost has affected women's lives in an enormous number of ways. This book can only cover some of its consequences. In chapter 8, Natal'ia Rimashevskaia sketches the background to the establishment of the first centre for gender studies within the Soviet Academy of Sciences. She points out that the process was difficult and that numerous problems remain. The concept 'gender' appears to have more critics, often silent ones, than supporters. Nevertheless, glasnost facilitated the introduction of gender studies as a new discipline. On a different note, Elizabeth Waters discusses fresh attention to the dire conditions in Soviet children's homes, previously taboo. Glasnost led to their exposure and condemnation in 1987. But the ensuing debate about the maltreatment of children included an attack on dissolute women who became pregnant and then selfishly abandoned their offspring. Images of 'cuckoo mothers' and of deviant and parasitic women were presented in the media. Glasnost neglected to devote similar attention to fathers. Then, in 1988, 'moral panic' calmed and a more sophisticated glasnost turned attention away from irresponsible mothers to scrutinise the social system and its poverty which accounted for their behaviour.

Greater openness also brought media discussion of different youth groups. Although new articles undermined the old image of young people as joyful builders of communism, they also, in Hilary Pilkington's estimation, left invisible the role of girls in youth cultural activity. In chapter 10, Pilkington shows how the spotlight of glasnost is highly partial and when it falls on girls, if at all, it portrays them as sex objects. Research, however, indicates that girls' roles vary according to the cultural group to which they belong. Girls who are *Stiliagi*, or lovers of rock'n'roll, for instance, are neither sexual pawns nor appendages to males nor passive.

In the last chapter, Barbara Heldt questions whether glasnost has resulted in more female voices being heard in literature, or whether the tradition of men speaking for women has been preserved. Heldt contends that the iconisation of the feminine, in fact, appears to be growing, complete with its patriarchal myth of the pure nature and abstract goodness of Woman, often symbolising the nation. Amid this conformity, some women, such as Tat'iana Tolstaia, Liudmila Petrushevskaia, Kira Muratova, Lana Gogoberidze, Natal'ia Sukhanova, Elena Shvarts, Valeriia Narbikova, Bella Ulanovskaia and others, contribute to what Heldt dubs 'gynoglasnost'.

Central questions which spring out of these chapters include the following: How can female unemployment best be limited in the transition from a command economy? To what extent did planners take women's preferences into account in the past and how likely is a market economy to meet them? What similarities and differences does economic reform bring to female labour in industry and in agriculture? What are likely to be the main benefits and disadvantages of a market economy for Soviet women as paid workers and consumers? What is the political significance of large reductions in the percentage of female people's deputies in a system in which most female political actors were token anyway? Would a reintroduction of quotas really aid women's role in political arenas? Which political and social organisations give women as political actors the greatest opportunities for influencing policy outcomes? Are the zhensovety politically impotent, or do they provide outlets for some constructive changes in women's everyday lives? What do women-only groups offer women in the 1990s and how significant are their disputes and divisions? What are the pre-requisites for the formation of a broad women's movement? What does nationalism mean for women and what could feminism contribute to nationalism? What is the significance of feminism's awkward status in Soviet society for social and political change and for women's studies? What positive and negative results has glasnost brought to women's lives? What is the significance of a burst of pornography into a society relatively unfamiliar with it? Why has glasnost prompted condemnations of mothers who leave their offspring in children's homes rather than of fathers? Why have recent newspaper articles obscured girls' participation in youth groups? What impact do the images of women, girls, men and boys constructed by the media, have on Soviet society? And why are female voices in literature and in the media still relatively silent? Is it useful to adopt the term 'gynoglasnost' when assessing the role of openness in fiction, poetry, plays and film?

Our purpose here is not to provide definitive answers to these questions, but to offer detailed analyses of the context in which they must be addressed with the aim of provoking further discussion.

NOTES

1 *Rabotnitsa*, no. 10, October 1990, pullout section, p. 4; *Rabotnitsa*, no. 12, December 1990, p. 4; *Rabotnitsa*, no. 1, January 1991, p. 31.
2 *Moskovskii Komsomolets*, 1 March 1991, p. 1.
3 *Moskovskii Komsomolets*, 5 March, 1991, p. 1.
4 Elizabeth Waters, 'Restructuring the "woman question": perestroika and prostitution', *Feminist Review*, no. 33, 1990, pp. 3–19; Elizabeth Waters, 'Changing views on prostitution in the Gorbachev era' in J. Riordan, ed. *Soviet Social Reality in the Mirror of Glasnost* (London: Macmillan, forthcoming); Elizabeth Waters, 'Sex and semiotic confusion: report from Moscow', *AFS*, no. 12, summer 1990, pp. 1–14; Sue Bridger, 'Young women and perestroika' in Linda Edmondson, ed. *Women and Society in Russia and the Soviet Union* (Cambridge: Cambridge University Press, 1992); Mary Buckley, *Women and Ideology in the Soviet Union* (Harmondsworth: Harvester/Wheatsheaf; Ann Arbor, University of Michigan Press, 1989), pp. 191–223; Mary Buckley, 'What does perestroika mean for women?' in Jon Bloomfield, ed. *The Soviet Revolution*

(London: Lawrence and Wishart, 1990), pp. 151–75; Mary Buckley, 'Gender and reform' in Catherine Merridale and Chris Ward, eds. *Perestroika: the historical perspective* (Dunton Green, Edward Arnold, 1991); Mary Buckley, 'Glasnost and the Woman Question' in Linda Edmondson ed. *Women and Society in Russia and the Soviet Union* (Cambridge: Cambridge University Press, 1992).

5 Norton Dodge, *Women in the Soviet Economy* (Baltimore: Johns Hopkins University Press, 1966); Michael Paul Sacks, *Women's Work in Soviet Russia: Continuity in the Midst of Change* (New York: Praeger, 1976); Gail Warshofsky Lapidus, *Women in Soviet Society: Equality, Development and Social Change* (Berkeley: University of California Press, 1978), pp. 161–97; Joel C. Moses, *The Politics of Female Labor in the Soviet Union*, Western Societies Program Occasional paper no. 10 (Ithaca, New York: Cornell University, 1978); Alastair McAuley, *Women's Work and Wages in the Soviet Union* (London: Allen and Unwin, 1981).

6 Gail Warshofsky Lapidus, *Women in Soviet Society*, pp. 198–231; Joel C. Moses, 'Women in political roles' in Dorothy Atkinson, Alexander Dallin and Gail Warshofsky Lapidus, eds., *Women in Russia* (Stanford: Stanford University Press, 1977; Hassocks, Sussex: Harvester, 1978), pp. 333–53; Barbara Wolfe Jancar, *Women Under Communism* (Baltimore: Johns Hopkins University Press, 1978); Genia K. Browning, *Women and Politics in the USSR* (London: Wheatsheaf; New York: St Martin's, 1987).

7 Gail Warshofsky Lapidus, *Women in Soviet Society*, pp. 232–84; Mary Buckley, 'Women in the Soviet Union', *Feminist Review*, no. 8, summer 1981, pp. 79–106; Barbara Holland, ed. *Soviet Sisterhood* (London: Forth Estate; Bloomington: Indiana University Press, 1985).

8 Mollie Schwartz Rosenhan, 'Images of male and female in children's readers' in Atkinson, Dallin and Lapidus, *Women in Russia*, pp. 293–305; Lynne Attwood, *The New Soviet Man and Woman* (London: Macmillan, 1990).

9 Mary Buckley, *Women and Ideology in the Soviet Union*. For discussion of women in the nineteenth and early twentieth centuries, refer to Richard Stites, *The Women's Liberation Movement in Russia* (Princeton: Princeton University Press, 1978) and to Linda Edmondson, *Feminism in Russia, 1900–1917* (London: Heinemann, 1984).

10 Mary Buckley, 'Social policies and new social issues' in Stephen White, Alex Pravda and Zvi Gitelman, eds. *Developments in Soviet Politics* (London: Macmillan, 1990), pp. 185–206.

11 Anders Aslund, *Gorbachev's Struggle for Economic Reform* (Ithaca: Cornell University Press, 1989).

12 For useful introductions to different aspects of political reform, refer to: Richard Sakwa, *Gorbachev and His Reforms, 1985–1990* (London: Philip Allen, 1990); Stephen White, *Gorbachev in Power* (Cambridge: Cambridge University Press, 1990); White, Pravda and Gitelman, *Developments in Soviet Politics*.

13 *Bakinskii Rabochii*, 31 January, 1987.
14 Larisa Kuznetsova, 'What every woman wants?' *Soviet Weekly*, 26
    November, 1988, p. 15.
15 Larisa Vasil'eva, 'Pervye lastochki na tsirkuliare', *Pravda*, 24 June 1989.
16 *Izvestiia TsK KPSS*, no. 12, 1990, p. 136.

Chapter 2

The industrial labour force[1]

Judith Shapiro

Journalist: 'And the last question, Valentina Nikolaevna: feminism and perestroika. What relationship do they have to each other?'
Valentina Nikolaevna Konstantinova: It isn't possible to give an unambiguous answer. On the one hand, we've received the right to express our point of view freely, which is a great blessing. But on the other hand, economic restructuring hits women first. Where there are cutbacks in staffing they are the first candidates; when there is a transition to *khozraschet*[2] they are taken on reluctantly, especially young women.[3]

Perestroika in industry

An analysis of the impact of perestroika on women in the industrial labour force is imperative because industrial labour[4] is the present centre of gravity of Soviet[5] women's paid labour and the need for a radical reform of industry was at the heart of perestroika. This chapter will examine whether perestroika has yet meant unemployment or redeployment for women industrial workers, the extent to which this is threatened and the likely pace of change. It will consider under what conditions women industrial workers labour, and how the women themselves react to them.

There is a broad sense to the word 'perestroika': the heroic period of Gorbachev's rule. This was to entail a radical and modernising transformation of Soviet society, economy and polity, but one which would not abandon the 'socialist choice' of 1917. There is also a narrow meaning of perestroika: economic restructuring. This chapter focuses on the latter. The economic reform process has never been fully coherently elaborated, and in life it has been even less intelligible. One deliberately blunt summary is that given by a leading American analyst of the Soviet economy, Ed Hewitt, to a reporter: 'Look, *perestroika* is a very polite phrase for firing a lot of people, moving a lot of people around and closing a lot of bad enterprises.'[6]

This is the plain meaning of a series of concepts. First, Sov
enterprises should seek to cover their costs (summed up in th
khozraschet, a shortening of the phrase for 'economic cost ac
ing'). Next, they should seek to invest out of their own earnings;
'self-financing'. An additional element is growing legal permissio
private economic activity, which began with the approval for coo ⌐-
ative firms and joint enterprises. For all this to work in any positive way
there would have to be radical price reform, since arbitrary Soviet
prices are no reflection of the cost to society of producing goods and
services. And there would have to be something resembling markets, so
that orders could be placed, supplies of items in high demand could be
expanded, and production of little-wanted goods curtailed. Underlying
at least the initial optimistic visions, was a hope that all this would lead
to the modernisation of Soviet industry, and to sharp improvements in
labour productivity.

The difficulty of carrying out such a restructuring in a reasonable
sequence, and the social resistance to it, would create problems for
even a very determined leadership with a great deal of legitimacy.
And it is questionable whether a partial marketisation can succeed
without the replacement of state enterprise as the dominant form of
ownership. As perestroika actually proceeded, the unintended consequences of a loss of central control of the economy, unaccompanied
by little compensating progress towards the market, have been far
more important for workers in the short run than any planned
rationalisation.

Work is virtually a universal for Soviet women now. Since 1970 the
proportion of working-age women in the labour force has been close to
the biological maximum, especially in the Slavic and Baltic republics. In
that year the proportion of women in the USSR aged 16 to 54 who were
employed or in full-time study reached a high 89.7 per cent.[7] And the
blue-collar worker[8] in industry is now the single most important
category of female labour in the USSR: the female exodus from the
farm has far exceeded the drift from the factory.

Soviet handbooks have been irritatingly coy about the proportion of
women engaged in industrial and manual work. The common table on
women's work divided into branches of the economy does not manage
nowadays to find space for 'industry.'[9] Fortunately, preliminary data
from the 1989 Census data are arriving to supplement our previous
deductions. These confirm that industrial labour remains a critical
focus of women's employment, despite a notable trend towards
alternative employment in the past decade.

Table 2.1. *Women in the paid labour force by broad sector, 1989 census*

	Number (thousands)	Per cent of total female labour force	Women as per cent of relevant labour force
Total in paid labour	67,997	100	48
Industry, transport and communications, construction	24,934	37	38
Agriculture and forestry	10,139	15	39
Trade, catering, material technical supply and sales	7,666	11	73
Health, physical culture, social services, education, culture, art, science and science education	18,321	27	73

Source: *Vestnik Statistiki*, no. 2, 1991, p. 39.

Of the 65 million Soviet women working outside the home in 1985, almost one-quarter (14.4 million) were blue-collar workers in industry.[10] It seems logical here to consider also women in construction and transportation. And, in industrial production proper, many white-collar jobs like 'economist' and 'bookkeeper', and even 'engineer' (especially in the lower grades) are heavily feminised. Taken together, these women formed 37 per cent of the female labour force in the 1989 census.[11] Table 2.1 shows the basic employment structure of women in the USSR by broad sector.

The proportion in industry is not dramatically different from, for example, Britain.[12] A key contrast derives from two significant facts. Rural life is still of far greater importance in the USSR, but the service sector is still of far greater unimportance. Thus Soviet women in industry remain more predominant in urban working life than their British counterparts.

One important conclusion from the emerging Soviet census data is that such contrasts are steadily diminishing. Soviet women are no longer a majority of the labour force, as they still were in 1979, but now constitute 48 per cent.[13] A far higher proportion of women than men survived the war years and this age cohort has now retired. The women of Soviet Central Asia, with a lower propensity to enter paid labour, are a growing share of the labour force. Table 2.2 shows significant

Table 2.2. *A guide to republican differences in Soviet women's work experience*

Percentage of each category which is female:

	Blue- and white-collar workers, 1988	Collective farmers, 1988	Directors of enterprises and organisations, 1 January 1989
Lativa	54	42	5.7
Estonia	54	41	2.9
Belorussia	53	43	5.8
Ukraine	52	45	5.3
Moldavia	52	47	4.4
Lithuania	52	45	5.5
RSFSR	51	40	6.5
Kirgizia	49	44	4.8
Kazakhstan	49	38	5.0
Armenia	48	48	0.9
Georgia	46	47	1.8
Azerbaidzhan	43	53	1.5
Uzbekistan	43	55	2.5
Turkmenistan	42	52	2.8
Tadzhikistan	39	52	2.7
USSR as a whole	51	45	5.6

Source: Zhenschchiny v SSSR 1990: Statisticheskie materialy (Moscow: Finansy i statistika, 1990), pp. 24, 25, 27.

Note that the proportion in column 3 had dropped abruptly from an all-Union 6.9 per cent in 1985 to 5.6 per cent. It is, however, almost certain that this is not an early negative result of perestroika, but rather the consequence of the retirement of the female-heavy war generation.

variation in the proportion of the labour force which is female in each of the fifteen union republics.

Soviet women are gradually shifting out of industry, and out of manual work. This is occurring even in fields where the labour force is expanding. Most branches of industry have shown a numerical decline in female labour, and virtually all witnessed a decline in the proportion of labour which is female. The exodus of women from construction, a drop of 23 per cent, over ten years, and from railway work, a drop of 29 per cent, is striking, though it does not rival the flight from the land.

Table 2.3. *Selected occupations of women in the paid labour force, according to USSR censuses, 1979 and 1989*

	Number thousands		Per cent of female labour force		Women as per cent of relevant sector of labour force	
	1989	1979	1989	1979	1989	1979
All women	67,997	66,994	100	100	48	50
Manual occupations	38,307	42,656	56.3	63.7	41	45
Metalworking and engineering	2,921	3,149	4.3	4.7	15*	17*
Chemical industry	466	452	0.7	0.7	58	60
Textiles	835	1,012	1.2	1.5	83	86
Clothing	1,920	1,981	2.8	3.0	93	94
Food	733	708	1.1	1.1	74	81
Communication	772	847	1.1	1.3	84	86
Sanitary personnel	1,931	1,841	2.8	2.7	97	98
Construction	1,198	1,198	1.8	1.8	21	26
Trade and catering	4,535	4,312	6.7	0.1	89	92
Services	3,913	3,843	5.8	5.7	89	91
Agriculture	6,873	10,879	10.1	16.2	43	52
Non-manual occupations	29,690	24,338	43.7	36.3	63	61
Technical and engineering personnel	6,542	5,638	9.6	8.4	50	48
Education and science	6,199	4,534	9.1	6.8	73	70
Medicine	3,908	3,033	5.8	4.5	86	88
Planning and accounts	5,886	5,421	8.7	8.1	88	87
Management of enterprises and their subdivisions	151	122	0.2	0.2	49	44
Office and secretarial	1,408	1,298	2.1	1.9	93	92

Source: Vestnik Statistiki, 1991, no. 2, pp. 39–40.
* Note that, as for Table 1, there are inevitably differences with previously published figures which were not produced by a population census. But in the case of metalprocessing and machine-building, however, this discrepancy is so great as to demand further probing on the basis of this calculation. Women workers in this sector have long been reported as making up a much higher figure, 42 per cent in 1985 (*Trud v SSSR*, Moscow, Finansy i Statistika, 1988, p. 106).

Women are leaving the declining textile industry even more rapidly than men. In the expanding chemical, food and printing industries, men are entering production more rapidly than women. At the same time, women are going into non-manual occupations in greater proportion than their male counterparts. Soviet women, in sum, are finding work in a pattern closer to that of their Western counterparts. This is a trend which began before perestroika. Table 2.3 presents a more detailed picture of the female labour force today, and contrasts it with 1979, the year of the previous national census.

Although the continuing importance of the industrial woman worker revealed here has been curiously absent from the statistics presented in the annual *Zhenshchiny v SSSR* (*Women in the USSR*), this booklet has become a catalogue of the plight of Soviet women. This is an ironic shift from its former role as an advertisement for the Soviet 'solution' to the woman question. Thus the 1990 edition[14] provides much which is informative, if unsystematic and depressing, confirming not only that women receive consistently lower wages (67 to 70 per cent of men's) and are under-represented in the higher skill grades[15] but that they are well distributed in the heaviest and least mechanised occupations, and even more so in especially dangerous work (they do 44 per cent of this work in industry). And they are over-represented on night shifts.[16] This bleak and frank picture tallies with the portrait drawn by careful Western research about a decade ago. Indeed, as seems characteristically Soviet these days, it goes even further than many, lamenting the 'Physically heavy, monotonous and wearing work, unsatisfactory sanitary and hygenic conditions of work, inconvenient hours, the lack of rhythm to the work (involuntary and unpaid) overtime, and also the unsatisfactory size of the pay packet.'[17]

But, if the official figures have virtually concealed the importance of female industrial labour, while not hiding conditions of work, a number of politically visible Soviet women were swift and eloquent in pointing to the potential negative effects of economic reform on women in the industrial labour force. The still rare, but growing, Soviet social science literature on gender issues also pays proper attention to the industrial worker.[18] But, in the absence of reliable global data, the task of evaluating the impact of economic changes upon this group is confined by the limitations of statistical sampling and unsystematic observation. The need for the newly formed department of statistics on women in Goskomstat, the State Committee on Statistics, is pressing. Despite the handicap of inadequate statistics, a fair amount can nevertheless be said. A new set of Soviet studies, investigative journalism,

and political discussion, have added to even the best of earlier Western analyses.[19]

Back to the home?

Scenarios for perestroika all reasonably involve a slimmed-down industrial labour force. The assumption is that there will be fewer workers, working more productively.[20] The general adoption by policymakers of the view that Soviet industry should not solve its problems by finding more or better workers, but rather needs fewer workers, is one milestone marking the transition, in 1987, to advocacy of radical reform.[21]

In fact, the overall number of workers in Soviet industry has not been expanding for nearly a decade. Nonetheless the proportion employed in industry, as a fraction of the non-agricultural labour force, is still comparatively very high. Whole sectors of industry are targeted for sharp contraction, and the work force will be trimmed to levels more in line with capitalist standards. Staffing levels are, in many cases, up to double comparable Western ones. Vladimir Shcherbakov, until recently the head of the State Committee on Labour, and latterly a deputy prime minister with responsibility for economic figures, suggested conservatively in an early 1991 estimate that 18 to 20 per cent of workers in Soviet enterprises are superfluous.[22]

This does not, of course, have to result in surplus labour overall. The service sector is badly in need of expansion – and its small size hurts Soviet women most. Retail and wholesale trade, for example, employs about half the proportion employed in the main market economies.[23] Within industry a shift towards consumer goods is sorely needed.[24]

But there is an evident fear that there will not be enough jobs, or the right kind of jobs, to redeploy everyone. Along with the expectation that cuts will fall first on women workers, has been a threatening companion argument: perhaps this is not such a bad thing. Thus, for example, a perusal of election ephemera finds a number of posters and platforms of male candidates repeating the call for the 'emancipation' of women from the double burden, by returning them to the home.[25] But a less categorical version can be found in the writing of serious sociologists:

It would seem that the high level of employment of women in social production is socially unjustified. It has had a negative effect both on the birth rate and on the upbringing of children. In the towns, and now sometimes in

the villages as well, the one-child family is becoming the prevalent model, which does not even ensure that the population reproduces itself.

This is the leading social scientist and now People's Deputy, Tat'iana Zaslavskaia, speaking.[26] It reveals, unfortunately, that Zaslavskaia's stress on the human factor has not stopped her from thinking about policy issues in such terms, which imply that the individual exists for the state. She does not even bother to justify the need for the population to reproduce itself.

The argument that female labour-force participation is too high was put forward by some Soviet scholars as early as the 1970s, essentially from a pro-natalist point of view.[27] Few had the interests of women, or even people, in mind. Rather they talked about the good of something called 'society' which needed a higher birth rate. Sometimes unsupported arguments about the allegedly baneful influence on children also surfaced. These arguments, highly reminiscent of the postwar US mood which accompanied American women's temporary retreat from the labour force, did not, however, find much resonance at that time. There was one important policy proposal to boost the birth rate which did coincide with the aspirations of many Soviet women: the proposal for more part-time work. This, however, was not implemented.

The right to choose

Zaslavskaia assumes, without offering any evidence, that significantly fewer women would choose to work if men's wages were higher. This is, after all, a critical issue. Assuming an 'optimal variant' of a reform scenario, would fewer women choose paid labour in a situation of growing prosperity? If so, perhaps outside observers might regret their choice, but still be pleased that they have the right to make it. It is difficult to quarrel with Galina Semenova, new Politburo member and former editor of *Krest'ianka*, that women should have the right to choose whether to work and whether to have children.[28] In deeply conformist Soviet society this choice was effectively very difficult. And the inability of most families to live at all reasonably on one income further narrows that choice.

But even if higher male wages could be assured quickly – an assumption which now seems distinctly doubtful – there is as yet no corroboration for Zaslavskaia's assertion that significantly fewer women would choose to work. It has long been popular to ask Soviet women under what conditions they would leave work. This approach is unlikely to get us very reliable predictions. But, for what it is worth, the great majority still insist[29] that they would want to work even in much improved material circumstances. This is altogether possible, even if women primarily work for money, not other goals. There are two conflicting forces at work in determining female labour-force participation when wages rise.

In such a situation women will, of course, be tempted, other things being equal, not to work. The alternative uses of their time, especially in Soviet economic conditions, are very attractive. The Soviet household still needs to make a wide variety of goods itself and perform services readily available on the market in other industrialised countries. Laundry services are primitive, and so are most home washing machines. Public launderettes would be a revelation. Tomatoes must be bottled for winter, fruit preserved. Some of the resulting products are splendid in comparison with our mass-production items, but we would be wise to repress any nostalgic longings when we observe the time and effort it takes to prepare them when they are not a hobby. And then good shopping in more normal days was still a time-consuming art. With a higher wage paid to the husband, a family could indulge this redistribution of resources from paid into unpaid work.

On the other hand, the prospect of higher wages, unless a 'men only' offer, must also make paid work relatively more attractive than before. Which of these two forces will be the stronger at any one time is an empirical question. The differing labour-force participation of women in the USSR by region today gives more support to the view that the higher the wage, the more likely women are to work, than it does to Zaslavskaia's assertion. But the actual outcome would be decided in a world in which, presumably, there would also be more services, more industrial preparation of foodstuffs, shorter queues, less need for the constant and alert search to obtain basics.

There is need for caution here, since many features of the present economic crisis make paid labour remarkably unattractive. Roubles are worth little to a growing number of families, who have found themselves with an increasing volume of largely unwanted savings. And, on the other hand, time has become much more precious, as the search for goods becomes more difficult and more basic in many areas. This is unlikely to be a permanent trend, but it does suggest a strong motivation for a number of women to cease paid labour at the present time. (This is, however, less true for industrial production workers, many of whom owe their sole access to goods in scarce supply to their enterprises). And once women have chosen this road, continuing along it may be more likely than before, even if conditions change.

Part-time work

Soviet regulations and decrees on the new employment situation urge women to be offered part-time work when redundancies and reshuffling occur. Many women would prefer part-time work, if it were available. Indeed it is often the enterprise which is resisting this more. Only a trivial 1 per cent of Soviet labour is officially part-time.[30] This minuscule number includes about as many men as women.[31]

In some Soviet professional and semi-professional jobs, a certain sort of hidden part-time work has evidently evolved. Schoolteachers, for example, have traditionally been badly paid, but the minimum work week is quite short. Additional optional duties are paid for, and men in these jobs do them rather more than women. Similarly, male doctors are more likely to hold more than one post. Women with children also choose jobs with the apparently punishing rhythm of a *dezhurnaia*[32] – one 24-hour period on, three off – above all for their free days.

In the first period in the new development of private production cooperatives in the USSR, there was hope they too might provide an outlet for displaced or dissatisfied female industrial labour, and would be congenial to working mothers.[33] But, as they have evolved in practice, 'the average *kooperator* [cooperative member] is a thirty-five year old male who formerly held a leadership post in a state enterprise.'[34] Cooperatives may have contract workers who are not members, and who do not share in the profits, and women may certainly be employed here. But Soviet cooperative activity remains an unreliable source of basic income and status. About one-half of workers in producer cooperatives have more than one job, and this half is very unlikely to be female. Many of the remaining half of the posts in this sector require a fuller or more arduous, not a shorter or lighter, working week.

There is, as well, a marked 'gender gap' in polled attitudes towards cooperatives. Women are significantly more negative. Thus *Fakt* found that 23 per cent of men and only 8 per cent of women considered cooperative members to be 'enterprising and businesslike people worthy of respect and support'. More than 25 per cent of men and 38 per cent of women considered them 'opportunists who bettered their own lot "at the expense of honorable labor"'.[35] Soviet cooperatives, in present conditions, seem unattractive to most women.

In industry itself there has been little official recognition of any desire for shorter work time, except for the use of homeworking. Recent discussion of the latter seems oddly innocent about the reputation homeworking has acquired historically as 'sweated' and 'exploitative'. Thus the journal *Okhrana Truda* (Labour Protection) published an enthusiastic account of the homework supervised by the Marat Knitwear Association in Tallinn. Touting the advantages of the system for women with young children, it chides the 'administrative-command mentality' for standing in the way of increased homeworking.[36] (In 1983 only 212,000, presumably overwhelmingly women, worked at home.[37] This was two-thirds of the tiny number working part-time.)

As for a more dramatic exit from the labour force, forecasts of the likely success of a voluntary 'back to the home' movement cannot be firm. The decisions women make depend upon a number of factors which include changes in overall wages, working conditions, relative wages and the development of a service sector. And it will depend also on a subjective factor, the preferences of women, influenced but not determined by social trends and public discussion. There is good reason to suspect that were radical economic reform to succeed, it would encourage a significantly lower labour-force participation rate for some time to come. But this is not a foregone conclusion.

If they won't jump ... unemployment

If women do not exit gracefully and voluntarily from the labour force in great numbers, will they be pushed? Today the overwhelming consensus is that they will bear the main burden of unemployment and of undesired reallocation to less attractive work. There have been comparatively few redundancies so far, but there is already supporting evidence for this hypothesis. According to Zaslavskaia,[38] women have made up 70 per cent of restructuring redundancies. Thus two women have lost their jobs for every one male. This is, of course, way out of proportion to their numbers in the labour force as a whole, and also to their weight in branches where dismissals have come first.

The journal *Okhrana Truda* reported a typical case in 1989. As a result of *khozraschet* and self-financing at the Kirov Apatit Production Association, 700 production workers and 125 engineering and technical personnel were made redundant, the majority of both groups being women. One machinist on a conveyer said, 'I'm forty years old and I've worked twenty of these years as a machinist on the conveyer line. When men were scarce we were needed, but now they're kicking us out.'[39]

Ironically, women workers are particularly threatened by progress. There are 4.2 million female industrial workers labouring without any mechanised assistance whatsoever. But, as the Director of the VTsSPS (Trade Union) Institute of Labour Protection in the textile town of Ivanovo acerbically noted:

Here a paradoxical situation arises. It is enough to mechanise a section for the stronger sex to begin ousting women from the work places. I see in this either total toothlessness on the part of the central committees of the trade unions or their conciliatory position.[40]

Trade-union central committees in turn blame the local trade unions for inaction. The union newspaper *Trud* (Labour) interviewed the Chair of the Central Committee of the Union of Workers in Textile and Light Industry in 1990, M. V. Ikharlova, who reported that workers had struck – though not generally about redundancies – in (predominantly female) light-industry enterprises in Moscow, Riazan, Briansk, Kemerovo oblast (in the Kuzbass, Siberia), Ukraine, Estonia and Georgia. She went on to complain that 'In most of these cases local trade unions showed little initiative in looking into or pressing workers' grievances.'[41]

International experience of resistance to redundancies suggests that active protest is the exception, not the rule. To date, it must be stressed, unemployment has generally been threatened rather than real. Even the rationalisation officially recorded has frequently meant redeployment within the same enterprises, though perhaps with lower wages or loss of special pension rights. Thus the most serious problems lie ahead.

The limited restructuring which has occurred has, by all accounts, hit women and children first. In *Sotsialisticheskii Trud* (Socialist Labour) one scholar reported:

The shift to self-financing, self-supporting and self-administration has worsened the position of women workers. Plans to make 16 million workers redundant by the year 2000 are hitting women first. ... The most defenceless are women with children, who have become the first candidates for discharge – because of sick children, or due to the unwillingness of management, or at times the impossibility due to economic difficulties, to grant them the rights and privileges accorded them by the law.[42]

According to sympathetic Soviet literature, the main cause of women's differential unemployment, actual and threatened, is not deliberate and wilful discrimination, but women's lower skills, lower worktime flexibility, and propensity to bear children.[43] There is some merit in this argument.

A squeeze on women also arises from one basic discrepancy. Soviet legislation on working women's rights remains generous in principle, but funding of these rights is to be shouldered by the enterprise. In the days when the latter had little incentive to economise on labour costs, this was a matter for sublime indifference. Suddenly it is not. And this abrupt confrontation between socialist-type legal entitlement and capitalist-type calculation produces a highly unpleasant outcome.

The terms of compensation decreed for the April 1991 price rises provided a sharp illustration of this. Women with children were given special additional increases to their pay – but enterprises, who pay the wages, were given no compensation. The Supreme Soviet's Committee on Women's Affairs, the Family and Children was quickly driven to writing an open letter to Prime Minister Pavlov declaring that enterprises simply could not afford the increases, and were releasing the women. They proposed that enterprises with large numbers of women workers be given central subsidies.[44]

If we leave aside the problem of the special costs of employing working mothers, there remains the common Soviet argument that women's already inferior position in the labour market is the basic cause of the disparity in impact of redundancies, rather than discrimination. There is supporting evidence for this, but an added degree of methodological sophistication is necessary. Are the women released genuinely less productive than their male colleagues, or is there a strong element of 'statistical discrimination' or worse? That is, are women actually less effective, or are they simply assumed by management to be so? As studies are only just beginning to reach the stage where reliable statistics are contemplated, more careful research can scarcely yet have been done.

The difference between enforced redundancies and a voluntary 'back to the home' trend should be clear. Economists differentiate clearly between those who are not seeking work at present, and those who are not working, but are seeking work, and are able and willing to work at the going wage rate. Only the latter make up the unemployed, still considered to be in the labour force. The abstract distinction is obvious. But in practice this division, which depends on how the woman defines herself, is not always simple to make. (It is further clouded in the USSR today by official and journalistic reporting which consistently muddles and conflates the two into unemployed, even though Russian possesses a more elegant way than English of marking out the *nezaniatie*, the non-working, from the *bezrabotnie*, the unemployed.)

The Soviet economy has not had open unemployment on a mass scale for six decades, albeit as the consequence of economic policies and structures which were costly indeed to human values. It had *de facto* even offered the effective right to continue at one job. This is one of the rights being renegotiated by perestroika. Economic reform undermines such job security.

While it is not an absolute law that cuts in staffing will hit women more than men, the historical exceptions are rare. One important and ironic example occurred in the USSR in 1932 in the heat of Stalinist industrialisation. Economic difficulties in this frenzied year led to a fall in employment, and to redundancies. (The redundancies were, however, very far from the level during the difficult 1920s, in which women were hit particularly sharply.[45]) Yet, as the archives of the Commissariat of Labour reveal,[46] the authorities continued to wage a campaign to attract and to retain women in industry. At the important Putilov works, for example, the policy of the tractor division administration was that if a woman was doing her job satisfactorily, she kept it and a man was let go instead.[47] In Ukrainian heavy industry, where the workforce was smaller by October 1932 than at the start of the year, the number of women workers actually rose by 14,469, and their representation in the total increased from 15.6 to 19.6 per cent.[48] To be sure, fewer women entered industry than had initially been 'planned'.[49] As an overall consequence of such policies throughout the Union, while the industrial labour force diminished, the proportion which was female actually continued to rise. The reasons are worth exploring. Was this simply inertia? After all, in the process of the campaign to recruit women for the ever-increasing labour demands of the First Five-Year Plan, watchdog committees and bureaucracies on women's labour had been created. Or was there rather more consciousness in keeping a second wage earner at work, an important means by which Stalinist industrialisation was able to lower real wages without pushing workers below actual physical subsistence?

In any event, nothing like it is being proposed now. Those, like Rimashevskaia and Konstantinova, who are concerned that women should not be fired first, have much less far-reaching aims, and are worried about attaining them if and when really serious redundancies – in the millions – begin. While few Soviet predictions on unemployment have been analytically clear, warnings like those of Nikolai Gritsenko, Chairman of the Supreme Soviet Committee on Labour, Prices and

Social Policy, who suggested that 5.3 million people will need unemployment benefits in 1991, may be only a little premature.[50]

What can be done to limit female unemployment? Employment bureaux and retraining facilities must work but nothing so far has given grounds for confidence in this. Vigorous development of the emaciated service sector could 'mop up' much female unemployment, while transforming the non-working lives of millions of Soviet women. Even in times of 'normal' supply, Soviet queues absorb unnecessary hours because there are not enough shops, and not enough cash desks. Dry cleaning normally requires the prior removal of all buttons. Of course, as in the West, these tertiary sector jobs might not pay as well as many of the industrial ones they replace. Nonetheless, for many of those who do the unmechanised drudgery on inflexible schedules in ancient Soviet factories, they might be a satisfactory alternative. Julia Szalai has stated that as of April 1991, Hungarian women, especially unskilled industrial workers, are less likely to be unemployed because they have found part-time work in the burgeoning service sector to their liking.[51] But, so far, the development of this sector in the USSR remains limited.

At the stage where women are first threatened with job loss, Rimashevskaia and Golodenko reasonably suggest that committees should ensure there are no unjust sackings of women.[52] But how much can committees and even legislation achieve, especially in Soviet circumstances? One striking reminder of how little the USSR is 'law-governed' is the contrast between labour law and reality. After all, it has been seven decades since women were banned from 'particularly heavy and unhealthy work, or on work underground'.[53] Night work for women is permitted only in 'exceptional circumstances'. And yet not only is the all-Union figure for women's shiftworking very high but, in some places, such as Moldavia, more than half the women working are on night shifts.[54] The RSFSR code is already very strict on paper in prescribing penalties for discrimination, especially against women. A manager can, it is legislated, be jailed for one year for sacking a pregnant woman. Given the evident lack of effectiveness of these codes, it is difficult not to be sceptical until a very different political culture is established.

Defended to death?

Is it entirely unfortunate that the splendid panoply of Soviet protective legislation for women workers has been a virtual dead letter for many decades? This is a complex matter. Certainly glasnost has brought to light the appalling conditions under which many Soviet women work. The newspaper *Sotsialisticheskaia Industriia*, for example, described the experiences of women textile workers at the Varentsovaia weaving factory in the textile town of Ivanovo, which is historically heavily female, and known as the 'Russian Manchester':

The noise in the shops is deafening. Women have to shout to make themselves heard. Not a single weaving or spinning loom, even the very latest, is in line with official norms for noise. The machinery is badly designed for women. It is, rather, suited for the statistically average male at the peak of his physical powers. Women must be extremely dexterous, fixing threads on some looms, 'coaxing' others, and then lifting heavy loads.[55]

Okhrana Truda adds that the danger of accidents from equipment in the textile industry has risen eleven-fold in the past fifteen years.[56] *Sobesednik*, a weekly newspaper for youth, visited a Moscow cloth factory, accompanied by journalism students. It found the conditions horrendous. Women have simultaneously to tend several machines and to hump heavy loads. The ventilation does not work, and the steam in the finishing shops burns women's faces. One woman told the young reporters: 'I'm twenty-seven and I shudder to think what I'll be like in two or three years.'[57]

Liudmila Telen' reports that in other branches of industry women are found in non-mechanised work 50 per cent more often than men.[58] In industry, 4.2 of the 14 million women work without the aid of machinery.[59] Of women working in industrial production 45 per cent are earning at least one special benefit ('privilege') for hazardous work: 32 per cent are getting higher rates, 7 per cent a shortened work day, 24 per cent accelerated pension rights.

That many of these jobs still exist for anyone, anywhere in the world, is regrettable. As *Rabochaia Tribuna* noted wryly, women foundry workers at Nyuchinsk iron works are still pouring pig iron into moulds by hand, just as workers did two centuries ago. The installation of electricity there seems to have been in vain. Khrushchev caught the same mood in 1962:

It is painful to see ... women armed with crowbars packing ballast under railway sleepers by hand. At a time when we have reached the Moon we have no machine to replace the worker's and equip him. In particular, I repeat, this applies to women.[60]

Nearly 4 million Soviet women are on night shifts, exceeding the male rate; 800,000 are officially exposed to excess noise and vibration;

400,000 are doing heavier than legal manual labour, precisely 1,230,000 are said to be exposed to excessive dust; between 20 and 50 per cent of female workplaces do not meet safety requirements; women are half of all workers doing unmechanised labour.[61] The catalogue is endless.

But how should it be ended? Even in the 1920s, some Soviet working women protested about the splendid protective labour legislation enacted by the early Soviet state. In conditions of high unemployment this was not necessarily a boon. Is it better, asked one woman delegate to the Sixth Trade Union Congress in 1924, to work in poor conditions or to trade oneself for a crust on the boulevard?

The present difficult position of women on the shop floor, which no one should idealise, is not necessarily the worst case. Women, by doing the heaviest and least attractive work achieved a certain monetary compensation, though quite often they cannot maintain this throughout their lives. (Thus women leave the most arduous textile jobs early.)[62]

There has been a cascade of exposés of the difficult life of women manual workers in the Soviet press. But the implication for policy of much of this writing has been that the choice to do this work should be removed from the woman worker. Yet it is clear that they regard shift work, heavy work, and even unpleasant and harmful work, as the lesser evil. Waiting lists to do such work are not infrequent.[63] Thus it is not surprising that in 1989 steps to remove women from positions in transport where they are formally banned were met with protests and even a large demonstration. They were not removed.[64]

What about the supposedly undesirable night shifts? The journalistic attitude towards this has been a model of exaggeration. Thus Shineleva ludicrously complained that the USSR was 'the only power in the world where women in production are occupied at this time of the night'.[65] Leaving aside such curious inversions of the old Soviet style of propaganda (in light of the fact that the Soviet rate of female night work is not all that remarkably high) there is still no doubt that some women must do night work without choice. But when the Ivanovo Institute for Labour Safety worked out an alternative to the traditional work roster, eliminating night shifts, this provoked opposition from the textile workers themselves. Women did not want to give up the extra money they earned from night work. The Institute added regretfully that this was also true of the receipt of danger money.[66]

A certain caution is necessary when chivalrous males, or crusading middle-class women, discover the abuse of women in industry. Are the majority of their proposals aimed at lightening the physical burden and increasing the skill content of women's work, or of legislating it away without compensation? It should be noted further that any new jobs opening in an expanding service sector are as likely to be as ill-paid as in the West. Soviet women who are allowed to choose may still select factory night shifts, and heavy lifting. But will they be allowed?

Perestroika and unskilled women workers

Soviet women industrial workers have found that taking monotonous and tiring jobs pays bonuses which compensate, in part, for the skill grades they lack. As Rimashevskaia found in her Taganrog study, women, who have not achieved the same skill levels as men, often move into jobs with heavy or harmful conditions in order to get better pay.[67] It is these jobs which will disappear first. And when they are mechanised and improved the key question will be: to whom will they go?

Given the present distribution of skill grades between male and female workers, modernisation would tend, without real moves towards equality, to harm women's job prospects. In engineering and metalworking, for example, 70 per cent of women workers are in skill grades one to three, and only 1.3 per cent in the highest (sixth) grade.[68] On the whole, the gap in industry between the average male and average female skill grade is .5 to 1.9 skill grades.[69]

Women who enter industry fail to get the on-the-job training which would give them the better jobs later on. The State Statistics Committee released the very depressing results of a 1990 survey of 93,000 women, which revealed that at least two-thirds of the time such training as did occur did nothing to improve a woman's pay, grade, or working conditions.[70]

Women in these 'normal' channels, as Filtzer has argued,[71] tend overwhelmingly to work in those areas where the work is most easily disciplined and where effective control by the workers over their own labour intensity has been the least. The textile industry is the archetype. Denied the more logical means of betterment, women doing the less pleasant jobs have, at least, the compensation of better pay and/or that certain degree of effective control summed up in 'We pretend to work and they pretend to pay us.' And many of these jobs would be the target of perestroika. It might seem retrograde to defend the repetitive lifting, the filth, the decibels, the dangerous chemicals. But it pays to underscore that the key question will be: what is to follow, and who will benefit?

A great tragedy for the older generation of unskilled women workers, the last 'reserve' of women to enter the labour force in the early 1960s, may be that any improvements will be for their daughters, not for them. There will be little place for them in a brave new world. Since in some of the longest-developed traditional work forces, such as the textile workers of Ivanovo, women say that they do not want their daughters to follow in their footsteps because the work is too nasty, this may be no small thing.

But how near is the threat?

Some have recently argued that unemployment and technological displacement are not a threat, since nothing much has been done. So far that is approximately right. Since 1987, 3 million have been re-deployed; this is a small number. It would cost 30 billion roubles, according to one estimate,[72] to install the necessary capital simply to rectify violations of existing labour legislation. And there is a strong mood which suggests that the first phase of perestroika has ended, and there is no real sign of radical reform. Instead, the most pressing problems for women in the industrial labour force seem to be in the failure of the initial conception of perestroika, not its success.

What was the conception of perestroika?

The attempt to change Soviet industry and Soviet industrial relations has been pivotal to the process which defined the era we came to know as 'perestroika'. How, we might ask, will future generations define this period? It may be seen as the interval of time which began when a Soviet leadership consolidated its power with an understanding that something far-reaching had to be done to rescue and modernise the limping Soviet economy. This leadership, led and symbolised by Gorbachev, embarked on this ever-more ambitious programme, which included economic, social and political measures. But it did so with a clear commitment to stay within the framework of the existing social order, the 'socialist choice'. When this seemed under threat, perestroika lost its momentum.

We will almost certainly never know what would have happened if a package of reforms which moved towards some sort of quasi-market economy had been introduced at one go by a leadership which retained political authority and a unified will to see things through. Instead, a set of remarkably partial and contradictory changes in the economic structures succeeded primarily in their destructive aims: undermining the old 'administrative-command' mechanism, the party and government, from a number of directions. Ministries effectively lost their power to command the enterprises; regions and towns made their own decisions. Moscow's writ ceased to run. But real markets and new and coherent political forces and programmes turned out to require far more.

Gorbachev's intensely pragmatic and centrist 'balancing act' has created its own massive economic problems, which are a caricature of the system it sought to replace. These, well on the way to hyper-inflation and a breakdown of the economy into barter of a pre-capitalist variety, are the dominant feature of the economic landscape as this chapter is written. Meanwhile, the usually simple but onerous routines of everyday Soviet life have been turned into a particularly nerve-wracking trial, a burden carried by a wide section of the population, but first of all by women workers.

What next? 'Workers can already feel the breath of unemployment on the back of their necks,' warned the deputy director of the Labour Statistics Administration of the State Statistics Committee in May 1991. This seems to be inescapable in all possible exits. Consider three alternative 'scenarios' projected by the Cabinet of Ministers of the USSR in April 1991. The first variant is to do nothing, and watch the economy continue to implode. Result: 15–18 million new unemployed. Their 'third variant', a dash to the market, they assert (in part to frighten), would cause the unemployment of thirty million. They insist there exists another variant, the 'second variant', in which unemployment is kept to 'manageable proportions'. This happy middle ground, whose very existence is in dispute, would apparently produce half as much unemployment as the first variant.[73]

Thus, even on these rigged scenarios, the alternatives, we can estimate, would provoke new female unemployment ranging from a 'manageable' rate of 9 per cent, to 18 or even 29 per cent of the female labour force. (The corresponding male rates would be about half. This would be the outcome *if* women continued to make up 70 per cent of the redundant, and *if* these women continued to want to work.) The sunny middle variant presumes an enhanced development of the service sector and of small enterprise to absorb some labour shed from industrial dinosaurs.

Thus, if the present arrangement of the economy is intolerable, the next steps in any direction will certainly be painful. The relative impact on women workers is likely to be heavy. Women in white collar posts will share the blows. When some dust has settled trends already visible before perestroika will have been reinforced. Factories, building sites and railways will be more male; services will be more female. Women's labour-force participation will have fallen towards Western levels. After six decades unemployment will be a factor. On 1 July 1991 eleven union republics begin to pay unemployment benefit, as part of a poorly worked out programme. When, finally, the queue for jobs has replaced the queue for goods, the women now in Soviet industry will themselves be able to assess the costs and benefits.

NOTES

1 This chapter has benefited greatly from consulting Donald Filtzer's unpublished work on labour under Gorbachev financed by the Leverhulme Trust. I have drawn heavily upon Filtzer's research on women in industry, and have gained much from debating with him the ideas in his forthcoming 'Soviet Economic Reform and the Labour Process' in Paul Thompson and Chris Smith (eds.), *The Labour Process Under State Socialism* (London: Macmillan, 1991). He, of course, is not responsible for any of the conclusions I have drawn from his work.

2 Khozraschet is 'profit and loss accounting,' or just rational cost accounting. First introduced during the period of the New Economic Policy in the 1920s, it essentially calls for organisations to cover their current costs. More ambitious 'self-financing' requires, in addition, that investment programmes be financed out of own earnings.

3 Interview with V. N. Konstantinova, Research Fellow at the Academy of Social Sciences of the CPSU Central Committee, 'My, feministki' ['We, feminists'] in 'Zhenshchina: zhizn' i sud'ba,' *Sotsial'naia zashchita* 1990, no. 2, p. 22. This new journal is published under the auspices of Goskomtrud, the State Committee on Labour and Social Questions.

4 Taken here to include blue- and white-collar workers in industry, and women in construction and transportation. Soviet industry normally includes, as well, mining and quarrying and much of the power industry.

5 The word 'Soviet' has to be used throughout as a description of the somewhat varied experience of women of different nationalities living and working on the territory of the USSR. In reality the Slavic (Russian, Ukrainian, Belorussian) situation dominates the picture quantitatively.

While women in the Baltic republics have, for the most part, a roughly
similar work history since incorporation into the Soviet Union, we are
increasingly aware of the very different position of women in Central Asia
and, to a lesser extent, the Caucasus. In these areas female labour force
participation is less than full, and opportunities for industrial work often
markedly less. Table 2 presents some contrasts between republics in broad
terms. But glasnost has only recently allowed a more serious debate on the
specifics of this. Thus it is still not yet clear what is the relative weight of
cultural and ethnic issues in labour supply versus economic factors in
labour demand in determining women's special problems in those regions.
See, for example, G. F. Morozova, 'Trudoizbytochna li sredniaia Aziia?'
Sotsialisticheskie issledovaniia, 1989, no. 6.

6 *Washington Post*, 6 November 1988.

7 G. P. Sergeeva, *Professional'naia zaniatost' zhenshchin: problemy i perspektivy* (Moscow: Ekonomika, 1987) p. 39. Note that this will include
women on maternity leave, even lengthy maternity leave. For this reason it
will be hard to quantify the casual observation that numbers of women
have been extending this leave in the past several years.

8 'Blue-collar worker' is used here as a term most commonly understood in
the West as the Soviet terminology for 'workers' as opposed to 'employees'.
Note that the Russian for what looks deceptively like 'manual labour',
ruchnoi trud, must be understood as literally that, work almost solely by
hand, or unmechanised labour.

9 For example, *Narodnoe Khoziaistvo SSSR v 1989 godu* (Moscow: Finansy
i Statistika, 1990) pp. 53–4; *Trud v SSSR* (Moscow: Finansy i Statistika,
1988), pp. 105–6).

10 This can be calculated starting from *Trud v SSSR* (1988), p. 105.

11 *Vestnik Statistiki*, 1991, no. 2, p. 39.

12 Especially before the latter's recent 'de-industrialisation'. In the 1971 UK
Census a quarter of all women were employed in manufacturing industry.
Half of these were in only four industries, not dissimilar to those in which
Soviet women are concentrated. R. Martin and J. Wallace, *Working
Women in Recession: Employment, Redundancy and Unemployment*
(Oxford: OUP, 1984) p. 36, citing the Census.

13 *Vestnik Statistiki*, 1991, no. 2, p. 39.

14 *Zhenshchiny v SSSR 1990* (Moscow: Finansy i Statistika, 1990).

15 *Zhenshchiny v SSSR 1990*, p. 4.

16 *Ibid.*, pp. 5–6.

17 *Ibid.*, p. 7.

18 And a reasonable proportion of the material on the impact of perestroika
on industrial workers has paid attention to gender issues. (It should be
noted that a number of the leading researchers on the social aspects of
economic questions are women.) See, as early as 1987, when the
"classical"' perestroika package was just being put together, the summary
of discussion in 'Ne slazhivaia ostrykh uglov (obzor)', *Sotsialisticheskii*

Trud, 1987, no. 7. Natal'ia Rimashevskaia, together with V. N. Golodenko, penned a sharp warning in 'Sotsial'nie garantii prava zenshchin na trud v usloviiakh povyshennoi trudovoi mobil'nosti naseleniia' (Social guarantees of women's right to work in conditions of higher labour mobility). *Izvestiia Akademii nauk SSSR*, seriia ekonomicheskaia, 1990, no. 1, pp. 97–101.

19 Mary Buckley, *Women and Ideology* (Harmondsworth: Harvester Wheatsheaf, 1989) provides the most recent scholarly survey. See also Lapidus, McAuley, Sacks and Atkinson, Dallin and Lapidus (eds.), cited in the introductory chapter. Following that time, the most important studies have generally come from Britain (also cited in the introduction) and have been informed by a greater depth of direct acquaintance with Soviet society.

20 See, for one good statement of this, I. D. Matskuliak, *Strategiia Zaniatosti*, Moscow, Ekonomika, 1990, especially chapters 2 and 3, pages 24–59.

21 The most important statement of this was by Vladimir Kostakov, Gosplan's foremost labour expert, 'Zaniatost': defitsit ili izbytok?' *Kommunist* 1987, no. 2.

22 Vladimir Shcherbakov, 'Rynok truda i zaniatost': sostoianie, problemy, perspektivy', *Sotsialisticheskii Trud*, 1991, no. 1, p. 9.

23 International Monetary Fund et al., *The Economy of the USSR* (Washington D.C.: World Bank, 1990), p. 38.

24 This was the subject of sharp debate in 1991 between RSFSR Prime Minister Siliaev and USSR Prime Minister Pavlov.

25 Collections can be found at the British Library and the Baykov Library, CREES, Birmingham.

26 See her *The Second Socialist Revolution* (London: I. Tauris, 1990), p. 94.

27 An interesting collection is to be found in Gail Warshofky Lapidus (ed.), *Women, Work and Family* (Armonk: M. E. Sharpe, 1982).

28 *Moskovskii zhurnal*, 1990, no. 11, p. 40.

29 See, for example, Zoia Pukhova, then head of the Soviet Women's Committee, citing a survey, *Izvestiia*, 2 July 1988. She cites a figure of 80 per cent, but a certain caution is needed of course, in interpreting any of these numbers.

30 *Trud v SSSR 1988*, p. 141. Over one-third of these were in industry.

31 Shineleva discusses the issue in *Sotsialisticheskii Trud*, no. 8, 1989, pages 64–5.

32 The *dezhurnaia* is the person on duty, most familiar to foreign visitors in the form of the 'key-lady' on a hotel floor. (There has been some tendency to rationalise these too.) These and similar duty-shifts, with long periods of inactivity, have evolved into a pattern of 24-hour duty, which does involve some possibility for rest.

33 Thus see *Moscow News*, no. 38, 1988.

34 John E. Tedstrom, 'The Reemergence of Soviet Cooperatives' in John E. Tedstrom (ed.), *Socialism, Perestroika, and the Dilemmas of Soviet*

Economic Reform (Boulder: Westview Press, 1990), p. 133, citing the survey by the cooperative FAKT in *Kommercheskaia khronika 1988* (Moscow: Mir, 1988), p. 5.

35 Tedstrom, 'Soviet Cooperatives,' p. 133.

36 *Okhrana Truda*, 1989, no. 9, p. 3.

37 *Naselenie i formy zaniatosti* (Moscow: Mysl', 1985), p. 5. If the report of a strike of homeworkers at a Moscow factory, making ribbon and carton labels, is at all representative, then most of these few must have been invalids. *Trud*, 25 November 1989.

38 University of Birmingham Centre for Russian and East European Studies Seminar on Women in Eastern Europe and the Soviet Union, 13 February 1991.

39 *Okhrana Truda*, no. 9, 1989, p. 2.

40 V. Zakharov, *Trud*, 27 October 1989.

41 Interview with M. V. Ikharlova, *Trud*, 10 January 1990.

42 See pp. 64–65 (L. Shineleva).

43 Thus see Rimashevskaia and Golodenko, 'Sotsial'nie' 1990.

44 Tass report, *Survey of World Broadcasts*, 8 April 1991, p. 1.

45 See J. C. Shapiro, 'Unemployment' in R. W. Davies (ed.), *From Tsarism to NEP: Continuity and Change in the Economy of the USSR* (London: Macmillan, 1990).

46 TsGAOR, (Central Archive of the October Revolution, Moscow), *Fond* 5515, *Opis'* 17, *Delo* 189. This contains 131 (typed) pages of reports collated by the Cadres Administration summarising the results on the introduction of female labour into industry, for the period up to October 1932.

47 TsGAOR (Central Archive of the October Revolution, Moscow) Fond 5515, (Commissariat of Labour) *Opis'* 17, *Delo* 189, pp. 13–13 *ob.* (*verso*). Despite this, the overall number of women released in the factory turned out to be greater than the number of men. The inspector excused this by the note that there were many engineering jobs to which women could not be redeployed, where a single piece to be machined weighed 30–40 kilos. (*ibid.*, p. 13 ob.)

48 TsGAOR, *Fond* 5515, *Opis'* 17, *Delo* 189, p. 23.

49 TsGAOR, *Fond* 5515, *Opis'* 17, *Delo* 189, pp. 17, 23, 24, 50, for example, contrast planned and actual figures.

50 Tass, *Survey of World Broadcasts*, 17 January 1991, p. C1/12.

51 Panel on East European Social Policy, BASSEES Annual Conference, London, 7 April 1991.

52 'Sotsial'nie,' 1990, p. 101.

53 KZoT article 129, *Sbornik*, p. 403.

54 *Zhenshchiny v SSSR*, 1990, p. 6.

55 Liudmila Telen', *Sotsialisticheskaia Industriia*, 22 January 1988.

56 *Okhrana Truda*, 1989, no. 9, p. 3.

57 *Sobesednik*, 1988, no. 23, pp. 4–5.

58 Liudmila Telen', *Sotsialisticheskaia Industriia*, 22 January 1988.

59 *Okhrana Truda*, no. 9, 1989, p. 2.

60 *Pravda*, 11 May 1962.

61 L. Shineleva, 'Nuzhna gosudarstvennaia programma resheniia zhenskogo voprosa' *Sotsialisticheskii Trud*, no. 8, 1989, p. 63–4.

62 *Trud*, 14 September 1988.

63 The head of the Department on Conditions of Work of the State Committee on Labour, L. P. Sharikov, reported this in a discussion summarised in *Sotsialisticheskii Trud*, 1991, no. 3, p. 8.

64 *Sotsialisticheskaia Industriia*, 15 June 1989.

65 Shineleva, '*Nuzhna gosudarstvennaia*' p. 63.

66 *Trud*, 27 October 1989.

67 Boldyreva, *EKO*, 1988, no. 8.

68 To simplify somewhat, the centralised wage-setting system which prevailed in the USSR, general wage scales were set throughout a given industry, most recently at just six levels. Job evaluation at the enterprise level then assigned a given post to a given grade. See Alastair McAuley, *Women's Work and Wages in the Soviet Union* (London: Allen and Unwin, 1981), pp. 78–86 for more on the potentially arbitrary nature of this process and the way in which this can result in vertical discrimination against women workers. McAuley's estimate of an average 1.4 grade gap between men and women seems to be well confirmed by recent evidence (p. 81).

69 Boldyreva, *EKO*, 1988, no. 8, pp. 142–3.

70 *Vestnik Statistiki*, 1991, no. 2, p. 55.

71 In Filtzer, 'Labour process,' 1991.

72 *Sotsialisticheskaia Industriia*, 22 January 1988.

73 *Ekonomika i zhizn'*, no. 18, April 1991, p. 6.

Chapter 3

Women and agricultural reform

Sue Bridger

By the fifth winter of the Soviet Union's much-heralded programme of reform, television viewers the world over watched in bewilderment as the first parcels of food aid arrived from the West. Even a casual visitor to the USSR could scarcely remain unaware of the parlous state of the country's food supply. Bare shelves in state shops and widespread rationing of essential items have become an all-too-visible feature of city life. The bumper harvest of 1990 bore eloquent testimony to the chronic shortage of farmworkers across much of the European USSR. Summer witnessed a rash of appeals to city dwellers to get out on to the land and bring the harvest in. The familiar sight of broken machinery standing idle as crops rotted in the fields was joined by the more bizarre spectacle of well-known faces, among them Sergei Stankevich, radical deputy chair of the Moscow City Soviet, lugging sacks of potatoes to their waiting cars. The blame for this state of affairs certainly does not lie with the farmers alone. Where the land yields an abundant harvest, the country's crumbling infrastructure has proved itself once more unequal to the task of delivering the food from the farm to the table. As central authority breaks down in the USSR, the battalions of students and workers who could once be ordered into the fields to bring in the harvest now stay at home, resisting even the bribes of such a popular figure as Boris Yel'tsin.[1]

'People judge us by what they've got on the table', announced one rural deputy at the first session of the Congress of People's Deputies in May 1989.[2] Without a reliable and adequate food supply, no amount of international acclaim can ensure President Gorbachev the trust and approbation of the Soviet population. The people of the countryside, for so long exploited, commanded and ignored, are moving to centre stage in the unfolding drama of the USSR's transformation. Without a willing and able-bodied workforce, the initiatives of the past five years

39

are destined to be added to the list of miracle cures that failed to revitalise Soviet agriculture. As the economic crisis deepens there are, however, signs that the voices from the land are at last beginning to be heard.

The crisis on the land: the role of women

One-third of the Soviet population still lives in rural areas: an astonishingly high proportion by comparison with other developed countries. As might be expected in such a vast and diverse land as the Soviet Union, however, the size and, more importantly, the structure of the rural population varies dramatically from one region to another. Over the last thirty years the Central Asian republics have experienced a high rural birthrate and very low levels of out-migration. By contrast, migration to the cities has been intense in the Russian republic, the Ukraine, Belorussia and the Baltic republics. The Non-Black Earth Zone of the Russian republic, a vast belt of land stretching from the republic's western extremities to the Urals and including both Moscow and Leningrad Regions, has been particularly hard hit. The result is a chronic lack of young, able-bodied workers, ageing villages and effectively bankrupt farms. As Soviet agriculture remains far more labour intensive than that of other developed countries, the loss of young workers has proved catastrophic for the country's food supply.

In many respects the reasons for the loss of workers in farming have been similar to those in other industrialising societies: higher wages in the expanding factories, a standardised working day, and the lure of the city itself with its promise of a rich social life and the freedom of anonymity. In their bitter attacks on the past, however, politicians and rural commentators point to a peculiarly Soviet phenomenon which has increased disenchantment with life on the land. The destruction of peasant farming through forced collectivisation led to profound psychological as well as economic damage – the 'alienation of the peasant from the land', as Gorbachev himself has termed the process. The strict control exerted by the Communist Party over each individual process in the agricultural calendar removed even elementary decision-making from those engaged on the land, exacerbating their sense of grievance at what they saw as preferential treatment accorded city workers. 'I'd swap the city for the village with pleasure', an erstwhile agronomist wrote to the press recently, 'but I still can't see any future in it. As long as they go on telling us farmworkers when and how to plough the land, what, where and how to sow and harvest, then it's all useless.'[3] There is, however, a further and perhaps decisive factor in the high levels of rural out-migration in the more developed regions of the USSR: the attitude of women towards agricultural work and rural life.

Contrary to the popular image, very few women have ever driven tractors in the USSR except at the height of the Second World War. An intensive recruitment campaign together with preferential working conditions for women led to a marginal increase in numbers during the 1970s. It also provoked an enormous amount of resentment from male colleagues and managers, leading to many cases of harassment and constructive dismissal. At the peak of female recruitment during this decade women still formed less than 1 per cent of Soviet agricultural machine operators. Extremely long working hours during the busiest times of the year, excessive levels of vibration, dust and fumes and loss of earnings caused by constant mechanical breakdowns all added to the catalogue of woe reported by women attempting to break into this traditionally male domain. Opposition from colleagues was certainly not the only factor inducing women to give up the work, but it could often aggravate the rigours of the job: though legislation provided for women to be assigned the newest machines, they were regularly given some old wreck to work on in the hope that their ambitions would be rapidly stifled.

Interestingly enough, many of the women who succeeded in making a career of tractor or combine driving, whilst not minimising the very real problems the work entails, have insisted that it is still considerably less demanding than the quintessentially female job of dairying. As one of them put it, 'No-one makes us choose a "man's job" – but where are the "women's jobs" in the countryside?'[4] The evidence of female migration shows that most young women entirely agree with her.

In its current state of development, the countryside has very little to offer in the way of office jobs or work in the service sector, particularly in the health service or in child care which are major employers of women in the cities. With work on agricultural machinery effectively closed to them, girls with secondary education are left with the choice of seasonal unskilled manual labour in the fields, usually tending vegetables or sugar beet, or work with livestock. The relatively high pay which many state and collective farms have offered their women livestock workers, and especially dairy women, is not regarded by young women as a sufficient incentive to perform the most time-consuming job in the Soviet economy. The traditional system of milking cows three times a day in the Soviet Union established an exceptionally demanding work regime in dairying. Women work from before dawn until late at night with short breaks between milking sessions. Days off and holidays, always a rarity in this job, have dwindled still further as migration has exacerbated labour shortages. Even where cows are milked only twice a day, hours often remain long due to breakdowns in equipment and a lack of automated feeding and watering systems. In 1987, it was reported that some 200,000 dairy women in the USSR were still milking exclusively by hand.[5]

The modernisation of agriculture is, paradoxically, not providing skilled work in acceptable conditions for women, but instead pushing them out of farming altogether. Where fully automated dairy units have been constructed, the work is viewed as an extension of the machine operator's job and is regularly taken over by men. The national machine milking competitions, once the preserve of women and proudly reported by *Krest'ianka* (*Peasant Woman*) magazine each year, are now dominated by male prizewinners.

With opportunities for acceptable employment dwindling, girls leaving rural schools are no longer interested in responding to the kinds of patriotic campaigns which used to send some of them to bale out ancient and dilapidated dairy units. Instead, their eyes are fixed firmly on the city and, if possible, a higher education which will keep them well away from the land. However much this may disturb the nation's politicians, economists and farm managers, young people leaving the villages have for many years gone with the wholehearted blessing of their families. Teachers and Komsomol officials have long complained that parents protect their children from farm work and encourage them to seek their future in the city. Far from being mere perversity or, as it is sometimes characterised, peasant pride in having a child with a city profession, the major reason for this phenomenon lies in a deeply felt sense of bitterness and resentment at the harshness of rural life, expressed only in pressing their children to reject it utterly. The force of this silent protest is well illustrated in a piece which appeared in *Krest'ianka* in 1987:

My friend Valia lives in a small district town. At one time she was a well-known dairy woman in the region. Her ageing mother had literally driven her into the town and is now left on her own in the village. Valia hadn't wanted to go anywhere, she'd insisted, but without success. One day her mother had set down in the middle of the kitchen a bucket of freezing water which she had carried a great distance and stated, or rather shrieked, the one argument which to her was irrefutable, 'I don't want your hands to freeze! I've had enough!' She'd been a dairy woman for 25 years and in all that time had never had a day off sick, had never once had a holiday. And she held out to her daughter pieces of ice which she scooped out of the bucket by the handful, as if putting into this one protest all the pain of her life.[6]

The plight of the ageing villages, where perhaps a handful of elderly women struggle on alone, is a tragic reflection of the inevitable consequence of this process.

In a socialised system of agriculture, involvement in running the family farm – the job of many rural women in Western Europe – has not been an available option for Soviet rural women. In a society in which it has been taken for granted that virtually all women will be in paid employment, simply becoming a housewife does not present itself as an idea for serious consideration in European areas. In any event, if working conditions fail to attract young women, living conditions do little to compensate. Whilst stocks in city shops have dwindled alarmingly, letters to the press indicate that many basic essentials have completely disappeared from rural areas, necessitating constant trips to the cities for food and consumer goods. Rural health care again often means long journeys to see a doctor and empty shelves in the chemist. Most rural housing still lacks mains sanitation or a mains water supply, gas and electricity supplies may be inadequate or non-existent. A lack of hard-surface roads, in the Non-Black Earth Zone especially, make many villages virtually inaccessible in spring and autumn. For women, on whom the major responsibility for the home and the family's welfare continues to fall, there is little here to retain them on the land.

The consequences of the mass departure of young women from the villages appear to have been largely unforeseen. Where farms have modernised and men have been attracted by the skilled work on offer, the farms have been unable to retain them for long: the lack of women drives them into the cities. The phenomenon has become so widespread that it even has a name: the 'bride problem'. Village girls born and bred have been making it very clear that if marriage is all the countryside has to offer, there are more interesting prospects in the towns.

Early in the process of perestroika it was recognised that massive investment in the rural infrastructure, with no guarantee of any immediate return, would be essential for the establishment of a stable rural workforce to secure future food supplies. Mikhail Gorbachev, himself a product of the Russian village, clearly had considerable personal sympathy with the plight of the countryside and spoke of the debt society owed to rural people and the need to provide a real change in living and working conditions.[7] By 1989, rural commentators and representatives were becoming increasingly impassioned in their demands for radical change. Watching the piecemeal reintroduction of rationing and seeing its implications for an increasingly unstable country, the 417 rural deputies to the First Congress of People's Deputies made the following appeal:

We urgently demand that, from this Congress onwards, the country's economy should be rapidly and sharply directed towards meeting the needs of the countryside. In the next few years rural living conditions should be brought closer in line with urban conditions, the continued construction of large-scale industry should be sharply reduced, together with expenditure on defence, space exploration and other prestige projects. The further growth of cities should be halted and the urbanisation of the country stopped. The funds, materials and labour which are released should be poured into the improvement of peasant housing and farms, roads, schools, hospitals and the entire social sector.[8]

The deterioration in living standards experienced at a time of unprecedented freedom of expression brought demands for an end to the state monopoly on land ownership and a new Land Law confirming the rights of peasants to own land. To many of those who lived and worked on the land the reforms brought by perestroika were little more than half measures incapable of tackling the magnitude of the country-side's problems. To bring people back to the land and to keep them there, far more radical measures would be needed. Above all, change was simply not happening fast enough. Yet significant moves had been made under perestroika to come to the rescue of the countryside: the introduction of leasing and a growing campaign in the media to start migration back to the land were the most important developments. What did these reforms offer women? And would it be enough to reverse the results of the years of neglect?

Leasing contracts and the concept of family farm

Since 1988 leasing contracts have been strenuously promoted as the most rapid and effective method of raising agricultural productivity. The system was intended not merely as a means of reintroducing direct material incentives into farming, but as the key to reestablishing a sense of personal involvement and identity amongst rural dwellers in the future of the land: 'Everything depends on how quickly we can get people interested and get work organised in leasing and contract collectives, how far we can attract rural workers into this process to make the peasant the true master of the land.'[9] Gorbachev's words at the 19th Party Conference were to be constantly echoed in the press and on television. The term 'peasant' itself, for so long replaced by the more progressive-sounding expression 'collective farmer', was now taken down from the shelf and given a new coat of varnish: to be a peasant was to be proud and independent, close to the land, the hands that fed the nation.

In practical terms, the system involves the leasing of land, buildings, equipment and livestock from collective and state farms by families, individuals or groups. Lessees pay rents and take full responsibility for production. The output is marketed either through the farm or at the discretion of the leaseholder, according to the type of contract negotiated. The vast amount of publicity which the system received was intended to overcome both widespread ignorance and, more importantly, mistrust at responding to yet another initiative from the party responsible for farming's ills. The rural press and TV programmes such as Sel'skii chas (Rural Hour) were full of features on highly profitable operations by leaseholders. Livestock units, in particular, often showed a spectacular increase in productivity when taken over by leaseholders and, as a result, the financial rewards of leasing could be substantial: reports regularly cited a monthly personal income of around 400 roubles at a time when the national average wage stood at 190 roubles a month. At least as important for those who took on leasing contracts was the sense of independence from petty authority which clearly came as a breath of fresh air for many of the movement's pioneers: 'Being independent, that's the main incentive,' was the highly typical comment of one Moscow Region leaseholder. 'Nobody interferes. I'm my own boss.'[10]

Within a year of the 19th Conference it had become all too apparent that leasing was not destined to have mass appeal to those who worked on the land. Letters began to pour into the editorial offices of the national press describing the less rosy aspects of the system. Top of the list were complaints of powerlessness in the face of collective and state farm managers – the lessors with whom the contracts were signed. Leaseholders were discovering that their contracts were unenforceable, placing them at the mercy of their landlords. Problems in obtaining credit, machinery, additional land and, above all, their own profits properly accounted for, were making some give up and discouraging others. In a country where over 20 million are directly employed in agriculture, by 1990 there were only 20,000 peasant farms, most of these in the Baltic republics and Georgia. In Russia itself there were just over 1,000. As Vladimir Bashmachnikov, vice-president of the newly formed Association of Russian Peasant Farms and Cooperatives, summed up the situation:

We need to give back to the peasant not the *feeling of being boss*, as some journalists love to describe it, but *ownership itself*. Only then can they become a real boss when they can combine the characteristics of worker and owner. The leasing system that we talk so much about is no answer. If you like, it's a form of deception of the peasant. After all, conditions are dictated to the leaseholder by the lessor, and that's the same old collective farm or agro-industrial complex. There's nowhere for the leaseholder to turn. There's no choice.[11]

The thorny question of private land ownership continued to be a source of heated debate throughout 1990, even after its acceptance within strict limits by the Russian parliament in December.[12]

The experiment with leasing has proved to be a transitional phase in the retreat from socialised agriculture. As such, it has clearly failed to attract either men or women. Nevertheless, the experience of those successfully working these embryonic family farms provides some indication of what may await women intending to take on the peasant farms of the future. Reports on leaseholders, and especially those working as a family on livestock units, repeatedly indicate that a 16–18 hour working day is commonplace with very few days off. Leaseholders face the classic dilemma of the small business of being too busy to be ill, or to be able to stop when too tired to work effectively. Being almost literally tied to the farm and obliged to keep going at all costs may become the lot not only of adult workers but of the children too. The typical working day of an Estonian couple and their two daughters of 10 and 14 on their family farm was described in the press in early 1989:

They get up at 6 a.m. Mart takes their daughters to school whilst Rina prepares feed for the cows and pigs. Then they milk and feed the animals. In the growing season Mart is out in the fields on the tractor until lunchtime while Rina works around the house. In winter there are trips to sort out contractual relationships, market their output and buy spare parts and fuel. Mart doesn't fetch his daughters from school until half-past five. The girls have a heavy load too – despite the fact that they are away from home virtually the whole day, Maira and Merle don't sit around in the evenings but help to milk the cows and clean out the sheds. Then they do their homework. In summer the grown-ups' working day ends at 11 p.m. after the evening milking. The girls finish two hours earlier.[13]

The extremely long working day characteristic of livestock workers employed by state and collective farms appears, if anything, to be extended by working as a family unit. Often one or two families will be taking over units previously staffed by several workers. Inevitably, the work they do becomes more intensive, as one journalist recently found on a Latvian family farm:

I was simply mesmerised by the intensive rhythm of work of the Kaleis family – Yuris, Irina, their nine-year old daughter Natasha and Yuris's mother. There was no shouting or urging each other on, just calm, half-whispered businesslike conversations. It was like a small ant hill – movement backwards and forwards, the sweep of a pitchfork, the rumble of the tractor, the clang of the streams of milk against the bottom of the pail, the swish of a scythe in the nearby meadow, the banging of doors, the lowing of the cattle . . . so it went on until late in the evening when the whole family gathered for supper.[14]

As this extract so vividly suggests, family farming marks a return to the past in more ways than one. The lack of small-scale mechanisation which has characterised the development of leasing and family farming is a major factor in the fatigue often noted by commentators on these latest innovations in Soviet agriculture. Just as important is the sense that 'the buck stops here'. When the care of the livestock is the family's sole responsibility and provides its livelihood, family pressure undoubtedly makes itself felt to ensure that everyone pulls their weight. Already reports have appeared from those who have been involved in family contracts since their inception suggesting the degree of moral pressure which may be felt by family members, not merely on a day-to-day basis, but in terms of their whole future. As children grow up, the question of whether or not they will remain on the farm, helping their parents and ultimately taking over responsibility will certainly become more acute if the farm is actually owned by the family and not merely on lease. In its concern to tackle the desperate problems of today's agriculture, this is an issue perhaps wisely left unexplored by the Soviet press. Photographs of Maira and Merle, the two young daughters of the Estonian farming family are happily captioned, 'the future heirs'. What happens if their talents and inclinations prove to lie elsewhere than in manual labour from dawn till dusk is left for the reader to speculate. Without ready access to small-scale technology and a radically improved rural infrastructure, it is difficult to see how anything but a deep sense of obligation would be likely to induce the young women of the future to remain on their parents' land.

The 'back to the land' movement

Over the last decade, increasing attention has been paid to the realities of city living for migrants from the village. The notion of a better life awaiting those who move to the towns has been depicted as a particularly powerful piece of rural mythology in a series of films and press articles on the experiences of migrants. It is not only in the capital that young women face cramped conditions and the jobs on building sites and in factories rejected by young Muscovites. In provincial cities across the USSR women from the villages share dreary rooms in workers' hostels, live out of suitcases for years on end, even raise children, frequently on their own, within the same hostel walls. The documentary shots of peeling plaster, dripping washing done by hand, the signs proclaiming, 'No husbands allowed in after 10 p.m.' must be all too familiar to thousands of former village girls in pursuit of the bright lights.

By the early 1980s it was already appreciated by some Soviet sociologists and demographers that the rate of out-migration in certain areas had been so intense that, even if all future school-leavers were retained on the land, labour shortages would still continue to beset the farms.[15] Studies of the adaptation of rural migrants to city life carried out around this period suggested that a significant proportion of this group could prove a potentially rich source of workers for the farms, given appropriate inducements to return. It was, however, noted that young men were considerably more receptive to the idea than young women: they valued the 'peaceful, unhurried rhythm' of rural life, work in agriculture and the 'openness of everyday relationships'. Women, by contrast, were highly critical of rural life and had a very different perception of its realities, in particular the lack of services in the village and, especially, the lack of basic facilities in rural homes. For these same reasons women adapted more easily than men to life in the city.[16]

Nevertheless, in September 1986, the first in a series of campaigns was launched in the national press to recruit city dwellers for permanent work on the farms. The Non-Black Earth Zone, the most critical area of labour shortage, became the focus of media attempts to turn back the tide of migration. *Komsomol'skaia pravda*, the daily newspaper of the Communist youth organisation, began its feature, 'I am choosing to live in the country', appealing for young people to move to farms with chronic labour problems. At the same time, the magazine *Sel'skaia nov'* began its 'Migrant' information service, publishing appeals for new settlers directly from the farms themselves. Readers wanting to move to the countryside were invited to write in advertising their skills. *Komsomol'skaia pravda* received 50,000 letters in response to its campaign within the first six months. The efforts of both publications resulted in over 20,000 people moving into Non-Black Earth Zone villages in 1987 alone.[17]

At the same time, the press began to publish not only its dismal accounts of hostel life, but also a series of articles and letters from former villagers writing wistfully of their life on the land. The letters speak eloquently of a desire to get out of the bustle of city life, of their own mistake in leaving their native villages, of the need to have a place they can call their own, with a patch of land and clean air. Many of these letters wax lyrical in their reminiscences of a lost former life: 'You shouldn't uproot yourself from the earth you sprang from. I dream of daisy-filled meadows, of the rains, the first patches of earth when the snow thaws, a Russian stove, a cat purring on the wall ...'[18] The evocation of the rural idyll, in the face of the very obvious hardships of life on the land, has become a recurrent theme in the attempt to induce people to return.

In May 1987, *Krest'ianka* joined forces with the campaign to repopulate the countryside, but from a rather different angle. *Krest'ianka*'s opening feature on Staritsa District of Kalinin Region focused on the demographic impact of the shortage of women workers on the farms. Across the district as a whole, a mere handful of women had their pick of over 1,300 unmarried men under 26 – three of whom were pictured in full colour on the front cover of the magazine. The response to this piece was little short of astonishing. In the first three weeks after publication, the magazine received 9,000 letters from readers interested in moving to the district and a further 1,000 simply turned up unannounced in Staritsa itself. What they found on arrival was rather less enticing than the army of eligible men. Neglected villages and dilapidated dairy units, the very conditions which had driven the district's young women to the cities, were inevitably waiting to greet the new recruits. Many left immediately, others, perhaps more cunning, or perhaps genuinely not appreciating the difficulties, accepted the proffered housing and nursery places and then applied for lighter, cleaner work than dairying within a month of arrival.[19] Yet despite these setbacks, responses to *Krest'ianka*'s campaign continued to develop dramatically. It soon became evident that the magazine had struck a significant chord with women from the countryside.

The overall picture emerging from these various press campaigns has been difficult to assess. Economists analysing this new wave of migration into the villages of the Non-Black Earth Zone have noted that precise information on the successes and failures of the campaigns can only be gained at local level. What is clear is that a significant proportion – perhaps between a sixth and a third – of people moving into districts such as Staritsa leave again within the first twelve months.[20] Not merely difficult working conditions but, just as significantly, a frequent failure on the part of farms to provide adequate housing as promised have driven many people away. By 1990 *Sel'skaia nov'* had introduced a charge of 500 roubles for farms wishing to advertise for workers in its columns in an attempt to avoid further ill-considered appeals for labour.

Additional problems of adaptation arise where new migrants are city born and bred – up to a third of migrants into Staritsa District by 1989 fell into this category. Press and television reports have commented on the numerous responses to the migration campaigns received from city dwellers who have absolutely no concept of what agricultural work is like. Some have become pioneers of the leasing movement in the Non-Black Earth Zone and received considerable publicity. Yet city people may need a huge amount of assistance and advice to make a successful transition to life on the land: a frequently declared desire to 'be your own boss' or 'find yourself' in the slower pace of rural life may not be enough to withstand the rigours of the Soviet countryside in its current condition.

It is perhaps in offering something more personal than a house, a job and a nursery place that *Krest'ianka*'s campaign has been most successful. In developing its 'Service of Hope' from the original Staritsa feature, the magazine set out quite deliberately to tackle the 'bride problem', rather than more general labour shortages. Introducing the service, the magazine asked local women's councils, farms and officials to put together information on the demographic situation in their region so that the magazine could then provide its readers with addresses of places where women workers were particularly needed and 'where there's a real hope of marriage and a family'.[21] By the end of 1989, the magazine was reporting that 1,500 people had moved into Staritsa District alone at their instigation, the first weddings had taken place and no less than 480 children had been born.[22] So, despite the fact that the conditions they found were far from perfect, the prospect of finding personal happiness was enough to persuade a significant number of women to stay.

A survey of 500 migrants into Staritsa District over a two-year period from 1987 found that three-quarters of those under 29 were women. The survey unfortunately gives no indication as to their marital status, yet, on the basis of *Krest'ianka*'s postbag, it seems safe to assume that a considerable proportion were single parents. Within five months of the original Staritsa article, *Krest'ianka* noted that the 'overwhelming majority' of responses, both to the magazine and directly to the district, came from women looking for 'a husband for themselves and a father for their children'.[23] *Krest'ianka* made no bones about the fact that its 'Service of Hope' was designed to tackle complex social and economic problems simultaneously: to end farming's labour shortages, create new families and, in the process, provide a basis for the introduction of family farming:

It is high time that we recognised just how close the links are between demography and economics, especially these days. After all, in some areas family contracts don't 'take off' for the very reason that there are so few families, especially strong and happy ones. Whilst, at the same time, there are more than enough women with children who have been left without husbands. If family contracts are the way to raise productivity, strengthen the family and boost the birthrate, then how hurtful that must be for those who find that road firmly closed to them, perhaps forever, because they have no family.[24]

Whilst it is clear that such an ambitious aim is not likely to be achieved overnight, particularly given the problems which have beset land reform and the introduction of family farming, the linking of the two main arms of the reform programme appears particularly significant at a time of economic crisis and heightened social tension.

Women and the market: a retreat to the land?

With the advent of cost-accounting and self-financing into Soviet enterprises, the shake-out of surplus labour has already begun. In the absence of sex discrimination legislation, women, especially those with young children, have become prime targets for redundancy. Official estimates suggest that some 32 million workers, around a quarter of the Soviet workforce, are in redundant posts. Inevitably, even with the promise of a completely overhauled benefits system, it is single parents who will be hit the hardest by the loss of employment. Already it is becoming clear that it is this group of women who are the least likely to be offered redeployment and will experience the greatest difficulty in finding alternative work.[25]

It is in this climate that the campaigns to encourage migration back to the land are now operating. Agriculture remains one of the few major areas of labour shortage in the Soviet economy. Yet the conditions it can currently offer have become deeply unattractive to women. Those who have moved to the city to escape farmwork and rural isolation are now being asked to return to the very conditions they so comprehensively rejected not so long ago. Advertisements from farms asking for 'brave girls' or 'girls who are not afraid of difficulties' make it clear that times have not changed for the better in much of Soviet agriculture. Even private land ownership, if it finally becomes a reality, cannot of itself rectify the living and working conditions which drive so many away. Indeed, the lack of small-scale mechanisation on the new peasant farms may even serve to make matters worse before they get better. So how realistic is it to expect women to return to the land?

Much, inevitably, will depend on conditions in the cities. If the economic crisis deepens, as expected, galloping inflation, chronic and persistent food shortages, unemployment and a hopelessly inadequate benefits system may well make a return to the land appear a very different prospect. For single mothers, in particular, the prospect of work, however hard, the opportunity to grow food for their children and a far greater potential for remarriage than the city can offer may come as a considerable relief. It is perhaps not too fanciful to suggest that psychological factors may play a decisive role: rediscovering rural roots and retreating into the family may appear highly desirable in a period of economic chaos, political uncertainty and increasing social tension. Providing the food the cities so desperately need may eventually bring a new generation of rural women the status and dignity they have lacked for so long. In the short term, as with so many of the USSR's problems, there are no easy answers. It will undoubtedly be many years before the countryside can offer young women, in particular, a future they will be happy to embrace.

NOTES

1 The Russian government, under its President, Boris Yel'tsin, offered special 'Harvest 90' vouchers to townspeople assisting with the harvest. The vouchers could be redeemed for goods in short supply, though there was evidently a lack of confidence that these goods actually existed.

2 *Izvestiia*, 1 June 1989, p. 8.

3 Mikhail Kaplunov, 'Vernulsia by v selo, no ...', *Sel'skaia nov'*, 8, 1989, p. 36.

4 N. Korina, 'O traktore i o sebe', *Krest'ianka*, 8, 1987, p. 16.

5 Liudmila Semenycheva, 'Za spinu rukovoditelia ne spriachesh'sia', *Kres-*

t'ianka, 1, 1987, p. 17. See also Susan Bridger, *Women in the Soviet Countryside* (Cambridge, Cambridge University Press, 1987), pp. 47–59.

6 Ol'ga Morozova, 'Iz derevni ili v derevniu?', *Krest'ianka*, 11, 1987, p. 12.

7 See, for example, Gorbachev's address to the 19th Party Conference, *Izvestiia*, 29 June 1988, p. 2.

8 *Izvestiia*, 1 June 1989, p. 9.

9 *Izvestiia*, 29 June 1988, p. 2.

10 *Sel'skii chas*, Channel 1 Soviet Television, 14 August 1988.

11 Aleksandr Rebel'skii, 'Udastsia li sokrushit' bastiony?', *Sel'skaia nov'*, 9, 1990, p. 7.

12 The drafting and consideration of new legislation on land tenure have been fraught with difficulty. The long-awaited USSR laws on land and ownership, approved in early 1990, failed to give the green light to private ownership of land and, later in the year, Gorbachev himself came out strongly against private land ownership. Nevertheless, in December 1990 the parliament of the Russian Republic reached a compromise decision allowing ownership rights but with limitations on sale. A Russian State Committee on Land Reform has been set up to implement the new law in the face of the expected local opposition.

13 Iurii Govorukhin, 'Stepen' svobody', *Sel'skaia nov'*, 2, 1989, p. 15.

14 Iurii Govorukhin, 'Stanovlius khutorianinom', *Sel'skaia nov'*, 1, 1990, p. 5.

15 See, for example, V. I. Perevedentsev, 'Migratsiia naseleniia i razvitie sel'skokhoziaistvennogo proizvodstva', *Sotsiologicheskie issledovaniia*, 1, 1983, pp. 54–61.

16 N. V. Evteeva, 'Kto i pochemu vozvrashchaetsia v selo', *Sotsiologicheskie issledovaniia*, 2, 1987, pp. 62–3; A. F. Ialalov, 'Adaptatsiia sel'skikh migrantov k gorodskomu obrazu zhizni', *Sotsiologicheskie issledovaniia*, 4, 1982, p. 115.

17 R. T. Nasibullin, 'Chitatel'skie pis'ma v redaktsiiu 'Komsomol'skoi pravdy' kak istochnik informatsii o dvizhenii naseleniia', *Sotsiologicheskie issledovaniia*, 5, 1987, p. 75.

18 *Krest'ianka*, 7, 1988, p. 7.

19 Valentin Sergeev, 'Nadezha', *Krest'ianka*, 10, 1987, p. 19.

20 Vladimir Trubin, 'V derevniu na zhitel'stvo – s nadezhdoi!', *Sel'skaia nov'*, 9, 1989, pp. 13–16.

21 Sergeev (1987), p. 21.

22 *Krest'ianka*, 11, 1989, p. 10.

23 Sergeev (1987), p. 21.

24 *Ibid.*

25 Igor' Bestuzhev-Lada, 'Torzhestvennyi marsh na meste', *Nedelia*, 23, 1988, pp. 9–10; Nadezhda Menitskaia, 'Ne khochu byt' bezrabotnoi!', *Rabotnitsa*, 7, 1989, pp. 10–12.

Chapter 4

Political reform

Mary Buckley

Political reform in the USSR had two immediate consequences for women's political activity outside the home: a drastic fall in the percentage of women elected to the soviets; and the emergence of an enormous range of women's informal groups.

The large reduction in the number of female people's deputies has prompted a great deal of soul searching among those committed to political roles for women, even though they are aware that in the past the high percentages of women on the soviets never indicated political power for women. Women deputies had always suffered from a higher turnover than their male counterparts and generally held politically unimportant posts, unlike male deputies.[1] Nevertheless, since 1989, the Soviet Women's Committee, women's groups and women's magazines have been debating whether quotas of female representation should be reinstated to guarantee women a political voice. And why, they frequently ask, had Western women like Margaret Thatcher, Benazir Bhutto and Corazon Aquino actively pursued political careers while many Soviet women still hesitated to try? What was stopping them? Kazimera Prunskene, Prime Minister of Lithuania until her resignation in January 1991, was viewed as a rare exception. The fact that Thatcher, Bhutto and Aquino were rare exceptions, too, was generally glossed over.

The formation of numerous women-only groups has meant that, for the first time in Soviet history, women are organising 'from below' around various concerns, without being told by the CPSU what they should be doing and why. But there is no unified women's movement. Different women have different goals; some activists describe themselves as feminists, others insist that they are not. Some groups are committed to economic reform and to democratisation, while others oppose a market economy and wish to see the 'leading and guiding' role

54

of the CPSU reinstated, not eroded. Many outside Russia are nationalists, but their concerns often vary. Women in *Rukh* in the Ukraine
embrace green issues, and some of them support feminism, whereas
women in Sajudis in Lithuania emphasise the importance of traditional
family life. While some women wish to promote religion, others
distance themselves from proselytizing. Some women's groups see
themselves as political, others prefer to describe their activities as
'social'. Some want to set up crisis centres, others aim to promote
zhenskoe nachalo (the feminine principle) in literature and in society.
Mothers and wives in various republics have organised around the
specific issue of trying to prevent their sons being sent to keep order in
troublespots wracked by nationalist unrest. Estonian, Latvian and
Lithuanian women want their sons to serve in Baltic armies on Baltic
territory. Likewise, the Committee of Ukrainian Mothers wants con-
scripts to stay in the Ukraine. Other women's groups pursue philanth-
ropic goals. The result is a vast heterogeneity of women's groups. While
women's role in conventional political arenas is less visible than before,
in small informal groups it is quietly growing, amid various degrees of
opposition from men.

The objects of this chapter are fourfold; first, to discuss the significance of electoral reform for women not just at the centre of Soviet
politics in Moscow, but also in the republics; second, to introduce
'new' arguments about women's political roles which, helped by the
growing strength of glasnost pre-dated the election results but were
subsequently fuelled by them; third, to provide an indication of the
span of activities currently pursued by women-only groups set up 'from
below'; and fourth, rather more generally, to assess how evolving
political agendas affect women, or reflect their concerns, and to
consider how women can best, if at all, influence these agendas.

Electoral reform

In December 1988 the Supreme Soviet passed a new electoral law
which ushered in 'active' voting for citizens, thereby ending the much
joked about system of the past in which voters could vote for one
candidate only. In elections to the Congress of People's Deputies in
March 1989, the people, in 1,116 out of 1,500 constituencies enjoyed a
choice of candidate. A minor experiment in free choice in elections had
taken place in 1987, but only 1 per cent of constituencies were
involved. The elections of 1989, therefore, represented a radical change
from the past, even though *demokratizatsiia* had failed to reach 384

constituencies, where only one candidate was nominated.[2] Then, in 1990, came elections to the Supreme Soviets of the republics and to the local soviets, the results of which, particularly in the Baltic states, exhilarated nationalists, who hoped for independence from Moscow. Women, however, fared badly in both the elections of 1989 and 1990. Throughout the fifteen republics, at all levels, fewer women were returned than in the past.

The new Electoral Law specified that the new Congress of People's Deputies would have 2,250 seats. Of these, 750 would come from local constituencies spread across the whole country and divided according to roughly equal populations. A second 750 would be chosen in constituencies broken down according to republic to ensure the representation of nationalities. Thus each citizen would have two votes. A third set of 750 deputies would be selected by social organisations. Effectively, these amounted to 'saved' seats. The CPSU and trade unions, for instance, each enjoyed 100. The Komsomol, zhensovety and other organisations had 75.[3] Many criticised these as undemocratic. But their significance for women was that the Soviet Women's Committee could put forward 75 women nominated by the zhensovety to be sent to the Congress of People's deputies. Yet this protection for women did not prevent a huge fall in female representation.

In fact, most social organisations, apart from the Soviet Women's Committee, chose men not women. Out of 168 scientific workers nominated by the USSR Academy of Sciences for its own internal second ballot, just three were women. But not one of these was chosen by the Academy's Presidium for the Congress of People's Deputies. Although 74 per cent of teachers were women, the Academy of Pedagogical Science and the Soviet Association of Pedagogical Researchers selected three men and one woman. Similarly, despite the fact that 66 per cent of doctors were women, of the ten mandates reserved for the Academy of Medical Science, just two were for women. A higher 23 per cent of the places reserved for official trade unions went to women – but women made up 51 per cent of Soviet workers. The CPSU gave 12 per cent of its seats to women, yet this was at a time when they comprised 29 per cent of party members. The proportion of women chosen as deputies by social organisations generally understated, quite radically, their presence within that organisation. And the percentage of women registered as candidates for election in all other local and national-territorial constituencies amounted to just 16.6 per cent.[4] Women were often reluctant to stand and others were hesitant to nominate them.

Table 4.1. *Number of women elected in 1989 to the Congress of
People's Deputies and to the Supreme Soviet*

	Number of women deputies	Percentage of women among all deputies
People's deputies	352	15.7
Supreme Soviet:	100	18.5
(i) Council of the Union:	44	16.2
(ii) Council of Nationalities:	56	20.7

Source: Zhenshchiny v SSSR: 1990 (Finansy i statistika, 1990, p. 21)

Just 352 women sat on the new Congress of People's Deputies,
amounting to 15.7 per cent of all deputies. A smaller Supreme Soviet of
542 was chosen from this larger Congress, of whom 100, or 18.5 per
cent, were female, compared with 32.8 per cent in 1984. Male representation increased from 67.2 to 81.5 per cent.[5] The Supreme Soviet is
divided into two chambers, the Soviet of the Union and the Soviet of
Nationalities. Table 4.1 shows that 44 women are members of the
former and 56 of the latter, amounting to 16.2 per cent and 20.7 per
cent of deputies respectively.

This fall in female representation was initially met with two
responses. Some argued that it was better for active women to take on
political roles than the old 'yes-women' of the past who always voted as
the leadership expected them to and rarely took independent initiatives. Fewer energetic women were preferable to a higher percentage of
hesitant ones.[6] Within a year this position sounded rather hollow.
Many female deputies still seemed reluctant to speak out or to assert
themselves in policy debate. There were exceptions, such as Galina Sta-
rovoitova, but the issue now shifted to how best to boost women's confidence in political arenas. Another response to the election results was
a deep regret at the much smaller proportion of women deputies, giving
rise to discussions about how to ensure that the same pattern did not
result in subsequent elections in the republics. In an attempt to deter a
repeat performance, the Soviet Women's Committee issued an 'Appeal
to Voters', published in daily newspapers, which called on citizens to
overcome their reluctance to nominate women as candidates. It asked
the media to give women candidates positive coverage and suggested
that the zhensovety should back women candidates through special
political campaigns.[7] Election results, however, were again bleak.

Female representation on the local soviets came crashing down from an average of 50 per cent to 35 per cent in Latvia, 34 per cent in Lithuania, 30 per cent in Kazakhstan, 29 per cent in Moldova, 25 per cent in Turkmenia and 23 per cent in Estonia. Thus women's presence on the local soviets declined by as much as 27 per cent. Similarly, women's presence on the Supreme Soviets of the republics fell from an average of 35 per cent to just under 15 per cent in Uzbekistan, 11 per cent in Turkmenia, 7 per cent in the Ukraine and in Belorussia, 5.4 per cent in the RFSFR to just 4.8 per cent in Moldova.[8] 'Saved' seats had been abolished in all but two republics on the grounds that they were undemocratic. This reinforced the decline in female representation.

These results provoked the anxiety that women's interests would be less seriously considered by parliaments than they had been in the past, notwithstanding the fact that numerous issues relevant to women's lives, such as the poor conditions in abortion clinics and the lack of contraception, had been ignored before. Concern about fewer women deputies fed into fresh arguments that had already begun to be aired in 1988 about the serious lack of women in the Soviet political leadership. Without glasnost and the additional boost given to it by the 19th Party Conference of 1988, these 'new' views may never have been openly expressed in public arenas.

Glasnost and women's political roles

In 1986 and 1987, glasnost prompted numerous critical articles on issues that affected women, such as poor working conditions, single parenthood, the lack of contraception, the humiliations of the abortion system and prostitution. It was not, however, until 1987, 1988 and 1989 that glasnost was wielded in damning remarks about the extremely low profile of women in top political jobs. Comments were directed at male domination of the CPSU, at the low number, generally, of women in ministerial positions and in top administrative posts, and subsequently at the poor election results.

At the All-Union Conference of Women held in Moscow in January 1987 Zoia Pukhova, then the new Chair of the Soviet Women's Committee (until 1991 when she was voted out and replaced by her deputy Alevtina Fedulova), observed that 'Women make up 7 per cent of party secretaries of obkoms and kraikoms, even though 29 per cent of party members are women'.[9] Men's upward mobility in the party was more successful than women's. Larisa Kuznetsova, in piercing journalism, noted a year later that: 'when we want to take part in

decision-making we are just "ladies". Otherwise, how is it that our
women workers – 51 per cent of the total employed – do not produce
professional politicians or stateswomen?' She added, 'the entire top
echelon is male, while women basically follow their orders: they are
yes-women'.[10] Soon after, *Sovetskaia Zhenshchina* (*Soviet Woman*)
carried an article entitled 'The right to decide' which regretted that 'In
all the socialist countries without exception the situation can be
presented in the form of a pyramid with a wide foundation. The higher
the echelon of power, the lower the representation of women.'[11]
Moscow News joined in the criticisms, noting 'restructuring has barely
affected the situation of Soviet women. During the 1970s and 1980s,
10 women have served as Prime Ministers around the world, and
several hundred more have headed government ministries ... in our
country woman very rarely holds the rank of Minister at the national
level'.[12] At a Plenum of the Soviet Women's Committee held in
October 1988, Pukhova argued that few women reached leading
positions because they received poor preparation lower down the
system which meant that there was not a pool from which to draw:

Let's take the example of Gosagroprom. Here women make up 2 per cent of
leaders and 8.5 per cent of main specialists. And where can they be taken from
if in practically every region of the country among economic leaders there is
just a handful of women. For example, in Altai territory out of 740 chairper-
sons of collective farms and state farms, there are only three women. And in
Lipetskii region – three. In Tadzhikistan also three. What a magic figure![13]

Pukhova regretted that social consciousness about women's roles has
still not changed.

These criticisms were all warranted. They were not, however,
allowed to be voiced so bluntly before glasnost. Khrushchev had noted
the low upward political mobility of women at the 20th Party Congress
in 1956 and Gorbachev had regretted it, too, at the 27th Congress in
1986, at the January Plenum of the Central Committee in 1987 and at
the 19th Party Conference in 1988.[14] But for most of the history of the
Soviet state, ideology and journalism loudly praised the thousands of
Soviet women engaged in politics, equal with men. Rarely were
comparative statistics cited, indicating with precision the huge gap
between the sexes in politics. The picture in 'high politics' was rather
bleak but never vigorously contested. Instead, ideology trumpeted the
high percentage of women on the soviets, in comparison with Western
parliaments, and suggested that male politicians defended women's
rights anyway since the USSR was a socialist society.

The political profile of women has always been relatively low in the powerful CPSU. In 1989 women made up 53 per cent of the population, but just 29 per cent of party members. The second woman ever to sit on the Politburo (Aleksandra Biriukova) was only named to it in 1988 in a non-voting capacity, thirty years after the first woman on the Politburo (Ekaterina Furtseva) had been removed from it after a short tenure of three years. Galina Semenova became the third woman to join the Politburo in 1990 when the 28th Party Congress resulted in a mass resignation of old Politburo members, including Biriukova. Semenova, however, remains the sole woman on this body.

Over the last ten years the percentage of women on the Central Committee has hovered between a mere 3.8 and 4.6.[15] The picture on the less powerful soviets has been quite different because fixed quotas of representation decided 'from above' ensured a much larger female presence. By the mid-1980s, women made up 32.8 per cent of deputies on the All-Union Supreme Soviet, an average of 35 per cent of deputies on republic level Supreme Soviets and 50.3 per cent of deputies on local soviets.[16] This presence, as already mentioned, is no longer guaranteed since quotas fixed 'from above' have been abolished in most republics and, in any case, failed to guarantee women many seats on the Congress of People's Deputies.

Before the 1989 elections, members of the Soviet Women's Committee were becoming edgy about a possible fall in women's representation. At the 1988 Plenum of the Committee, Pukhova explained how the new system would work and asked 'Are we ready for this?'[17] She encouraged the zhensovety to work with women candidates and with voters, suggesting: 'We must put forward the most active and resolute, able to defend the interests of women.'[18] Women able to compete well with other candidates should be found. Pukhova urged the zhensovety to take initiative: 'the zhensovety must not sit and wait for orders from above, but must actively apportion the preparation for the election campaign through all channels – the press, radio, television, meetings – to start to prepare society to support their candidates'.[19] In an interview with Pukhova in Moscow in June 1990 she told me that, in fact, the zhensovety had worked 'badly' in the election campaigns.

The new elections highlighted several problems for women's political representation. First, women were much less likely to be nominated to stand as candidates than men, and were also probably less eager to be put forward. Second, many voters expressed the view that they would rather vote for men. Alevtina Fedulova, when still first deputy chair of the Soviet Women's Committee, told *Izvestiia* that research showed that women candidates were seen by voters as among 'the least desirable'.[20] Third, those women who did stand could have benefited from better-run campaigns (a point relevant to male candidates too). As a result, the Plenum of the Soviet Women's Committee held in November 1989 debated these and other issues. Various views were aired. There were regrets that many regions and territories did not really bother to put women candidates forward for the 75 'saved' seats for the zhensovety.[21] There was support for the view that 'we must create for our candidates support groups which include sociologists, psychologists and journalists'.[22] The Congress of People's Deputies also came under fire: 'With great regret neither at the Congress of People's Deputies, nor at the sessions of the Supreme Soviet not one woman question has been tabled and not one solved.'[23] Many subscribed to the view that special quotas for female representation should exist, not along the old Soviet lines, but following the example of some Western states. There appeared to be some confusion, however, about how different parties in the West attempted to put forward female candidates and how this affected final legislative outcomes. A year later, Tat'iana Khudiakova writing in *Izvestiia* stressed the same point, indicating growing popularity among women for quotas of representation. 'Guaranteed quotas in election organisations and in higher organs of power', she argued, would help to increase women's participation in politics. These were not the 'sad' old quotas that guaranteed women one-third of the seats on the soviets, nor 'ladies' subterfuge', but rather 'a generally accepted world practice'. 'In the parliaments of the developed countries', she continued, 'and in a great number of ruling parties, a guaranteed number of seats are reserved for women. This is the root of the feminization of world politics.'[24] Rather an overstatement of political reality, her argument nevertheless showed a concern on the part of Soviet women to win legitimacy for the idea of quotas not from the stagnant Soviet past, but from Western arenas, now viewed as more credible.

Various opinions about the political significance of the zhensovety were also aired at the Plenum of the Soviet Women's Committee. One held that because they were organised 'from above', they could not become genuine women's mass organisations. Another maintained that, on the contrary, they were formed 'from below' by women and for women.[25] Genia Browning's chapter analyses their role in detail. They are worth mentioning here, however, since their place in women's political activity is controversial. The Soviet Women's Committee, at the apex of the zhensovety, had, 'from above' assigned them the task of promoting women candidates. But many women failed to take the zhensovety seriously and preferred to set up their own informal groups to tackle issues not necessarily connected with elections. By 1991, it was clear that some zhensovety were formal and inert, whereas others were relatively dynamic and in the process of redefining their purpose.

Independent women's groups

Gorbachev's policy of *demokratizatsiia* allowed groups and movements independent of the CPSU to form. Although women's groups were slow to emerge in comparison with broader popular fronts and nationalist movements, by 1991 many had sprouted around an enormous range of concerns. They fell into five main categories: first, those which formed women's sections within broader nationalist movements, already in existence; second, women-only political groups or parties; third, professional women's groups; fourth, women-only consciousness-raising groups; and fifth, women's self-help groups.

Some women who were already members of nationalist movements decided to meet separately from male nationalists in order to address issues specific to women which they felt larger, mixed-sex meetings ignored. Solomea Pavlychko in chapter 6 discusses the women's group of Rukh in the Ukraine. Women members of Sajudis in Lithuania also organised separately. They were concerned, in particular, to contest the political indoctrination received by their children in schools, which they saw as imposed by Russian domination. Describing themselves as not a feminist movement (but probably not aware of the different strands of Western feminism and reacting more against a stereotype than a reality), they championed independence for Lithuania, an enhanced status for mothers and a serious overhaul of the education system.[26] When I spoke to representatives of the group in March 1989 they believed that men in Lithuania should conduct political struggle for independence whilst women should make beautiful homes for the new sovereign state.

Women-only political groups or parties became established a little later. In 1990, for instance, the Christian Democratic League of Women of Moldavia formed. Its aim was to draw women 'irrespective of nationality and belief, into activity for the spiritual rebirth and democratisation of society'. Its members believed that 'a primitive understanding of emancipation as equal rights for men and women' had resulted in 'a hidden form of exploitation of women' and had brought 'harm' to society. They argued that society would benefit from

greater recognition of differences between men and women. Democratisation, however, was also one of their official goals.[27] By contrast,
those who organised around 'Women for a socialist future for our
children' wanted to see the CPSU retain a leading role in society. They
held a three-day conference in 1990 in Kuibyshev, rallying around the
motto 'I want to see the Motherland happy' ('*Khochu videt' Rodiny
schastlivoi*'). The main organiser and group leader was L. Morunova, a
mother of several children. This group opposed a market economy for
the USSR and wished to defend women from the threat of unemployment. Polozkov, the hard-line leader of the Russian Communist party,
expressed his support for them.[28]

Different again is the United Party of Women (*Edinaia partiia
zhenshchin*) which registered in Leningrad. Its main task is to prevent
the exclusion of women from participation in discussions about the
future of the country. Vera Kuril'chenko, leader of the party, declared
that 'our organisation expresses the strong spirit of women'. Through
promoting women candidates in elections, the United Party of Women
hoped to encourage 'personal dignity and responsibility for peace,
progress, culture, the rights of women and ecology'.[29] These three
examples of women-only political groups illustrate their diversity.

Further variety is found among women's professional groups which
were set up a little earlier. These include the Federation of Women
Writers within the Writers' Union, the Association of Women Scholars,
the Club of Women Journalists and the Union of Women Cinemato-
graphers. Unlike the nationalist women or women-only political
groups, these gatherings grew around narrower work concerns.
However, their aims were not necessarily narrow ones. The founding
conference of the Federation of Women Writers declared its commitment to confirming the 'feminine principle' (*zhenskoe nachalo*) in
society and in literature, to changing the climate of society, to affirming
the feminine principle in writing and, finally, to strengthening relations
among women writers. Although their main creative activity was
writing, these women nevertheless felt that women writers had a duty
to transform society through feminine values.[30]

Smaller feminist groups constitute a fourth category of women's
political activity. Ol'ga Lipovskaia describes these in the next chapter.
They are more common in large urban areas, but are beginning to fan
out into smaller towns. Initially, they lacked ties with each other, but
these are now growing. Meetings in Moscow in 1990 and in Dubna,
just outside Moscow, in 1991, attempted to draw them together.
Awareness of discrimination against women unites these groups.

Different views about suitable strategies to address discrimination divide them. Numerous meetings are likely in future years, as are disagreements, controversies and splits. Although it is premature to analyse the new feminism in the USSR, it is worth stressing that its style, content and aspirations remain predictably distinct from the several strands of Western feminism.[31] This was also the case in the nineteenth century and in the late 1970s.[32]

Alongside these more overtly political groups have emerged various self-help groups, such as 'Women for Social Renewal' (*Zhenshchiny za sotsial'noe obnovlenie*). This group became officially registered in September 1989. Its goal was to bring about 'radical changes in the social status of woman and her role in the life of modern society', by encouraging women to develop self-respect and dignity. The underpinning philosophy was that women should help themselves and take initiative in order to improve their own economic, social and political position.[33]

With this end in mind, Women for Social Renewal advertised a competition for the best women's social initiative. One winning idea was the setting up of a crisis centre to give moral, psychological and material support to poor women who might otherwise sink into lives of alcoholism and drug addiction and reject their children. They applauded another crisis centre being set up with the backing of the Soviet executive committee of *Oktiabr'* district in Moscow in order to help women whose jobs were being taken over by the new technology. Members of Women for Social Renewal hope that these centres will spread by example. They are also seeking advice from those with work experience in crisis centres in Italy. The group, therefore, looks outside the USSR for inspiration. They have set up a 'woman's fund' to help finance various crisis centres, giving special backing to a centre to help single parents, whether mothers or fathers.[34]

In a similar spirit, when Russian women refugees left Azerbaidzhan, Women for Social Renewal liaised with other organisations giving material and medical help. They are also examining how children's homes are run and have distributed a questionnaire with a view to improving them. A completely different project adopted by Women for Social Renewal is the production of cheap and fashionable clothes for women and children. They voice special approval for the 'theatre of children's clothes', already set up by the director Liubov' Grechishchikova.[35]

Financial help for the activities of Women for Social Renewal has come from the new cooperative sector. At the outset, a construction

firm agreed to donate a portion of its profits to help the group get off
the ground. They then gave financial advice about how the women
themselves could enter the business world in order to be self-financing.
The women subsequently set up a firm, *Tvorchestvo* (Creativity) and
became involved in four other small firms. They have an interest, for
example, in a firm called *Briz* in Nizhni Novgorod which makes garden
sheds and children's play areas. In Latvia they are involved in a firm
which makes ecologically sound products.[36]

In sum, Women for Social Renewal is an entrepreneurial group,
pursuing diverse projects which cater to different aspects of women's
lives. By comparison, the women's group of Sajudis is more focused,
directing attention at improving selected aspects of the lives of Lithuanian women. Various groups of Soldiers' Mothers in the Ukraine
and in the Baltic States also have very specific goals – to demand that
troops serve only within their own republic and that killings and
brutality within the army be investigated. Ol'ga Lipovskaia's work in
Leningrad is different again, devoted mainly to producing the journal
Zhenskoe Chtenie which translates Western feminist writings and
provides expressive comments on personal themes such as maternity,
male/female relations and lesbianism. Women's professional groups
have very clearly defined memberships, but their goals can embrace
radical transformations of society at large.

Despite the recent proliferation of women's groups, many Soviet
women are unaware of them, or unsure about how to become involved.
The women's magazine *Rabotnitsa* (*Working Woman*) claims to
receive many letters in the following vein: 'All this is very good: a
women's movement, personal self-awareness. I would, of course, with
joy become involved in this work. But I do not know how, or with
whom to talk.'[37] Others complain 'Our economic level' prevents Soviet
woman from taking advantage of democratisation because 'she devotes
all her strength to the elementary survival of her family.'[38]

For many women the tiring problems of *byt* (daily life) are para-
mount. Queuing for food, especially at a time of sharp shortages,
takes up a great deal of time. In this context, many women lack the time
to become involved in politics. And frequently the inclination is lacking
because many do not believe that their lives will improve as a result.
Over and over again in the USSR, women say 'our lives cannot get
better until the economy improves'. So political activity for many
remains a self-indulgent luxury. As consumers and shoppers, women
are worn down by a system which makes these roles extremely difficult
to perform efficiently. By 1990, the increasing scarcity of food,

especially in Moscow and Leningrad, topped with rationing and rumours of impending famine, made women feel increasingly helpless in a system unable to deliver basic necessities. This feeling intensified after sharp price increases in April 1991.

Evolving political agendas

Soviet political agendas between 1985 and 1989 offered women brief hope of economic improvement and greater democracy. The 27th Party Congress in 1986 had stressed the former and the 19th Party Conference of 1988 pushed for the latter. But, by 1990, reality had delivered failed economic reform and increasing political chaos. As consumers women felt cheated. Even bread, the symbol of successful agriculture, disappeared from Moscow's shops for three days in September 1990. By December, milk was hard to come by in some districts of the capital. Food could be bought more easily in private markets, but at prohibitive prices. The cooperative sector offered restaurants out of the reach of most purses, and more stylish clothing. But a predictable supply of food was lacking. Sharp price increases in 1991 left many women stunned, anxious about how they could best feed their children. Political reform did not appear promising either. Not only had female representation fallen, but female people's deputies seemed reluctant to speak out to defend women's interests.

The proliferation of new movements and parties often seemed to offer women little, since many of their programmes ignored women's issues or suggested that women should be allowed to return to the home. This led to such consternation at the Soviet Women's Committee that representatives of new groups and parties were invited for discussions to explain how they viewed the 'woman question'.[39] New movements gave women political outlets for activity, but did not necessarily promise new policies for women. The results of surveys suggested that women felt powerless to influence high politics. Writing in *Izvestiia*, Galina Sillaste cited one survey (as is often the case, without sample size or selection procedures) which reported that only 6 per cent of women felt they could influence policy of the country as a whole, 8 per cent believed they could influence policies in their republic and 10 per cent considered they could have an impact on the policies of their territory or region. Optimism increased at the local level: 20 per cent of women believed they could affect the policies of their town or district; a larger 50 per cent felt confident about shaping the decisions of their work collectives and 60 per cent their workplace. Sillaste concluded that 'Democratisation and glasnost have not led to substantial change for the better in the position of women. In addition, their alienation from power has intensified.'[40]

In this context, the Soviet Women's Committee is attempting to educate more women into political roles. As Fedulova put it in May 1991, 'If women do not enter politics, policy will not change. We need to find women who are willing to be politicians.'[41] To be successful political actors, Fedulova believed women should display their knowledge, be confident and possess the ability to argue well. A *politklub* within the Soviet Women's Committee had been set up to develop these skills among women. Women from different parties were invited to attend its meetings. The general aim was to build women leaders. The Committee was also organising a 'School for Women Leaders' with the help of Finnish sponsors. Finns would give lectures on various topics geared to organising for the next elections.

The role of the Soviet Women's Committee is clearly changing due to political and economic pressures. At its conference due to be held at the end of 1991, brought forward from 1992, it will adopt a new charter after debate about its changing function and new strategies. But women in independent groups criticise it as a conservative organisation, as a product of the communist past, and as attempting to maintain its monolithic grip over fresh women's groups with all the financial and organisational advantages of the CPSU itself. Fedulova objects to these criticisms. 'I am a realist', she stressed in 1991. 'New groups exist and we do not wish to control them. Those who want to work with us, please join us. Others will go their own way.'[42] With one-third of its budget slashed, the Soviet Women's Committee is currently searching for sponsors to finance its various projects. Help has already been found to fund open lectures on business. Dutch and Australian sponsorship has been forthcoming for courses to train businesswomen. The Committee's own Business Club for Women also hopes to instruct women how to compete in new markets.

Despite these activities, many of the 'new' feminists, who are also active in promoting courses to draw women into business, either dismiss the Soviet Women's Committee as a prop of the old system, or criticise it for its already developed institutional base and budget – an advantage it enjoys over new groups, despite its cut-backs. In response, Fedulova points out that thousands of Soviet women turn to the Committee for free legal advice every year. In 1991, the Committee's hot-line rang constantly as women sought information about how to receive financial 'compensation' from workplaces which were neglecting to pay it. These new payments had been decreed in order to soften the blow of price increases. Clearly, the Soviet Women's Committee provides necessary services which the new feminist groups cannot yet fund, and which women need. But it does not advocate feminist politics. 'What is women's politics?' asked Fedulova. 'Politics is politics. And it includes men. We have a different understanding of women's politics from the independent women's organisations.'[43] Herein lies the main division.

Most multi-party democracies enjoy a range of women's political groups. A diversity is now developing in the USSR, with the result that women are organising around different and overlapping concerns in different structures. They are conscious of each other and critical of those whose ideas, goals, strategies and politics they question. Some of these groups are competing with each other for Western sponsors.

Conclusion

Demokratizatsiia under Gorbachev has not brought a proliferation of lively female parliamentarians defending women's interests, but it has given women the political space to form women-only groups independent of the CPSU, a freedom denied to them for seventy years. The scope for women's political activity outside the home has broadened considerably in terms of the opportunities available. Whether or not women chose to pursue them is a separate question, and linked to a range of other issues such as scarce time, motivation, inclination, confidence, social attitudes and forms of discrimination.

Although new opportunities have presented themselves, it seems to be men who are seizing them, particularly in more conventional political arenas, and men who will be deciding the fate of many aspects of the woman question. Due to pressure on the CPSU from the Soviet Women's Committee, a women's section has been set up within the Council of Ministers. But its budget in 1990 seemed uncertain, as did its likely course of action.[44] The Committee of the Supreme Soviet responsible for women and children may, like its predecessor, successfully promote some positive legislation for women, but be powerless to guarantee its implementation.

Glasnost has definitely led to more open discussions about the significance of women's absence from 'high politics'. In the past, this was a non-topic, kept off agendas. Refreshing reflections on it, however, do not deliver instant results. The two main suggestions for injecting more women into top jobs are quotas for women and support groups for female candidates standing in elections. As yet, the appears to be little receptivity to the former outside the pages o women's magazines or outside the walls of women's political meetings. Admittedly, some Soviet male politicians, particularly those who have travelled to the West, now seem aware that the relative absence of women from top decision-making is an issue; in the past, they regularly dismissed the suggestion with amusement. As the West has become a popular reference point, Western criticisms of the dearth of women in top jobs are heard. But again, serious commitment and decisive action by male leaders to alter the picture is wanting. And whether female support groups for candidates running in elections can affect election results depends, in part, on the energy and astuteness of the zhensovety, new women's groups and new women's parties, but also on the willingness of voters to choose female politicians. In many traditional communities, this may take time to happen, and will be influenced both by the policies and personality of the candidates, and also the cultural values, views and prejudices of the electorate.

NOTES

1 Gail Warshofsky Lapidus, *Women in Soviet Society: Equality, Development and Social Change* (Berkeley: University of California Press, 1978), pp. 202–8; Mary Buckley, 'Female workers by hand and male workers by brain: the occupational composition of the 1985 Azerbaidzhan Supreme Soviet,' *Soviet Union*, vol. 14, part 2, 1988, pp. 229–37.

2 Stephen White, *Gorbachev in Power* (Cambridge: Cambridge University Press, 1990), p. 46.

3 *Zakon Soiuza Sovetskikh Sotsialisticheskikh Respublik o Vyborakh Narodnykh Deputatov SSSR* (Moscow: Izvestiia Sovetov Narodnykh Deputatov SSSR, 1988).

4 L. G. Strukova ed. *Trud, Sem'ia, Byt Sovetskoi Zhenshchiny* (Moscow: Iuridicheskaia literatura, 1990), pp. 22–3.

5 *Zhenshchiny v SSSR: 1990* (Moscow: Finansy i statistika), p. 21.

6 I. Skliar and O. Laputina, 'Vremiia doveriia', *Rabotnitsa*, no. 1, January, 1990, p. 19. For an earlier attack on the 'yes-women', see Larisa Kuznetsova, 'What every woman wants?' *Soviet Weekly*, 26 November 1988, p. 15.

7 *Bakinskii rabochii*, 30 November, 1989, p. 1.

8 I am grateful to Irina Kovrigina of the Soviet Women's Committee for these statistics.
9 *Izvestiia*, 2 July 1988, p. 10.
10 Kuznetsova, 'What every woman wants?', p. 15.
11 *Sovetskaia Zhenshchina*, no. 1, 1989, p. 4.
12 *Moskovskie Novosti*, no. 44, 30 October 1989, p. 12.
13 *Materialy plenuma Komiteta Sovetskikh Zhenshchin* (Moscow, Komitet Sovetskikh Zhenshchin, 1988), p. 14.
14 Mary Buckley, *Women and Ideology in the Soviet Union* (Hemel Hempstead, Harvester Wheatsheaf; Ann Arbor, Michigan University Press, 1989), chapters 4 and 6.
15 Genia K. Browning, *Women and Politics in the USSR* (London, Wheatsheaf; New York, St Martin's, 1987), p. 28.
16 Mary Buckley, 'The woman question in the contemporary Soviet Union' in Sonia Kruks, Rayna Rapp and Marilyn B. Young, eds. *Promissory Notes: Women in the Transition to Socialism* (New York: Monthly Review Press, 1989), pp. 251–81. Before electoral reform, the soviets were effectively run by the CPSU and were not powerful institutions in their own right.
17 *Materialy plenuma Komiteta Sovetskikh Zhenshchin*, p. 15.
18 Ibid., p. 16.
19 Ibid.
20 *Izvestiia*, 30 December, 1989, p. 2.
21 Skliar and Laputina, 'Vremiia doveriia', p. 19.
22 Ibid.
23 Ibid.
24 Tat'iana Khudiakova, 'Zhenshchiny idut v politiky', *Izvestiia*, 21 October, 1990, p. 2.
25 Skliar and Laputina, 'Vremiia doveriia', p. 18.
26 For further details, see Mary Buckley 'Gender and reform' in Catherine Merridale and Chris Ward, eds. *Perestroika: The Historical Perspective* (Dunton Green, Edward Arnold, 1991).
27 *Rabotnitsa*, No. 1, January, 1991, p. 5.
28 Ibid.
29 Ibid.
30 Larisa Vasil'eva, 'Zhenshchina. Zhizn'. Literatura,' *Literaturnaia Gazeta*, 20 December, 1989, p. 7. For further discussion, see Mary Buckley, 'Gender and reform'.
31 Buckley, 'Gender and reform'.
32 Richard Stites, *The Women's Liberation Movement in Russia* (Princeton: Princeton University Press, 1978); Linda Edmondson, *Feminism in Russia, 1900–1917* (London, Heinemann, 1984); Alix Holt, 'The First Soviet Feminists,' in Barbara Holland ed. *Soviet Sisterhood* (London: Fourth Estate; Bloomington, Indiana, 1985), pp. 237–65. Mary Buckley, 'Soviet religious feminism as a form of dissent', *Topic*, Journal of Washington and Jefferson College, vol. 40, Fall, 1986, pp. 5–12.

33 *Rabotnitsa*, no. 9, September, 1990, pp. 14–16.
34 Ibid.
35 Ibid.
36 Ibid.
37 *Rabotnitsa*, no. 9, September, 1990, p. 14.
38 Ibid.
39 Khudiakova, 'Zhenshchiny idut v politiky'.
40 Galina Sillaste, 'Kuda dvizhetsia zhenskoe dvizhenie?' *Izvestiia*, 30 October, 1990, p. 3.
41 Interview with Fedulova in Moscow, May 1991.
42 Ibid.
43 Ibid.
44 Interview with Pukhova in Moscow, June 1990.

Chapter 5

New women's organisations

Ol'ga Lipovskaia

Perestroika has not brought positive changes for women. The economic situation coupled with social and political tensions make the everyday lives of women even harder. Shopping and childcare mean emotional stress. Family ties are breaking, the young do not want to understand their elders, and women as mothers suffer this distancing.

A patriarchal tradition prescribes women's roles and place in society. The Soviet mass-media, generally, reacts in tune with party ideology. Most publications on the 'woman question' are influenced by gender-role stereotypes. In this context, propaganda to send women home is strong. From conservative writers, the Church and the media come the familiar charge that the high divorce rate, juvenile delinquency and alcoholism can be directly attributed to women's absence from the family.

So widespread cultural attitudes about 'woman's place' limit women's sense of collective oppression; disparate treatment does not necessarily generate moral indignation. As a result of very scarce information about Western women's movements, feminism is almost unknown, or rather associated with the state exploitation of women in the labour force, where they work in unskilled jobs for low wages. The total responsibility of women for childcare and domestic chores is never questioned.

Social and political changes, though, have not broken the silence on the woman question. Many of the new political groups, organisations and parties have ignored women's issues. Not one of them, so far, has included women in their programmes and platforms. So the ideas of democracy have not yet been extended to questioning male power in the USSR. Nevertheless, quite a number of women's organisations have been formed in recent years. They can be divided into three types: formal/official; informal/unofficial; and feminist organisations.

Formal/official women's organisations

Formal/official women's organisations include two subgroups: nomenklatura institutions, transformed into supposedly 'new' organisations, and new organisations formed 'from above'.

One example of the first type is found in the new name for an old structure of the local Soviet Women's Committee (SWC) in Leningrad. It is now called 'The Association of Women of Leningrad and Leningrad District'. The ruling organ consists of the same 'apparat' of the SWC. Its function is almost the same, except that its economic status is now based on sponsorship from state companies. It also makes money by publishing a women's newspaper entitled *Leningradka* (Leningrad Woman). Since any kind of publishing activity is very difficult due to a lack of paper and access to printing presses, we can deduce their strong connections with the CPSU – still an extremely powerful organisation which controls all the means of printing and publishing and, as well, enjoys a state supply of paper.

The new organisations formed 'from above' could be called a 'new nomenklatura' since they are successfully using a pretence of concern for women with the aim of creating connections with the West. These include various professional women's clubs, such as 'Women writers', 'women journalists' and the Soviet national department of the international organisation of women in cinema (KIWI) which has departments in many cities of the USSR. The aim of these organisations is usually purely pragmatic – to make money, to travel abroad and to find new business contacts in professional spheres.

Herein lies the important factor of cultural misunderstanding between East and West. Most of the Western women's organisations have very little knowledge of the reality of Soviet life. They sometimes mistakenly assume that any organisation of women is feminist, or at least is developing in that direction. Sometimes, though, the members of these organisations are taking advantage of the old contacts and connections used by Soviet women of the 'nomenklatura' in order to achieve economic profit with the help of similar representatives from the West.

Various conferences provide examples of the use of these sorts of connections, such as the 'Women's Summit' in the USA in May 1990 and the Soviet–American conference in Alushta in November of the same year, where a lot of different official women from the USSR met with American feminists. The results of these meetings have, unfortunately, had very little impact on the lives of millions of ordinary Soviet women.

Sometimes there is a real confusion of purposes and activities. When the Women's Press Club was organised in Moscow in 1989, Western women journalists who were invited to the opening ceremony could not understand their Soviet colleagues. The Western members arrived expecting a serious discussion on the problems of women in professional spheres. For their Soviet sisters it was only a pretext for attracting publicity for this club. Even the way they were dressed was different. Westerners were dressed for business and Soviets were dressed for the party. Ironically, the final part of the ceremony was the election of 'Man of the Year' – the honour was given to Nikolai Ryzhkov, the Soviet prime-minister...

The list of organisations in this category is very long. They include: the Association of Women of Leningrad and Leningrad Region; the Association of Women 'Creativity' (with departments in Moscow and Leningrad); the Women's Department of the Leningrad State Management Training Centre (which was recently opened by the Leningrad Regional Committee of CPSU); the International Centre entitled 'Future of Woman'; KIWI – International Association of Women in Cinema; and various zhensovety in all areas of work. The leading organ is now called the Union of Women of Russia (*Soiuz Zhenshchin Rossii*).

Informal/unofficial women's groups

Informal/unofficial groups include various kinds of women's organisations of different orientations. They are numerous and can be divided into the following subgroups: political, business and social/charity/humanitarian.

Sometimes, however, their purposes mix, and a business organisation may also deal with cultural and charity issues. A typical process throughout the country is for some zhensovety to be transformed from official nomenklatura organisations, formed from above, into informal, independent groups geared to social and political activity. This indicates a process of transformation of the old totalitarian structures into new ones, forming a new system of relations, which is a necessary part of the process of building a civil society.

The largest subgroup here embraces all kinds of business groups, courses, enterprises and clubs. Activities include the organisation of small businesses for single mothers at home, the provision of different funds to help single mothers or mothers with large families (three or more children). These organisations vary in type and scope – some of them are local, even for just one district, some are national. Women in the USSR seem to be concerned with the economic problems that are awaiting us during the period of transfer to a market economy. As a mouthpiece for these new concerns, a newspaper called *Business-woman* appeared in October 1990 (*Delovaia Zhenshchina*). This newsletter is closest to feminist issues. It interviews women politicians and focuses on the active participation of women in the country's political, social and economic life. Other new papers include *Lenin-gradka, Natali* and *Polina* in Leningrad and *Moskvichka, Women over 18* and others in Moscow. These are still searching for their identity, confusing patriarchal material with more or less 'emancipated' ideas.

Single mothers organise small traditional women's businesses, like knitting and making clothes. Big family groups (organised mainly by mothers) tend to start cooperative farming since women are concerned about the ecological problems of big cities, as well as how to feed three or more children, in current circumstances.

Many groups are organising to protect women from unemployment. Such is the concern, for example, of an organisation called VERA in Leningrad. VERA is comprised of women working in the system of higher education (teachers, professors at universities, as well as students). They have a small enterprise and a cultural programme, but they are a non-profit organisation. Defending women from unemploy-ment, they organise courses for retraining women and help find alternative jobs for them. Also their programme includes 'cultural development'.[1] In fact, it has become a very popular slogan now to return 'spiritual values' to our society, to 'revive culture'. Many women's and humanitarian organisations include them in their platforms.

Some of the zhensovety deal with these problems too, particularly those which are transforming themselves and gaining an 'informal' status. One zhensovet in the town of Zhukovskii, near Moscow fits this description. It is led by Ol'ga Bessolova and its members organised a women's political club in 1989. They were active in the election campaign for the Congress of People's Deputies and supported the well-known journalist Larisa Kuznetsova, as their candidate (who was unsuccessful). The group, however, is developing very well.

Political organisations constitute another large subgroup. There are two women's political parties: *Edinaia Partiia Zhenshchin* (United Women's Party) in Leningrad; and *Partiia Zhenshchin Suverennoi Rossii* (the Party of Women of Sovereign Russia) founded in Tomsk, in Siberia. The Leningrad party has a rather vague platform, declaring as its goal a total change of politics and society, but does not explain how this will come about. It recognizes that discrimination against women exists in the USSR, but its programme does not make clear how to tackle this. In fact, the Programme is a mixture of universal humanitarian ideas and outcries against discrimination against women. It argues that women should be equally represented in the institutions of power, but how this should, or could, happen is not indicated. The idea of 'uniting all women in one powerful political party', expressed by its leader Vera Kuril'chenko in slogans like 'all grains of female intellect should be brought together' seems to find few supporters among women.[2] She is not very popular in the media. Most of her interviews on television, radio and in the press have been rather critical of her, despite being done exclusively by women. The party was registered in October 1990, but since then it has achieved little. According to Kuril'chenko, its major concern now is to collect enough money for effective political activity. So members are trying to organise an enterprise as well as fundraising. How large the party is remains unclear, since it lacks serious public relations.

It is hard to say how well this organisation fits into the definition of 'party'. But in Soviet political life, lack of any political education or knowledge of theory is typical. Soviet society is now at the stage of learning politics in practice. It could be called a process of becoming subjects of politics out of being its objects.

The Women's Party of Sovereign Russia seems to be more effective and less demagogic. Its members' desire to stay independent of other male-dominated political organisations creates a basis for a future feminist movement. Unlike the United Party of Women, they do not wish to grow into a huge organisation which unites all women, despite their differences. Their tactic is to be careful; to think first, then act. The only organisation with whom they agreed to liaise on some political matters is the Popular Movement of Tomsk, which is quite flexible in structure and in organising principles.[3]

The Committee of Soldiers' Mothers is a more specific women's organisation, initially formed in Moscow and Leningrad in 1989 by mothers of veterans who fought in Afghanistan. They came together to provide war invalids, usually young and severely injured men, with some kind of social security. The mothers wanted the men to receive qualified medical help, wheelchairs, artificial limbs, jobs and pensions. They organised demonstrations and campaigns with these goals in mind. Later these women were joined by mothers of soldiers serving in the regular army. This was after a campaign raged in the media about *dedovshchina* – the system of brutal slavery and discrimination to which soldiers in their first year of service are subjected by soldiers in their second year. This phenomenon is widespread in the Soviet Army and includes hard beatings, rape and even the murder of young soldiers. The Moscow group of the Committee is particularly strong and managed to organise a demonstration outside the Kremlin demanding protection for their sons. Its representatives were even received by Gorbachev.[4]

Among various women's groups there are many who are preoccupied with cultural activities. There are collectives of mothers with children, organised around art and dance or gymnastics and sports. There are also women's clubs like *Preobrazhenie* (Transfiguration) in Moscow, whose programme is based on better self-realisation of women's creativity.

There are also women's organisations of an anti-feminist orientation, or organisations based on conservative, patriarchal values – like *Caritas* in Lithuania. *Caritas* is pro-life and pro-family. One anti-feminist group in Leningrad is called *Rossiia* (Russia). Its size is unknown, but its leader is Ekaterina Miasnikova – an artist and political activist. *Rossiia* is part of a conservative (nationalistic) movement called the Movement of the Spiritual Rebirth of Russia (*Dvizhenie za Dukhovnoe Vozrozhdenie Rossii*). According to their programme, a woman is first of all a mother and a wife and she is responsible for the spiritual education of children and men. Her femininity is a necessary trait, needed for spiritual revival (similar to the position of American Mormons). Part of their programme is the 'restoration of the Russian Home', which means some kind of traditional community. Most of their ideas are characteristic of the Russian nationalist movement.[5]

Feminist organisations

I refer here to all groups that consider themselves feminist, notwithstanding the meaning they give to that term. The first group that called itself 'feminist' was SAFO (*Svobodnaia Assotsiatsiia Feministskikh Organizatsii* – the Free Association of Feminist Organisations) which was formed in May 1990. A group of ten to fifteen women came together as a result of a conference in March 1990. The conference and an exhibition of art called 'Women as Subject and Object of Art' was organised by three women from Moscow. One of them, Natal'ia Philippova has become a leader of SAFO. The group issued a declaration which describes the position of women in the USSR as one of discrimination and suggests ways of changing this predicament.[6]

The main activity of the group is consciousness-raising, based on the system of Re-evaluation Co-counselling advocated by the American Harvey Jackins. This is a form of person-to-person communication, aimed at bringing out human distress. It eventually helps individuals better to realise their creative and intellectual capacities. The basic idea of co-counselling is that every human being is genuinely talented and capable of being creative. However, in the course of growing up, behaviour patterns develop which are based on early distress and bad personal encounters. The group is gradually extending and new sections are being organised. There are women-only as well as mixed groups forming.

Another organisation was formed in the summer of 1990 as a result of an open seminar on 'Women in Politics and Policy for Women' which was held at the Centre for Gender Studies in Moscow. The Centre itself was founded in May 1990 under the Academy of Sciences of the USSR, with Anastasiia Posadskaia as Director. Women who attended the seminar decided to organise a movement called NEZHDI (*Nezavisimaia Zhenskaia Democraticheskaia Initsiativa*, or the Independent Women's Democratic Initiative), an acronym also meaning 'do not wait'. NEZHDI was formed in the town of Naberezh-nye Chelny since most of the participants at the seminar were from the Kamaz truck factory there. It currently deals with women's problems at work, such as defending them from unemployment and trying to change their hard working conditions. In addition, NEZHDI holds political seminars and discusses the position of women in Soviet society.[7]

'The New Feminist Forum – "Beauty will Save the World"' is another organisation. Its fifteen members are located in six cities of Russia. Their leader, Nikolai Rogozhin, lives in Sochi. While calling themselves feminists, they seek harmony and salvation of the world in the maternal ideal of a woman. It is an idea about matriarchy. Their ideological point is that women are closer to nature and essentially 'better' than men, so they should rule the world. The general idea is that men destroyed the world, and women will save it.[8]

Another initiative of a similar sort is the idea of 'breeding' a woman president, expressed by a man named M. Pilshikov. A group of people, mostly men, calling themselves 'Coordinating Centre for the Defence of Women's Rights in Social and Political Activity' are working on a project to train women to assume high positions in the institutions of power.[9]

So far, these are the only organisations whose members consider themselves feminist. But this increase in women's activity all around the country gives one hope that women are ready to start a women's movement, defending their rights as women, seeking real equality with men.[10]

A recent event, the First Independent Women's Forum, which took place in the town of Dubna from 29–31 March 1991, proves that the process of consciousness-raising in Russia has begun. Discussions on many political, social, cultural and economic issues were based on feminist theory. Some basic feminist issues were raised, such as violence against women, rape, discrimination against women in professional and in political spheres and gender-role stereotypes in family life.

Conclusion

A feminist movement has not yet started in the USSR. It is difficult to predict when it will and from what base. Politically and sociologically, the soul is ready to accept grains of a women's movement. There is enough dissatisfaction among women with their lives and their place in society. But there is not enough recognition of discrimination against women in society as a whole and among women in particular. Speaking in feminist terms, one could say that there is no sisterhood yet. Compared to Western history of the last wave of the Women's Liberation movement, Soviet reality lacks a so-called 'civil society' – a society that consists of rather independent individuals, who are aware of their individual rights, who are familiar with the legal and political concepts and structures of democracy and who are capable of organising themselves. So women's liberation in the West enjoyed a much more suitable and propitious starting point. For a large-scale and mass Soviet women's movement to start, some kind of impetus, or a stimulus is needed. It might be an anti-abortion campaign or a law that would seriously affect women's position, leading to an obvious deterioration for the majority of women. Something like that is already happening in Poland, Czechoslovakia and possibly in other East European countries. In the Soviet Union, the Orthodox Church, which is gradually gaining power, has not yet succeeded in its goal of implanting conservative values in society.

Another relevant point is the sheer ignorance about feminist issues and movements. Not one feminist book or piece of serious feminist research has been published in the USSR. Only recently, beginning in 1989, a small number of feminist articles appeared in the Soviet press, mostly in specialised sociological and political journals. Alongside the lack of information about feminism, a huge number of sex and erotica newspapers (dozens of them appearing new every month) popularise and extend the traditional masculinist view on women. The popular image of woman now is either a beautiful sex-object, or a rather unpleasant, 'overemancipated' 'Soviet-type' shrew. The voice of feminism is still unheard by the majority, but the message of its opponents is clear – women should know their place. Feminism, then, is not tainted by Western images. Few women have any notion of real liberation. And ideas about 'emancipation' are associated with the state and its coercive power.

Nevertheless, the reality, the everyday ordeal of Soviet women confronted with economic difficulties and with an image of pretty doll or a happy housewife, cannot but leave them confused. How can she combine her reality with this sweet dream of 'real femininity', or 'purely womanly mission'? Since there is not a real answer to this paradox, feminist developments are unavoidable. The only question is, how?

In many ways, women's problems are at the heart of a changing political and social culture of the USSR. Referring here to the specifics of Russian culture, the traditions of patriarchy, we now observe the emergence of so-called 'male democracy', in which women, long associated with the home, are simply not seen in this newly emerging civil society. On the other hand, at least some of the economic independence gained by Soviet women under socialism cannot be dismissed so easily. It is hard to imagine Soviet women gladly shedding their independent economic status. The emergence of so many women's enterprises and women's organisations based mostly on the real need to survive in a market economy, is obvious proof of that. Soviet sisters just need to keep, to maintain and to improve their economic position. But the strong myth of Mother Russia will keep Soviet women attached to the family. This is a very serious part of Russian culture – communal activity and community ties are very strong. And, despite the fact that the divorce rate is increasing due to understandable dissatisfaction on the part of women (two-thirds of divorces are initiated by women), the importance of the private sphere is still there. This means that most feminist activity and the development of feminist ideas will be located in the family. There will be much less emphasis than in the West on separatism and division between the sexes, much more desire to find compromises in the realm of family life.

This does not necessarily mean that women will have less to say in political and social spheres, only that their active participation in those areas will probably have to wait. It will be delayed for the time needed to recognise that nobody, except women, can solve their own problems. These problems have yet to be named. In this respect, Soviet feminists will definitely need to draw on the experience, terminology and knowledge of their Western sisters. We do not need to 'reinvent the wheel' since there are universal women's issues, global problems shared by us all, such as reproductive rights, sexual violence, sexual harassment, professional discrimination and the masculinist tradition of objectifying women – all these expressions, terms and problems will have to find names and solutions in Soviet society.

NOTES

1 As described by VERA's president, N. Andreeva, at the First Independent Women's Forum, Dubna, March 29–31 1991.

2 *Programma Edinoi Partii Zhenshchin* (Leningrad, July 1990).

3 Speech of the party leader, Tat'iana Frolova, at the First Independent Women's Forum, Dubna, 30 March 1991.

4 Interview with Leningrad journalist, Tat'iana Zazorina, a member of the 'Committee for the Defence of the Rights of the Military', April 1991.

5 Speech of E. Miasnikova at the First Independent Women's Forum, Dubna, 30 March 1991.

6 *SAFO Declaration* (May 1990).

7 *Occasional Newsletter*, no. 1 (Moscow Centre for Gender Studies, September 1990).

8 Speech of Nikolai Rogozhin at the First Independent Women's Forum, Dubna, 29 March 1991.

9 *Pravda*, 9 December 1990.

10 A 'samizdat' magazine *Zhenskoe Chtenie* (Women's Reading) has been published since the beginning of 1988. Ol'ga Lipovskaia is the main journalist and translator. The magazine, so far, has six issues with between thirty and forty copies of each. Each edition has about 100–140 pages of typewritten text. It declares itself to be feminist. Part of *Zhenskoe Chtenie* consists of translations of extracts of Western feminism. It also publishes articles on women's issues in the USSR. Another part covers women's literature – poetry and prose by unknown and unofficial women-writers. There are also sections on 'Women in History', 'Documents' and 'Humour'. Now the magazine is going to be published on a more professional scale with a much larger circulation of 5,000 to 10,000.

Chapter 6

Between feminism and nationalism: new women's groups in the Ukraine

Solomea Pavlychko

In October 1990 the Second Congress of Rukh – the main opposition force in Ukrainian politics – took place in Kiev. At the Congress the name of this mass organisation was changed from the Ukrainian People's Movement for Perestroika (or *perebudova* in Ukrainian) to the People's Movement for the Revival of the Ukraine. By then, the movement had between 5 and 6 million members and supporters.

'There is nothing to restructure', proclaimed the Congress. We must start building a new independent and democratic Ukraine. So it is appropriate to ask what will be the role of women in the new Ukraine? In fact, what has it been for seventy-two years? Are there any changes in women's lives, self-understanding and social status comparable to the radical changes in society at large? Do women plan to influence the political and social life of their country and how will they formulate and protect their own interests?

It may seem that in the Ukraine nobody is really interested in answering these questions, even women themselves. Everything concerning women has traditionally been treated as secondary. Women's studies does not exist as a scholarly discipline. Sophisticated sociological investigations among women or concerning women's issues were never carried out in the Ukraine. An independent women's movement is only just emerging. And it does not yet have a clearly formulated feminist ideology, or a really strong leadership.

The position of women in the Ukraine

The life of women in modern Ukrainian society is unenviable and grey. Moreover, attitudes towards women are abnormal. Women have never tasted the fruit of the equality of sexes under socialism, as proclaimed by all three Ukrainian Constitutions adopted during the seventy-year

82

period of socialism. The alleged constitutional equality was underpin-
ned by economic exploitation, easily shown by statistics. The numerous state laws protecting women and forbidding them to work at night
and in dangerous industries were never implemented. Thus, women's
rights as mothers were protected mostly on paper.

Women make up 54 per cent of the Ukrainian population and 51.5
per cent of workers and employees in the Ukraine. However, 35.7 per
cent of women are engaged in heavy physical labour.[1] Millions of
women are working in conditions that violate the labour code and 25
per cent of women in the Ukraine work in conditions dangerous for
their health. Every third woman in Ukrainian industry works nights.
For hard physical labour women receive wages from 25 to 30 per cent
lower than average. The situation is similar in other Soviet republics.

Soviet Ukrainian society is structured with a dual role for women:
one is that of worker in a plant or on a collective farm, usually for a
small salary: the other, as a housekeeper at home and a mother,
responsible for feeding and bringing up children. Women were never
admitted to the economic or political elite in this society and they are
not admitted now. The Soviet state inherited a system of feudal
bureaucracy that never accepted women. And the communist patriarchy was always suspicious of women in any kind of leading role.

The number of women among the supervisory personnel of plants in
the USSR is very small – just 12 per cent. On 1 January 1990, only 5.3
per cent of women worked as directors in Ukrainian industry and
agriculture.[2] Consequently there was never a female minister in the
Ukraine and there is no prospect of having one in the near future. A
feminisation of certain fields has also occurred. For instance, 75–80 per
cent of school teachers and cultural workers in the Ukraine are women.
The reason is obvious. For decades, the job of a school teacher was
treated as secondary and the salary was low.

Approximately 30 per cent of the members of the Supreme Soviet of
the Ukraine of the 10th convocation (1985–1989) were women. This
percentage was fixed 'from above' by the Communist party and was
repeated with little variation every five years from one convocation of
the Supreme Soviet to another. And it was easy to do this, because the
deputies were not really elected, but appointed. A woman in the
Ukrainian parliament played a token, symbolic role and was not
accepted in the leadership. At the same time, the Ukrainian Supreme
Soviet played a secondary role, compared with the Central Committee
of the Communist Party of the Ukraine and even the Ukrainian Council
of Ministers. That is why it became possible for a woman, Valentina

Shevchenko, to be the Head of the Ukrainian Supreme Soviet from 1985 to 1989. Her position, however, never reflected equality of the sexes, but served merely as propaganda. She never posed questions about the position of women in the Ukraine and was among the toughest of communist party hard-liners in recent times.

The Communist party in general, and its Ukrainian subdivision in particular, never admitted women to its highest ranks. The participation of women in various elected party organs and boards was strictly regulated and also approached 30 per cent. But these were regional, raikom, city and obkom party bureaus. The number of obkom and raikom first secretaries was obviously far less than 30 per cent, though this statistical information was never published.

Misogyny and sexism are deeply rooted in modern Ukrainian society. They find expression in numerous psychological clichés, in behaviour patterns, in political and popular culture, in literature, art, elitist painting, poetry, street posters and in dirty jokes.

This misogyny appears in different forms – women's beauty and loving heart are idealized in poetry, written by men. In fiction, women are usually depicted as emotional creatures with a longing towards 'true love'. The walls of the subways in big cities are plastered with pornographic posters. Numerous beauty contests have become a major television entertainment. And among the new subjects of political rock music are children who have been left by their mothers in orphanages (fathers, by the way, are never mentioned). This list goes on. Unfortunately these phenomena have not yet been properly studied. Their roots, however, lie not only in the legacy of seventy-two years of communist regimes, but also in a strong peasant ethos, in Christian traditions and in certain aspects of Ukrainian history and culture specific to a non-sovereign country.

Political change in the Ukraine

After Gorbachev became General Secretary of the Communist Party in April 1985 and launched perestroika, it was not particularly noticeable in the Ukraine for its first five years. People joked that with Vladimir Shcherbitsky as the head of the Ukrainian Communist party, the Ukraine would remain a Brezhnevite sanctuary for ever. But the process of change, although much slower than in Moscow or in the Baltic republics, could not be stopped. By 1990, it had become radical in the Ukraine.

The year 1990 marked the beginning of the transition period from

the old socialist society of economic stagnation and political oppression of individuals to some sort of new democratic society in the
Ukraine. In 1990, the democratic forces were intellectually and politically strong enough to proclaim that the second-largest republic of the
USSR should become an independent state, subject to international
law.

So the period of swift political change started in 1990. The first free
elections to the Supreme Soviet of the Ukraine took place in March.
Founding congresses of new parties and political organisations happened in the Ukrainian capital, Kiev, nearly every month. Miners'
strikes took place and, in the autumn, students went on political hunger
strikes. There were huge rallies in most Ukrainian cities every other
Sunday, as well as numerous meetings and discussions. Most important, 1990 was the year of radical shifts in people's views, ideas and
consciousness.

The clichés started to crumble in people's minds and this was the
major 'territory' of this peaceful revolution. Women progressively
became involved in the ecological, educational and cultural movements
for the revival of the Ukrainian language and culture, for the protection
and restoration of Ukrainian architectural monuments, and for a safe
environment. The idea of national revival of Ukrainian sovereignty and
independence became the most appealing for women activists.

At the beginning of perestroika, one might have supposed that
women as members of the newly formed democratic political organisations, and as demonstrators in huge street rallies and demonstrations,
would come to occupy at least some leading positions in the official
political structures of the Ukrainian republic. However, the results of
the first free elections to the Congress of People's Deputies of the USSR
in 1989 and to the Supreme Soviet of the Ukraine in 1990 demonstrated that the role of women in the leadership actually decreased.

In the Ukraine, 38 women (16.3 per cent) were elected to the
Congress of People's Deputies, 6 of whom were given 'saved' seats by
the Soviet Women's Committee. Mariia Orlyk, the former Deputy
Prime Minister of the Ukraine and the Head of the Ukrainian Women's
Committee, was one of those delegates. Alla Iaroshyns'ka, a journalist
from Zhytomyr, who won her position following a severe struggle with
the head of the local party organisation, became the only woman-
deputy, representing the democratic wing in the Ukrainian delegation
and the only Ukrainian woman member of the Interregional Deputies
Group – the official opposition.

In the first free elections in the Ukraine in March 1990, only 13 women were elected to the Supreme Soviet's 450 seats. Five of them were running in the elections on the Rukh platform and joined the opposition minority – Larisa Skoryk, a Rukh activist and one of the most popular deputies in the Ukrainian parliament, Irina Kalynets, a former political prisoner from L'vov, Mariia Kuzemko, a journalist from Ternopil, Katerina Zavads'ka, a school teacher from Ternopil region and Tatiana Iakheieva, an economist from Cheernikiv. Six were members of the Communist party and joined the conservative majority in Parliament.

There were 939,070 women in January 1990 in the Communist Party of the Ukraine (28.5 per cent of party members). At the 27th Congress of the CPSU in 1986, 27.7 per cent of the delegates were women. And, in 5 years, at the 28th Congress of the CPSU in June 1990, only 7 per cent were women. The reduced number of women among the Communist party congress delegates may suggest that women are no longer interested in party activities and, according to my own observations, they are actively resigning from the Party. The mass process of resigning from the Communist party started in the spring of 1990.

The membership of women in different oppositional structures also turned out to be very small. Rukh is the largest opposition political body. Its founding Congress took place in September 1989, at which there were 98 women delegates out of a total of 1,109 (8.8 per cent). Not a single woman made a speech or participated in a discussion. Only 3 women were elected to the executive bodies of Rukh (Larisa Skoryk, an architect, Mariia Kuzemko, a journalist, and Halyna Antoniuk, a chemist), along with 45 men. The Coordinating Council of the Kiev Regional Organisation of Rukh consisted of 75 men and 5 women and included Skoryk, Antoniuk and also Lina Kostenko, a poet, Katerina Zelenska, a journalist and Aleksandra Fedoruk, a scholar.

At the Second Congress of Rukh the situation was similar. Out of 2,020 delegates, 10.24 per cent were women but only 2 women were speakers (Larisa Skoryk and Liudmila Truchmanova). I do not include those women who addressed the Congress merely with greetings, such as the chairwomen of different émigré women's organisations. The Congress elected the central leadership of Rukh. Only two women won posts – Larisa Skoryk and Mykhailyna Borodai who is also deputy of the Head of the Kiev Rukh Board.

The membership of the Ukrainian Parliament and the delegates of the recent Communist party congress and two Rukh Congresses shows that women were not able to compete successfully with men in free elections to a soviet or to a party conference of any level. Oppressed economically and politically for decades with their double burden as professionals and housewives, Ukrainian women were not ready to compete with male politicians. And society did not encourage them in such competitions.

Society, moreover, obviously did not want any more women politicians of the old type. During the elections to the Congress of People's Deputies of the USSR, two women workers were running for election in one of the Kiev electoral districts. Both of them lost because people no longer trusted women deputies from the working class, usually appointed by the apparatus and obedient to its requests: a female puppet who may be of working-class origin, but who reads speeches written in the raikom.

Such stereotypical female speeches at any major political meeting, congress or conference consisted of criticism of some minor, usually economic item, and of expressions of gratitude to the party and of support for its external policy (e.g. 'We women-mothers support the peaceful policy of our party because, as women-mothers, we need peace to bring up our children' etc.). The tone of such speeches has now changed, but the main ideas are preserved: namely, motherhood and all the problems connected with it, are primary for women. One most recent example from Kiev political life is a speech delivered at a communist celebration of the 73rd anniversary of the Great October socialist revolution by a young woman collective-farmer from Kiev oblast. She condemned Rukh and praised the 'socialist choice' of the country.

During 1990, a wide range of political parties formed and officially registered in the Ukraine. These parties declared themselves an anti-communist opposition. There were, however, few women in the leadership or on the executive boards of these newly formed political parties (Republican Democratic, Christian-Democratic, People's, Social-Democratic, etc.).

Most of the parties' documents neglected to mention women's problems and interests. Only the Peasant-Democratic party paid attention to women and women's issues. In the Declaration of the Main Principles of the Ukrainian Peasant-Democratic Party, sections 11 and 12 were wholly devoted to women: the cult of mother and child and widows, orphans and single mothers, respectively. The authors of the declaration first urged society to take care of women and children in the contaminated environment of the Chernobyl area. But then they made pathetic and rather mythical statements. The republic must revive the ancient cult of *Berehynia* – the main goddess of home cosiness, the cult of the mother (keeper of the family and nation) and the cult of the child. The word cult is repeated three times. This general cult of women is the continuation of the traditional orthodox cult of the Holy Virgin (the religious background is very strong in the declaration which even finishes with a section called The Prayer). There is also the cult of the Ukraine which is traditionally associated with a whole range of female images from folk and romantic poetry (primarily that of Taras Shevchenko) to images of a widow or a mother who is left or betrayed by her ungrateful children. Then the declaration stresses the resolution to protect widows, orphans and single mothers. And, in the same section, it says that the party wants to improve labour and safety conditions for men and to increase men's salaries in order to provide them with the possibility of feeding their families and keeping them healthy.[3]

Sometimes the understanding of women's interests by the so-called 'rights' (communist party bureaucrats) and democrats is strikingly similar and patriarchal in its essence. The newly elected Supreme Soviet voted for the formation of a special commission dealing with the problems of women, called the Commission for Women's Problems, Protection of the Family, Motherhood and Childhood. The very title reflects the concept of the commission's activities – women's concerns are supposed to be exclusively identified with the welfare of the family and children. Although communists speak about an abstract Soviet family, nationally conscious peasant-democrats are concerned with a genuine Ukrainian family.

Obviously motherhood, and more so childhood, must be taken care of by the state, especially when the situation is critical. And it is critical. There are 70,000 orphans in the Ukraine and the material state of the children's homes and orphanages is dreadful. Medical care in maternity hospitals is another big problem. The infant mortality rate in the Ukraine was 14.5 per 1,000 in 1987.[4] The mother mortality rate during childbirth is also high.

The best treatment for these social diseases, as they are understood by the Supreme Soviet and by some political spokespersons, is to help women to return home to their primary and natural obligations. During the debates on the title of the commission and its functions, one of the deputies said: 'We should restore her [woman's] role in society as the main carrier of the genetic code and hereditary information about the traditions, customs, culture, etc. ...'[5] When the deputy Valerii Khmel'niuk (the first secretary of the Odessa city communist party council, who was running in elections for the head of the Supreme

Soviet of the Ukraine in July 1990) was asked about his attitude towards women's problems he said:

We shouldn't deceive and fool ourselves any more claiming that emancipation saved women from slavery. A whole range of laws should be adopted, which would forbid a woman to work more than 4 hours per day. That's the most urgent question ...[6]

As for introducing women to political activities or economic administration – this is out of the question.

Thus emancipation is considered something evil and unnatural. But the system of Soviet or communist patriarchy which gave woman a false liberty, which permitted her to work physically but never allowed her into the ruling elite, which never tried to persuade men that family obligations and child rearing do not lie only in the sphere of women's interests, was not considered evil or unnatural. Some politicians would like to create a false enemy called emancipation, as if unaware that Ukrainian women never enjoyed real emancipation in the Soviet Union.

Emancipation and feminism are rather unpopular terms. Even two years ago, feminism as a notion was never mentioned. Now it is sometimes mentioned, though mostly critically. Women, except a narrow circle of women writers or literary scholars, do not know for sure what it signified. In 1990, for the first time, they tried to start a broader debate, to study the Western intellectual experience in this field, to work out their own concepts and to apply a feminist approach to society and culture. The reaction of male-dominated scholarship towards this attempt was rather hostile.

'Emancipation is nonsense' – a respected Ukrainian literary scholar told me in a private discussion. 'Feminism is a dead and destructive theory, already forgotten in the West', declared a prominent economist and Rukh advisor. When a woman scholar criticises her male colleague, he may ignore or dismiss her criticism. 'As a woman she is too emotional and neurotic,' said a member of the Ukrainian Academy after being severely criticised by a woman scholar for his works on Marxist–Leninist theory of literature. Even in the Supreme Soviet, the speaker sometimes stresses that women deputies are listened to because they are women, not because they are reasonable. The general public, and even journalists, usually ascribe to the activities and statements of women-politicians certain mystical features of female psychology. 'A woman is a woman', wrote the newspaper of the Ukrainian Communist party *Radians'ka Ukraina*, commenting on the resignation of the British Prime Minister Margaret Thatcher as the decision of a true woman ready to sacrifice her own interests to the interests of the party. The strangest thing is that the article was also written by a woman.[7]

Ukrainian women's organisations

Now for the first time in the history of the Ukraine, women have started their own organisations with obvious political and feminist orientations. These organisations were formed in opposition to the official women's organisation of the pre-perestroika and perestroika period – the Republican Women's Committee. For decades it was politically conformist, operated under the control of the communist patriarchy and played a secondary and propaganda role. It is an all-Union structure with its centre in Moscow and with local zhensovety in every Soviet republic. It was, and it is, an unimportant, 'token' organisation which never raised the question of real equality – political, economic or professional – for women.

There are 57,000 zhensovety (zhinocha rada in Ukrainian) in the Ukraine. I remember quite clearly how they were formed. After Gorbachev's speech at the 27th Congress of the CPSU when he called on the country to strengthen the women's movement, the Institute of Literature of the Academy of Sciences of the Ukraine (a research institution for literary scholarship where I work) received a command from the local raikom to form a zhinocha rada, to elect its board and to report immediately to the raikom about the results. It caused certain animation in the Institute, men invented sexist jokes, women were embarrassed, but the board was elected and the raikom obtained the necessary information. From that time on, nobody in the Institute ever mentioned the existence of this body.

The Republican Women's Committee has its own journal, which is the single women's journal in the Ukraine, published under the title *Radians'ka Zhinka* (Soviet Woman). It was founded in 1920 and reached a circulation in 1990 of 2,085,500. In 1989 and 1990, it published poetry and fiction, usually love poetry and fiction of a romance style, some general political material, articles about Chernobyl and the economic problems of women workers at some Ukrainian factories and farms. It has never, however, raised questions of political equality; it has never published statistics on the number of women employed in dangerous industries, such as the chemical industry, or the number of women working now at the Chernobyl nuclear station and its effect on their health. It has never raised the question of feminism, feminist theory and feminist studies.

The first independent women's organisation formed in 1990 was the Ukrainian Women's Union (*Soiuz Ukrainok*) which was originally founded in L'vov in 1917, became a large movement of more than 50,000 members and existed until 1939. It was reestablished by the Ukrainian women's conference held also in L'vov on 21 February 1990. Later that year, branches of the Union appeared in Kiev and in other Ukrainian cities, though mostly in the Western Ukraine. The first paragraph of its Statute declares: 'For centuries a Ukrainian woman was the guardian (*Berehynia*) of the home hearth, took care of the customs of the ancestors, national language, morality, ethos, education, culture, participated in the struggle for the high ideals of Ukrainian statehood.' The main goal of the Ukrainian Women's Union is to take care of the formation of national consciousness, to engage women in public activities and to elevate the spirituality of Ukrainian women.

The term *Berehynia* mentioned in the Programme of the Peasant-Democratic Party and in the Statute of the Ukrainian Women's Union is relatively new and also an offshoot of perestroika. Probably it is one of its paradoxes. It became widespread after a popular book of the same title by the Ukrainian ethnographer Vasyl' Skurativs'kyi.[8] The book described Ukrainian rural culture and was actually written to call on people to preserve it. So *Berehynia* is the main symbol of this rural culture, the home hearth itself, the peasant house with all its attributes, towels and pillows with embroidery, hand-made rustic furniture, rituals of the rural holidays, folk costumes, etc. A woman singing folk songs, sewing a folk blouse, teaching the same to her daughter and granddaughter is the centre of this idyllic world of the lost and adored past.

The paradox of this book, and of an entire range of similar publications, is that the salvation of rural culture, which is considered identical with the whole national culture as such, means restoring its peasant patriarchal structures. The book provides not only thorough depiction of ethnography, but also makes an attempt to revive a certain ideology. The author often scolds modern Ukrainian women for not being able to sing a folk lullaby or to embroider a towel, reproaches them for preferring modern rock music to folk songs. And the women, especially in the rural regions of the Ukraine, are taken in by such propaganda. They are eager to revive forgotten domestic industries. They believe themselves to be the only bearers of folk culture. They come to their meetings wearing folk costumes, though most of them do it not to show that they are able to make a costume themselves, but to confirm their willingness to struggle for the Ukrainian cause.

The primarily cultural and educational goals of the Ukrainian Women's Union are, in certain respects, successors to those of the pre-war Union and to the movement of Galician women of the 1880s. Martha Bohachevsky-Chomiak analyses them in her book *Feminists Despite Themselves: Women in Ukrainian Community Life 1884– 1939*. The main dilemma of the movement is reflected in the title of the book. The activists of the first Ukrainian women's groups usually denied that they were feminists, subordinated their interests and the struggle for their rights to the general cause of the Ukrainian nation. Thus the family never became an object of their criticism. On the contrary, it was viewed as the institution which deserved strengthening, a sort of national opposition. One can speculate that while for Europeans and Russians the family was seen as an extension of state power, for the Ukrainians (as for some other subject nationalities) the function of the family was perceived as the preservation of the cultural autonomy of the nation against the encroachment of the state.[9]

Just recently when national culture was threatened by Russification, family remained the only refuge where parents taught their children the national language, traditions and even religion (in the case of the Uniates in the Western Ukraine). At the same time, with perestroika and the creation of different cultural societies such as the Taras Shevchenko Society of the Ukrainian Language, women faced the need to formulate their own spheres of interest and values outside the domain of the family. Increasingly, they rejected the very idea of traditional peasant family subordination – women to men, young to old, children to parents.

These two tendencies in the new women's movement in the Ukraine, emerging feminism and national self-assertion, which sometimes go along with the protection of traditional values, are reflected in the first issue of the new women's newspaper, *Halychanka* (Galician Woman), published in L'vov, in October 1990 with a circulation of 10,000. The newspaper is planning to publish twice a month. An editorial on the first page stresses the need to struggle for real equality, the last page gives recipes for good housewives. A picture of a smiling young woman in national costume is on the cover. The traditional image of a Ukrainian woman, often publicized in most Ukrainian journals and newspapers of the recent period, is also promoted here.

In February 1990, a small group of women Rukh activists (Mariia Vlad, Lilia Iaremenko, Halyna Antoniuk, Katerina Moschchych,

Mariia Drach and others) started the first independent political women's group – Women's Community of Rukh (*Zhinocha Hromada Rukhu*). It began its activities stressing the ecological problems of Kiev. The main task was to organise women's efforts to save children of the Chernobyl zone from the damaging effect of radiation. In May and June, lectures by women scientists on radiation problems held in the Ukrainian Writers' Union gathered a great number of listeners. On 15 May 1990, when the first freely elected Ukrainian parliament started its work, activists of the Women's Community of Rukh were on the square in front of the Parliament building with slogans and demands that the Chernobyl question be added to the agenda of the parliamentary session, that the Chernobyl nuclear plant be closed immediately, that food should be checked in Kiev and the Chernobyl area, and that children be given the possibility of spending summer vacations outside contaminated areas. Later in the summer, the women's group working through Rukh, sent the rest of Chernobyl children outside the contaminated districts. The Women's Community also supported all political initiatives of the democratic forces, the student's political hunger strike in October 1990 and participated in demonstrations against the new Union Treaty.

The weakest item in the ideology of the group concerned women's interests. While the political aspect was quite clear, the feminist remained vague. There were continuous debates in the group about its future activities. Some of the activists, and even 'ideologists' of the Community, believe that women should be politically active only during the present state of unrest in the country but in the future, when the goals are fulfilled and the Ukraine is independent, women should return home to fulfil their primary maternal obligations.

A minority in the group believed that women need equal positions in all spheres of social and political life, and that the road to emancipation is only beginning. The advocates of the first view say: 'Emancipation is good for the West, but it is not adequate in our country, when we face the danger of the ecological disaster of Chernobyl and the national disaster of Russification which in the future, if the Soivet empire manages to survive, might reduce the Ukrainian language and culture to ashes. Do we need equality of sexes in a country which is the colony of another country?' Larisa Skoryk, a member of the Parliament, formulated her attitude to this problem in an interview for *Radians'ka Zhinka* in the same fashion: 'Why did I struggle so persistently for a place in Parliament? If the editors of the women's journal hope that I'll say that I wanted to promote the problems of women, I shall disappoint them – no, I did not. I think that these problems are important and we shall push them forward. The main thing is to solve the problems of the whole society, to solve the problems of the Ukraine.'[10]

The contradictions of the movement, or its dilemma, may be perceived in an article by Sofiia Maidans'ka, a poet and a member of Rukh, where she outlines her view of the most urgent tasks for the Community. It consists of fourteen items which deal with cultural, educational and medical issues. Sofiia Maidans'ka stresses that the former women's organisations of the beginning of the century put forward not feminist but genuinely national tasks[11] and that we should continue this tradition. So the cause of governing the state should be left for men; and the family and culture – for women. She expresses, however, her discontent at the way Ukrainian men ran the state both in the very distant past and today.

In October 1990, nonetheless, the members of the Women's Community of Rukh adopted their statute, which indicates a different attitude to women's interests as such:

The Women's Community of Rukh calls on women to reject the patriarchal values of the past, to fight for genuine equality of women and men in society, in guarding the home hearth, in bringing up children, and in political and social activities. The traditional patriarchal division of roles has already brought, and will bring again, devastating results to the whole Ukrainian society.

So the Community, concentrated mainly around the Ukrainian Writers Union, and comprising a number of women writers, showed that it was ready to examine feminist ideas and to understand that nationalist and feminist ideas do not necessarily contradict each other. Yet little is known about feminist ideas and Western feminist experiences because no feminist ideas ever penetrated through the ideological iron curtain which separated the USSR from the West.

Another important group in the Ukraine is the Organisation of Soldiers' Mothers. From its inception, it became the most politically powerful women's group. Mothers (not the parents or fathers!) of soldiers who had died or who had been killed in the Soviet Army contacted one another to demand investigations and trials. Then the mothers of soldiers who had not perished but who, for example, had been beaten by their officers or who had served in regions of national conflicts in the Soviet Union like the Central Asian republics, Armenia and Azerbaidzhan, also joined the movement. Mothers started to demand that their sons serve only on Ukrainian territory. Students who were on hunger strike included this in their own package of demands. After long debates, the Supreme Soviet decided that the citizens of the Ukraine should serve in the Soviet army only on the territory of the Ukraine or go to other republics on a voluntary basis.

The founding congress of the Organisation of Soldiers' Mothers of the Ukraine took place on 8–9 September 1990, in Zaporozhe. Its Resolution appealed to the Supreme Soviet of the Ukraine not to sign the new Union Treaty, to form the Ukrainian National Armed Forces on a professional basis and to recruit citizens to the divisions of KGB and Ministry of Interior strictly on a voluntary basis. These and fourteen other demands were political in essence. The Soldiers' Mothers demanded the formation of a special Supreme Soviet commission to investigate the deaths of Ukrainian citizens while serving in the army.[12] Liudmila Trukhmanova, the mother of two soldiers, became the head of the organisation.

The significance of the group was stressed when Trukhmanova became a member of the official parliamentary delegation of the Supreme Soviet of the Ukraine at the negotiations between the Ukrainian Supreme Soviet and the Soviet Defence Minister, Iazov, in October 1990. Trukhmanova spoke about this mission at the Second Congress of Rukh. She stressed the women's resolve to struggle for their demands. She said: 'We are the strongest and the most dangerous movement, because we are a women's movement.'

Activists of the Women's Community of Rukh and Ukrainian Women's Union joined in the activities of the Organisation of Soldiers' Mothers, in particular in helping to hide deserters from the Soviet Army, and in organising press conferences and meetings in Kiev in order to attract more public attention to the state of affairs in the Soviet army.

Paradoxically, the mothers' movement which embraced women of different nationalities (those from the Eastern Ukraine are mostly Russian speakers and Liudmila Trukhmanova is Bulgarian) and of various strata (workers, intellectuals, collective farmers, etc.) from the beginning tended towards both feminism and nationalism. Mothers were galvanized by the will to protect their grown-up children. They addressed an issue ignored by society. They proposed a solution far from either traditional or feminist women's concerns. Never interested in any theory of liberation, they challenged society and asserted both their political maturity and ability to articulate the feminist agenda.

Conclusion

On the old Kiev hills close to the ancient monastery of the twelfth-century Pechers'ka Lavra stands a huge monument – a woman more than 100 metres high with a shield and a sword. The statue, hated by the citizens of the city, has a dreadful face, full of anger. It was erected in 1980 to commemorate the thirty-fifth anniversary of victory in the Great Patriotic War and was meant to symbolize the Motherland. This fearful, strong, merciless goddess of the atheist society differs greatly from a timid home guardian of peasant ethos and from Holy Mary, specially worshipped by the orthodox Christians. The woman idol with a sword demonstrates the total lack of femininity, being a symbolic macho-woman of the male-dominated society. In order to survive, Soviet women had to become such machos – mothers and housewives, doomed by their men to manual labour and inferiority, who lost their femininity and instead acquired profound and unacknowledged psychological problems. The road to assuming a visible role in Ukrainian life and to developing a feminist ideology will probably take many years but the first women's groups of 1990 give at least some hope that Ukrainian women have already chosen it.

NOTES

1 N. Koval's'ka and T. Oleksandrova, *Zhinsky Radians'koi Ukrainy* (Kiev: Politvydav, 1990), p. 8.
2 'Social'na statystyka', *Pid praporom Leninizmu*, no. 4, 1990, p. 48.
3 *Literaturna Ukraina*, 5 July 1990, p. 7.
4 *Zhinky Radians'koi Ukrainy*, p. 32.
5 *Persha sesiia Verchovnoii rady URSR dvanadtsiatoho sklukannia* Biuleten' 38. p. 42.
6 *Persha sesiia Verchovnoii rady URSR dvanadtsiatoho sklukannia* Biuleten' 73. pp. 52–3.
7 *Radians'ka Ukraina*, 25 November 1990, p. 1.
8 Vasyl' Skurativs'kyi, *Berehynia* (Kiev: Radians'kyi Pys'mennyk, 1988).
9 M. Bohachevsky-Chomiak, *Feminists Despite Themselves* (Edmonton: CIUS, 1988), p. xxii.
10 *Radians'ka Zhinka*, no. 8, 1990, p. 3.
11 Sofiia Maidan's'ka, 'Poku maty u tobi zhyva' *Literaturna Ukraina*, 9 August 1990, pp. 3–4.
12 *Literaturna Ukraina*, 11 October 1990.

Chapter 7

The Zhensovety revisited

Genia Browning

The zhensovety were created from above as an outlet for woman's activity. They were not, and will not become, a women's mass organisation.

The zhensovety are organisations created from below, by women themselves for women. They have a long history.[1]

Why the zhensovety?

The zhensovety (zhenskie sovety), or women's councils, are the women-only groups earmarked by Gorbachev to 'help resolve a wide range of social problems ... confronting women and their families'.[2] In this time of momentous, devastating change, it could be argued that consideration of these institutionalised women's organisations is misplaced. The above conflicting perceptions expressed at the 1989 plenum of the Soviet Women's Committee (SWC), however, underline the complexity of the zhensovety and hence the need to examine, not to dismiss them.

One of the fledgling sounds of perestroika has been the voice of women. For those long concerned with the under-representation of women in the power structure, it has been exciting to witness Soviet women's articulation and analysis of sexism in Soviet society. Larisa Vasil'ieva, for example, has referred to the CPSU itself as a contributory factor, and identified the nomenklatura system as a barrier to women attaining positions of power, yet dismissing present female party functionaries for not representing the 'living female soul'.[3] The need for women to have 'a sorority' has been recognised and acted upon.[4] Furthermore, women's voices contend that their problems cannot wait until the economic crisis is overcome, but must be confronted now. As Vasil'ieva has pointed out, it is women who are in the front line of the crisis, it is women who will be the first to be dismissed from their jobs, it is women who stand in queues to feed their

97

families.[5] What is there to prevent the zhensovety taking up the demands of these voices as they become louder, less strange and more visible? It is these voices, though, which tend to reject the zhensovety as 'old forms' which 'are not attracting' women because they are 'too bureaucratic'.[6] In the view of feminists like Valentina Konstantinova, the zhensovety are 'distributors of food', not 'raisers of conscious-ness'.[7] This perceived irrelevance and rejection of the zhensovety is, in part, a rationale for the variety of alternative women's groups now emerging.

It is tempting for Western women, informed by the history of our own women's movement, to presume that it is the unofficial groups which are of real relevance to women, and hence only these which are worthy of study. But we do a disservice to our potential understanding of the Soviet system if we ignore the statutory bodies. Despite apparent ineffectiveness, despite lack of dynamism, they are part of the fabric of society and contribute to the maintenance of the system. We also do a disservice to those many, many Soviet women who give their time and energies to these formal organisations and to those among them who maintain a positive commitment to their activities in the zhensovety. The reasons for their ineffectiveness, their staying power, and their potential for change, are all issues to be addressed. We therefore re-visit the zhensovety, look at their current activities and at the organi-sational, relational and attitudinal changes taking place. Particular reference is made to zhensovety in the town and district of Ivanovo.[8]

The zhensovety before perestroika

Although some consider the zhensovety to be new organisations,[9] they do indeed have a long history. Some existed pre-war. Others were established during and after the Second World War in a number of towns, including Ivanovo.[10] Their main growth was during the Khrushchev period of the late 1950s, and they were again the focus of attention in 1975, International Women's Year. The lack of knowledge about their history is a reflection of their lack of status. They are located throughout the USSR at republic, oblast, raion and local level both in the work place and in residential areas. The higher the level, the larger the committee or *aktiv* tends to be. Committees at republic level are likely to have fifty members, at oblast they have about thirty, towns and raions fifteen to twenty and local groups as few as five members.[11] Their work is divided into sectors which typically include mass political work, production, daily life, culture, work with children and social work. Their role in the past has been characterised as mobilising women for implementation of the current economic plan, and acting as a social welfare organisation. Although these were often the dominant features, the zhensovety did fulfil other roles.[12] Under Khrushchev, the aim was to raise women's political consciousness in the context of strengthening party influence among women. It was this aim, and their description as 'spontaneous', 'independent women's organisations', whose activists work on their own 'initiative',[13] which initially led to my interest in the zhensovety. Research suggested though, that such characteristics had to be seriously qualified. 'Initiatives' tended to emanate from the republic or oblast zhensovety and were passed down to the local groups. The tasks undertaken indicated not spontaneity but uniformity, albeit the lack of a central directive did provide some diversity. 'Independence' described the lack of a formal, structural relationship to a parent body. Where links were formalised, they varied. Sometimes ties existed with the local soviets, or the trade union organisations, but more frequently with the appropriate committee of the CPSU. Party 'guidance' meant that ultimately 'independent' organisations operated within the parameters defined by party ideology. This was accomplished by leading activists being members of the CPSU, and through the general political culture.

The zhensovety and perestroika

The proposal at the 27th Congress of the CPSU to re-activate the zhensovety had three main effects. Firstly, the zhensovety came under the umbrella of the Soviet Women's Committee which afforded them a national status for the first time in their history. Centralisation had been argued for by activists in the past as a means of strengthening the zhensovety. Now the Soviet Women's Committee holds plenums and annual regional conferences to co-ordinate their work. Whereas initiative has always been limited, streamlining is likely to make activity more uniform. Anna Mel'nik, chair of the Moldavian republic zhensovet, recognising this possibility, has warned that the structure should not be formalised on conventional lines.[14] So far, restructuring has had a more immediate effect on the status of the SWC, since it now has responsibility for internal issues as well as its previous concern with international affairs.

The second effect was the allocation of seventy-five seats for the zhensovety on the Congress of People's Deputies. The future of this allocation is already uncertain though, and its effectiveness limited.

The third effect was to extend the number of zhensovety and to reactivate existing ones. By early 1988, 236,000 were reported, and 240,000 in April 1989.[15] In the Tartar region in 1990, there were 2,319 zhensovety.[16] In Ivanovo, a regional zhensovet was formed after 1987, whereas the town and local zhensovety existed already. The Suzdal raion and town zhensovety were organised at the end of 1987 and the beginning of 1988. The composition of zhensovety committees continues as before. This is evident from a kolkhoz zhensovet in the Ivanovo district: 'For the past ten years the zhensovet of the kolkhoz has included a milkmaid, vet, teacher, librarian, book keeper, and laboratory assistant.' It has four sections: mass work, ideological and moral education of women, improving living and working conditions, strengthening the family and raising its role in the education of the younger generation.[17]

Although now answerable to the Soviet Women's Committee nationally, local relationships between the zhensovety, the soviets, trade unions and party remain. Officially the CPSU retains its 'guiding role'. Many leading activists are party members. N. L. Kovaleva, the chair of the Ivanovo town zhensovet in 1989, was a second secretary of the regional party committee. But the dramatic change occurring in the political culture means the parameters are no longer clearly defined. The CPSU is losing its authority to set these parameters. According to a survey of women's attitudes conducted in 1990, only 2 per cent named the party as having authority.[18]

This loosening of control does not inevitably lead activists to determine their own agenda. For many it has left a vacuum which they feel ill-equipped to fill. When pressed about alternatives to the current guidelines of work, the chair of the Ivanovo zhensovet spoke of the difficulty of no longer having clear directives. Many zhensovety, therefore, continue to follow past patterns. Although at the 1989 plenum of the SWC, groups from a variety of republics – from Latvia and Lithuania, to Kazhakstan and Uzbekistan, as well as Russia and the Ukraine, were praised for their 'useful and necessary' activity,[19] and activists compared their present work favourably to that of the old zhensovety, it is difficult to discern any marked change.

Indeed many articles about current activity present a picture that is startlingly similar to that of the earlier zhensovety. Mel'nik, who was involved before 1987, wrote in *Partiinaia Zhizn* that the zhensovety of the 1990s must learn from experience. Yet, although she claimed that the restructuring of their work has 'breathed new life into zhensovety initiatives, new creativity and innovation', and that their role was

'hotly debated' by activists at a pre-congress meeting of the 4th
Moldavian Republic Women's Congress, the examples provided of
current work closely resemble those of the past.[20] Assessments anyway
should not necessarily be taken at face value. A current member's
description of the old zhensovety in Ivanovo as 'useless and ficti-
tious',[21] bears no relation to how a former member of the town
zhensovet perceived their activity. Her own role had been to provide
women with reading material. She spoke enthusiastically about the
zhensovet; clearly she had loved her work, had been committed to it,
and considered it worthwhile.[22]

The major change that has taken place is in the attitude of women
themselves to the zhensovety. There have always been those who
criticised them for their ineffectiveness. Now the criticism is far more
extensive, notably sharper, and explanations are being seriously
sought. In discussion in 1989, representatives from the Soviet Women's
Committee referred to the failure of the zhensovety to deal with
important issues, whereas in 1980 correspondence from one of these
same representatives presented them as unproblematic. Zoia Pukhova,
when chair of the SWC, chastised the zhensovety, claiming that they,
'still struggle half-heartedly ... Not all of them understand their role,
nor realise what their place is in society under the new conditions.'[23]

These weaknesses are generally acknowledged. Amongst those who
seek to retain the zhensovety, two main approaches can be identified.
The first is to strengthen the zhensovety within their existing guidelines.
Attention is focused on their relation with other organisations,
resources, internal structure and activities. Pukhova and Galina
Galkina, from the Soviet Women's Committee, have both pointed to
lack of support from other organisations. The hypocrisy of official
attitudes, which had always applauded 'women's initiative' whilst
de-valuing it because it was women's, has not changed. The soviets,
CPSU and trade union organisations reflect, as before, a general male
indifference to women's organisations. Pukhova was already com-
plaining in 1988 that not all party organisations seriously support the
zhensovety.[24] A year later, Galkina repeated the claim, 'The zhensovety
work side by side with others, the party, trade unions and workers'
collectives, and I must say that sometimes there is not a correct attitude
... this fault is widespread.'[25] In Moldavia, the people's universities
have assisted the zhensovety, not the trade unions and party organisations.[26] Whereas independence from such bodies might be desirable,
Krylova, editor of Rabotnitsa has pointed out that the problems
confronting women are too extensive to be resolved by the zhensovety

alone.[27] The volume of work facing a factory zhensovet in Ivanovo, for example, has meant that 'regretfully' activists have had to try to involve disinterested factory foremen and supervisors.[28] Pukhova's response in 1988 was to try to strengthen the relationship between the zhensovety and the local party organisations.[29]

Lack of resources is commonly raised. Activists complain that the zhensovet is 'a social organisation which hasn't its own purse. We can only ask, beg, demand'.[30] Moreover, 'resources are controlled by the CPSU'.[31] Nor do the zhensovety have the power to affect legislation.[32] A further weakness lies in the content and organisation of their activity. They have also been criticised for a lack of focus and too diverse a range of tasks.[33] At the Tartar Women's Congress in 1990, delegates called on the zhensovety to 'reconstruct' their own activities.[34]

The second approach is more radical. Whereas there are those who want further centralisation under a republic zhensovet of the RSFSR[35] others seek more fundamental 'reconstruction'. Larisa Kuznetsova has argued that the only viable future for the zhensovety is to find 'their own leaders', and to separate themselves from other organisations.[36] Aleksandra Lugovskaia from *Rabotnitsa*, in discussion with Galkina, challenged the continued reliance on such 'unpopular, archaic forms' as seminars and plenums, pointing out that these are forms associated with the inaction of the old administration.[37] There is, nevertheless, recognition of the dilemmas facing the zhensovety. As noted in *Rabotnitsa*, 'Women are being asked to do an impossible job – reconstruct society. But, reconstruction is not working for women, thus the zhensovety face an unresolvable conflict.'[38]

The criticisms of the zhensovety should be qualified by their achievements, by the support they provide women, by the extent to which they operate as a pressure group, and by the new consciousness which some zhensovety are generating. Evidence prior to 1987 suggests the zhensovety helped to ease women's 'double burden' by establishing kindergartens, by challenging factory managements and by providing facilities.[39] As will be shown by zhensovety in the town and district of Ivanovo, such activity continues. Galkina has pointed to research conducted by the zhensovety among women about their working day. As a result, women can now opt for a reduction of 1½ hours at the beginning or end of the working day, an extended 2-hour lunch break, and additional leave.[40] Glasnost has prompted the zhensovety to add ecological issues to their list of concerns. At the women's conference in the Oktiabr' raion of Ivanovo, the building of a nuclear power plant in the region caused particularly sharp exchanges amongst participants.[41]

In Iakovo, Siberia, the zhensovet claimed to have organised successfully against the building of a nitrogen fertiliser plant.[42] In Tomsk, following meetings and demonstrations, zhensovety collected 15,000 signatures on the 'Day of the Defence of Children' (1 June 1988) against the siting of a harmful industrial enterprise.[43]

Furthermore, perestroika and glasnost have provided the space for consciousness raising and independent initiatives to emerge. In the 1989 elections to the Congress of People's Deputies, zhensovety could nominate committee members for selection by the Soviet Women's Committee for the seventy-five reserved seats. The zhensovet of the Central Aerodynamic Institute in Moscow headed by Ol'ga Bessolova, nominated its own alternative candidates, including publicist Larisa Kuznetsova. Although the candidates were declared invalid by the Moscow zhensovet,[44] the attempt was subsequently dubbed 'the first women's sponsored election campaign'.[45] The experience transformed Bessolova's zhensovet into a 'socio-political, civic women's association'.[46] In another example of independence, a work-place zhensovet in Dubna defied the town zhensovet by hosting the First Independent Women's Forum.[47] Ol'ga Bessolova was one of the participants. Groups attempting radical change, though, face a dilemma. As Bessolova herself has recognised, the traditional activities of the zhensovety which 'assist, demand, procure and distribute'[48] are in themselves of value to women and from this, 'there is no escaping ... After all, the women who elected us expect help, which is why we must deal with canteens, recreation rooms ... as well as women's working conditions ... benefits ... and children's education.'[49]

Two points of note arise. Firstly, the traditional activities of the zhensovety have validity. Secondly, as women-only groups, the zhensovety can challenge existing assumptions about female roles. Can the independence shown by Bessolova's zhensovet be replicated? Does the centralisation of the zhensovety aid their effectiveness? Or does it stifle potential local initiatives? To explore such questions we focus on the current activities of the zhensovety in the town and region of Ivanovo.

Have the zhensovety changed? The case of Ivanovo

Known as 'the town of single women' because of its predominantly female workforce, Ivanovo is the centre of the textile industry. In November 1989 when I met members of zhensovety in Ivanovo and its environs, there were 6,000 activists in more than 800 zhensovety throughout the region.[50] A meeting with committee members of the town zhensovet took place in the bar of the women's club of Oktiabr' raion. The evening began with a fashion show by students from a textile institute arranged by a lecturer who was on the zhensovet committee. The members of the committee represented a similar cross-section of society to those on other zhensovety committees. Alongside Kovaleva in the chair, and the lecturer in textile studies, was the Director of the 8th March Textile Factory, Head of Social Services, a doctor, deputy chair of the local soviet, secretary of a factory party committee, a journalist, and two heroine mothers.[51]

Kovaleva introduced the zhensovet by citing Gorbachev's description of their role, itemising, 'motherhood, protection at work, health, and easing the burdens of housework and daily life' as the main problems facing women. She believed women joined from a two-pronged concern for working conditions and their children. Committee members described their tasks in the familiar terms of easing women's double burden and offering emotional support.

Political and economic activity

In the new era of perestroika and glasnost, raising political consciousness is the role of the zhensovety which probably has the most potential for change. One of the first questions put to the committee members, therefore, concerned their level of political activity. Their response referred to little else than their work to improve facilities in particular factories and to supplement the meagre state benefits to heroine mothers. It seemed the only difference to the past was Kovaleva's belief that they now had more strength to face up to management.

Nor did it appear there was much change in public attitudes to women activists. Committee members suggested that men are still taken more seriously, 'because men are tougher – more like warriors' and that this spills over into the world of work where women are not perceived as managers. An enquiry as to how their husbands viewed their involvement in the zhensovet drew a lively response. It was generally agreed that they were 'not against their wives being socially active, so long as there was still time for housekeeping and their supper was on the table.' Some admitted that 'It's a problem, [you] have to select a patient husband.' Members distinguished between political activity which took place in the Komsomol, the party or trade union, and social activity in the zhensovet. Yet they considered that their reserved seats to the Congress of People's Deputies, despite its limitations, afforded them a potential voice and more direct political participation in national policy. There was general agreement that the present representatives were inadequate, but they were determined to select women in future with a commitment to change.

Explanations for women's apparently low level of knowledge of politics and economics has shifted since the 1950s, when blame was put on religion, or party inertia, to the poor quality of women's lives. According to a journalist I interviewed, 'the conditions for women are so poor that political activity is virtually impossible', but, at the time, she was optimistic that perestroika would change this as 'Women feel more free now and can express themselves more.'[52] There was little evidence that the zhensovety in Ivanovo, though, are explicitly raising political consciousness. Their reports make little reference to political education. Where there are such sectors, they have a clearly defined role which is as limited as those of earlier zhensovety. The task of the political sector of the zhensovet in the Krasnaia Talka factory is to inform women about the factory's history, mark the *rites de passage* associated with joining the Komsomol, and arrange exhibitions in the factory museum on themes like women's role in the war.[53] Some of the earlier zhensovety suggested a broader approach to raising women's political consciousness and this too was evident in the present aims of a kolkhoz zhensovet in Gavrilov-Posad raion: 'We try to ensure that our women know more, read more, are more interested in politics and the cultural life of the country through talks, literary discussions, and oral newspapers.'[54] But in Ivanovo this approach appeared to be an isolated case.

Women's working conditions, the long hours, night shifts and unmechanised labour, have always been of concern to the zhensovety. Despite the achievements of individual groups, poor and illegal conditions remain. At a conference of the Oktiabr' raion zhensovet in 1988, participants were still calling for women to be taken off night shifts.[55] At the town meeting, the director of the 8th March Textile factory cited the recent reduction of hours from forty-one to thirty-eight per week and committee members were adamant that women wanted shorter working hours. It seemed that the zhensovety in Ivanovo worried primarily about the minutiae of working conditions instead of addressing fundamental issues like unemployment. In the changing Soviet economy, women are likely to be the first to lose their jobs, especially women with large families.[56] Although initially highlighted by women, there was no evidence that either this, or other inequalities, were being confronted by the zhensovety in Ivanovo.

Consolidating the Soviet family

The main focus of activity of the zhensovety at every level during this period appears to have been the family. This follows Gorbachev's view that the family should be consolidated and support be given to women's 'maternal duties'.[57] Although the official role of the zhensovety embraces women's living and working conditions, as evident in Kovaleva's address to members of the Oktiabr' raion at their 1988 conference, it is the family which takes centre stage,[58] and the context in which other areas of activity are located. The Ivanovo report of work during 1989 and 1990, for example, declared that 'the aim is to enable women to work to their full strength whilst combining this with their family commitments.'[59] It is not surprising, therefore, that since 1987 the family appears to have been the prime target of the zhensovety in Ivanovo. Members of the town zhensovet see it as one of the main areas of their work, the 'fundamental issue'.[60] Conferences held by the zhensovety on the family in the Iuzha raion and elsewhere, report that many local people are now 'thinking about how to improve the family, how to make it happier and stronger'.[61]

What purpose does such attention to the family fulfil? Does it challenge the present inequality of gender roles or, in strengthening the family, does it reinforce these inequalities? The activities of the zhensovety in Ivanovo suggest it is the latter. As the title of Sinitsyna's report from Pestiaki raion in Ivanovo oblast shows, ideology of the family has not been an area for reconstruction. In 'A strong family – a strong state', she writes that the family is not only a circle of close people, but the cell of society,[62] thus echoing the Family Code of 1968.

In this context, efforts are being made to prevent family breakup. The town zhensovet pointed out that of the 500 new families formed each year, more than 40 per cent, most of them with children, are likely to split up within two years.[63] Drunkenness, differing interests and infidelity, are identified as the main causes.[64] Many zhensovety in Ivanovo, therefore, provide counselling and practical help to 'problem families'. Members of the Shuia raion zhensovet, for example, have reported that their work with 'unfortunate' families concentrates on the reasons for poor family relationships. 'If necessary the husband and wife have been invited to meet the trade union committee. We try and help those that need it, do repairs in the flat, arrange pre-school places and offer good advice. People do not always know what to do and so go to court for a divorce, but if offered counselling [they] stop and think again, about the children, about the family ...'[65]

Young families, in particular, are viewed as vulnerable. Zhensovety have organised events such as 'The week of the young family', and attempts have been made to time the holidays of young mothers to coincide with those of their children.[66] The club for young women at the Krasnaia Talka factory has held lectures on marriage and the family,[67] whilst the zhensovet at a machine-building plant has reported that its advice to young married couples has helped prevent family breakdown.[68]

Although the rationale for such activity is to strengthen the institution of the family, the counselling probably does help individual family members. But it is debateable whether it should be the responsibility of untrained volunteers. Evidence suggests that activists do much to support women within the family and do more than sloganise and pass resolutions. A number of the local zhensovety refer to starting 'a family document or passport', a detailed list of families in their area or place of work. Thus, at the 1989 women's conference in Oktiabr' raion, the chair of a factory zhensovet reported, 'Our zhensovet isn't big – it only has twenty members', but it has documented all the large families, one-parent families and 'problem families' in the area to co-ordinate activity with that of the administration, schools, and social organisations.[69] Surveys conducted by zhensovety indicate the extent of the problem facing them. The findings of the Iuzha raion survey, for example, referred to in its report 'Happiness – to each home', showed that, 'Out of 14,400 families living in the raion, there are 362 large families, 283 poorly provided, 437 single-parent families, and a further 166 problem families needing moral and financial support.'[70] In Ivanovo, the over-population of women makes single parenthood a particularly acute problem: forty-nine one-parent families with three or more children were identified in the survey. Between 1987 and 1989, the zhensovet helped twenty-five of the large families, using the children's fund to provide items such as washing machines.[71] In one of the villages of this raion, the zhensovet focused on a large family on the sovkhoz, noting that 'Everyone in the village knew they lived poorly, but it's one thing to know, another to do something about it.'[72] The zhensovet organised a round table on the practical implementation of its programme which resulted in the family being given a larger flat. Support to single parents and large families is nothing new. Zhensovety have always helped individuals by supplementing state benefits but, as these examples illustrate, needs are so extensive that voluntary efforts can only produce limited results.

Whilst all the zhensovety in Ivanovo pursued work on the family, they varied in their area of emphasis. Alcoholism has been one of the long-standing explanations for family breakdown. This aspect of work combines issues of the family with female responsibility for 'moral order'. The zhensovet in an Ivanovo building plant, for example, 'keeps an eye on families where a parent has a drink problem'.[73]

Other zhensovety focus on young people. The zhensovet attached to a pedagogical institute, together with members of the Commission of Home and School, regularly visit children's schools. According to its report, members talk to teachers 'about the children's progress, about discipline, about their attitude to social work and, of course, how the parents themselves relate to the education of their children – whether they regularly visit the school, attend parents' meetings, and support the school'.[74] Its survey on the relationship between parents and children showed that it was particularly children in the older classes who were, 'less under their parents' control' who required special attention.[75] The zhensovet confronted the problem by inviting the children to an 'open doors' day at the institute and to meetings honouring their parents' work. The aim was to foster closer contact between parents and children and deeper understanding. Other zhensovety addressing similar problems have held lectures on child rearing and arranged courses for parents about problem areas in education. To help enhance children's status within the family, exhibitions, such as 'Children – our pride' mounted by the zhensovet in a furniture factory, depict children who study well.[76]

In keeping with traditional gender roles, zhensovety activists have always been expected to act as mediators between family and school. The zhensovety take a two-pronged approach to this work, the general, as instanced above, and the particular. Thus, in certain cases, a zhensovet singles out individual families for attention, as in a weaving factory where 'Serious discussion has taken place with ... a weaver, about her daughter's education.' The same zhensovet counselled a family in which 'The children ... are often out of control' with positive results: 'now the situation is normal and the family has kept together'.[77] Not surprisingly, zhensovety have retained responsibility for visiting the families of children in children's homes and boarding schools.[78]

This traditional caring role of women is likewise replicated in attention to the elderly. One factory zhensovet, in a mood of self-criticism, reported, 'We talk a lot about kind-heartedness, of helping people, but don't do much more than talk.' To amend this situation, the zhensovety ran the operation 'Caring' to re-establish contact with retired women workers.[79] Other zhensovety have invited pensioners to social events and helped them at home.[80] At the kolkhoz *Druzhba*, the zhensovet organised an 'Evening of remembrance' with veterans of the Second World War, at which everyone 'drank tea together, danced, and sang'.[81]

As women, activists are expected to extend their maternal role to young women as well. Ivanovo uses labour from all over the USSR. Fifteen- to seventeen-year-old girls are housed in hostels. Members of the zhensovety have a responsibility for the welfare of these young female workers and encourage them to keep in touch with their parents.[82]

Thus, the demanding, time-consuming activities of the zhensovety aimed at being supportive of women, serve to reinforce segregated gender roles. Locating women's social activity within the private sphere of the family contributes to the existing conceptualisation of the family. The state's reliance on female activists suggests that its concern for the family is ambiguous. The strain imposed on family relationships by harsh living conditions cannot be resolved by voluntary work. Zhensovety involvement appears to absolve the state, whilst at the same time, the necessarily limited achievements of zhensovety members dubs them meddlers in the lives of others.

Fresh emphasis on the need to include men in family activities could challenge such views. According to the report 'Attention to the family', 'The zhensovety should help accustom men to help their children, especially their sons.'[83] But the activity described in the reports suggests that it further reinforces gender demarcation. This is particularly apparent in the activities of clubs and festivals organised by the social sectors.

Social activity

Judging by the zhensovety in Ivanovo, their traditional concern for women's rest and leisure now centres on leisure within the family. Thus the report of a factory zhensovet headed 'Don't forget about rest', stipulates that whilst it has done much to improve working conditions for women, 'it has to be remembered that a woman is still a mother, a wife, a housewife, and needs to rest'. It recognises that women have little time for leisure due to 'the many cares on their shoulders',[84] but the problem is addressed by the 'days of family rest' organised by the social sector to unite the collective and the family.[85] The family as a nuclear unit is affirmed by such activities as competitions like 'Papa,

Mama and Me – a sports family' which are replicated elsewhere in family festivals, for instance as in the Pestiaki raion. Here 'Rest for all the family' replaced the traditional 'Day of the Factories' with a series of events following International Women's Day, focusing on different aspects of family life. One Sunday, for example, the theme was 'All the family to the library'. Families were invited to a film *Mama, Papa and Me*. A competition, 'Papa, Mama and Me – a reading family', followed. The library held exhibitions on family themes including 'Parents, children and leisure' and 'The Ul'yanov family'.[86]

As women, activists like those in a factory zhensovet in the Puchezh raion recognise that 'home responsibilities' give women 'too little time to mix with one another'.[87] Their 'solution', though, hardly seems appropriate. They organised a competition, 'We did it ourselves – with our own hands' based on women teaching their daughters traditional skills, and fathers instructing their sons.[88] Much of the activity in clubs is along similar lines.

Zhensovety in the past referred to their 'search for new forms of work'. This search continues. The zhensovet in the kolkhoz *Druzhba*, Solkol raion, reported that 'under the leadership of the party organi-sation, activists constantly search for new forms of activity'.[89] In Ivanovo, this search had produced little that was new. The 'new forms' cited are clubs and festivals – both long established. Furthermore, in keeping with family policy, many clubs either cater for all members of the family rather than women specifically, or provide activity which serves to reinforce segregated gender roles. The club 'Young Family' attached to *Druzhba*, for example, organised its first event 'Getting acquainted' on a non-working day so that parents and children could come together. Women brought along their favourite dishes, jams, tarts and salads, in order to appraise each others' and to exchange recipes.[90] Such domestic activities are judged to be most popular,[91] and so under the common theme 'Women and family', competitions regularly occur like, 'Manager – with golden hands' held by 'The Contemporary Woman' club.[92]

What emerges from these reports is two main roles for the zhen-sovety. On the one hand, they are engaged in strengthening the very institutions which serve to contribute to women's problems whilst, on the other, they are attempting to alleviate the problems which emerge from that same activity. As Novikova has said, the tendency to resolve existing problems by 'sending women back to the family' is not 'emancipation' but 'dooming' women to 'play a dependent role'.[93]

Although much of zhensovety activity has concentrated on the family, it does not represent the total picture. There are activities arranged for women only which address wider issues. The women's club in the Oktiabr' raion has its own museum, meeting rooms and a most comfortable and congenial bar. The club's activities for 1988–9 included women's 'universities', or study sessions, on particular themes. One session on education consisted of a lecture and film. Another on the social services tackled questions like, 'Why are there queues at the hairdressers?' A general session on perestroika 'Time for questions and answers' was held. The club also arranged consultation sessions with economists and other specialists.[94] Although both the activity and the themes embraced appear to remain within the confines of what is considered legitimate for women, the import of women coming together and having space for discussion should not be devalued. The club formed at a kolkhoz in the Gavrilov-Posad raion, for example, under the slogan: 'All the best – for women', combined activities for old and young alike, proclaiming that 'the life experience of the one and the energy of the other, combine well',[95] and its courses on women's health and household economy appear to have been successful. The zhensovet reported that the women spoke little at first, but 'by the third class you couldn't stop them'.[96] We are informed also that a 'most interesting' discussion ensued following the film 'Young Wife'.[97]

The zhensovety in Ivanovo appear to differ little from their predecessors. Although they list their achievements these, as always, have to be put in the context of a volume of multitudinous problems. When asked about the similarity of claims before and after 1987, Kovaleva answered that the new did not invalidate the old, gains had been made, but there was still much to do. As problems were dealt with, others arose. It is clear that the predominant role of the zhensovety remains that of social welfare, with activists engaged as unpaid stopgaps for the system. Raising women's political consciousness is secondary. The zhensovety use women to cover the responsibilities of others. As Bessolova clearly recognised, 'We have to patch up holes, do other people's work – too much effort is spent in vain.'[98] In Ivanovo, the effects of streamlining the zhensovety appear to have led to more uniformity, but not increased their power. In the early days of the zhensovety some activists were concerned to raise women's status, 'stir up all women, even the most reticent, and establish women's rights in the home and at work.'[99] However, in the main, their own reinforcement of gender roles contributed to the very sexism that prevented the zhensovety from bringing this about. As we have seen, much of the activity conducted by the zhensovety from 1987 to 1989, especially the emphasis on familiar roles, continues to contribute to women's inequality.

A future for the zhensovety

The official role for the zhensovety clearly illustrates the unreconstructed attitude towards women. As aptly stated by Belyaeva, 'Perestroika lacks the women's point of view. It is not women's hands that are missing, but women's minds'.[100] Hence the widespread feeling amongst women that the zhensovety are powerless, time-wasting organisations. The zhensovety have lost the legitimacy afforded them, however weakly, by the CPSU, but have yet to replace it with their own legitimacy. It is feasible that the former well-established existence of the zhensovety in Ivanovo contributed to the continuity in patterns of work. There remain, though, committed women actively seeking ways in which the zhensovety can contribute to change. Concern with the conditions of women's lives is genuine. Solov'eva, Chair of the Iuzha raion zhensovet, concludes her report of work with solicitude for women's happiness and the belief that, 'it is possible to nudge the thought of it, the feeling and the need on its way'.[101] The increasing articulation of the inter-connection between male roles and women's problems was evident amongst members of the Ivanovo town zhensovet. Their dissatisfaction with the People's Deputies nominated by the zhensovety shows there is a demand for women's issues to be put on the political agenda. Questions are being asked: 'What kind of zhensovety can pose and defend the interests of working women, the family and children?'[102] Are the zhensovety superfluous to the emergent radical organisations? The zhensovet of the Central Aerodynamic Institute has shown that providing a base for women to gather together, can lead to consciousness-raising. Despite her brush with officialdom, Bessolova was adamant that given the existence of the zhensovety, they must not be rejected.[103] In *Rabotnitsa*'s report of the SWC plenum in 1989, it was pointed out that the kind of relationship between the new organisations and the zhensovety is yet to emerge. Representatives from the Soviet Women's Committee and the zhensovety at the plenum maintained that there should be, 'the closest contact ... however varied they are, whatever issues they raise'.[104] This is a major step forward given the generally hostile attitude to any alternative women's groups prior to perestroika. It remains to be seen how current developments in Soviet society will affect these sentiments.

It is also less likely that the emergent feminist groups will themselves want to associate with the SWC and the zhensovety. Both are tainted with the officialdom of the past. Is there sufficient will and means amongst the present zhensovety activists to shed that image, and to use their resource of access to women throughout the USSR, to act as their voice? If they fail, we must regret this missed opportunity for radical change.

Whether the zhensovety participate, or it is left to alternative women's groups, the demand for radical change in the position of women, and the recognition of the need for women themselves to bring about that change, is now on the agenda of Soviet women and hence will grow.

Increasingly, women like Larisa Kuznetsova recognise that, 'Work amongst women is specialist, separate ... It is work to raise women's consciousness, in order that women themselves can seek, find and form a programme improving their lives ... it must be a women's organisation for women, an organisation for women with wide social and political tasks ...'[105]

NOTES

1 I. Skliar and O. Laputina, 'Vremia doveriia', *Rabotnitsa*, no. 1, January 1990, p. 18.

2 M. Gorbachev, 'Report to Congress', 30 May 1989, *Current Digest of the Soviet Press*, vol. 41, no. 25, 1989, p. 4.

3 Larisa Vasil'ieva, 'Post congress reflections', *Current Digest of the Soviet Press*, vol. 41, no. 25, 1989, pp. 33–4.

4 The First Independent Women's Forum was held in Dubna, 29–31 March 1991.

5 Vasil'ieva, 'Post congress reflections', pp. 33–4.

6 Ibid.

7 Valentina Konstantinova, Moscow Centre for Gender Studies, discussion, London, April 1991.

8 Much of the information on zhensovety in the town and region of Ivanovo comes from a visit to the area in November 1989.

9 According to Svetlana Kaidash the work of the zhensovety 'had been reduced to nought by the early 1930s'. 'On the "women's problem"', *Moscow News*, no. 33, 198.

10 A. A. Muzygia, V. V. Kopeiko, *Zhensovet: opyt, problemy, perspektivy* (Moskva: Politizdat, 1989), p. 15.

11 A. S. Stoiankina, *Zhenskie Sovety* (Moscow: Sovetskaia Rossia, 1962), p. 7.

12 This point is discussed in Genia Browning, *Women and Politics in the USSR: Consciousness Raising and Soviet Women's Groups* (Sussex: Wheatsheaf Books, New York: St Martin's Press, 1987), pp. 120–9. For further discussion about their role see Mary Buckley, *Women and Ideology in the Soviet Union* (Harmondsworth: Harvester Wheatsheaf; Ann Arbor: University of Michigan Press, 1989), pp. 209–19.

13 Browning, *Women and Politics in the USSR*, p. 56.

14 Anna Mel'nik, 'Zhensovety-vazhnaia forma razvitiia, trudovoi i obsh-chestvennoi aktivnosti zhenshchin', *Partiinaia Zhizn*, no. 2, 1987, pp. 59–63.

15 *Sovetskaia Zhenshchina*, no. 4, April 1988, p. 18; *Rabotnitsa*, no. 11, November 1989, p. 4.

16 Nadezhda Os'minina, 'Pereput'e ili povorot?', *Rabotnitsa*, no. 7, July 1990, p. 14. Comparison with the number of zhensovety before 1987 is not possible. There was no systematic data for individual republics. In 1979, 18,000 were recorded in the RSFSR; in 1975, 4,000 in Lithuania and, in 1965, 9,000 in Kazhakstan; Browning, *Women and Politics in the USSR*, pp. 142–4.

17 S. Senicheva, 'Esli zhivesh v sele', *Iz praktiki raboty zhenskikh sovetov oblasti* (Ivanovo: RIO uprpoligrafizdata Ivanovskogo oblispolkoma, 1989), pp. 13–14.

18 G. Sillaste, 'Zhenshchiny o samikh sebe', *Rabotnitsa*, no. 11, November 1990, p. 7.

19 I. Skliar and O. Laputina, 'Vremia doveriia', p. 18.

20 Mel'nik, 'Zhensovety-vazhnaia forma razvitiia', p. 61. In the Belitskii Furniture Factory with a work force that is 75 per cent female, the zhensovet plays 'an important role in raising production, the quality of goods, and improving working conditions'.

21 Interview with Tat'iana Preobrazhenskaia, reporter and committee member, Oktiabr' raion zhensovet, Ivanovo, November 1989.

22 Interview with a hotel dezhurnaia (key lady), Ivanovo, November 1989.

23 Zoia Pukhova, report of 19th All-Union Conference, *Izvestiia*, 2 July 1988, p. 10.

24 Ibid.

25 Aleksandra Lugovskaia and Galina Nikolaevna Galkina, 'Zhensovet: drug, pomoshchnik? Da!', *Rabotnitsa*, no. 11, November 1989, pp. 4–5.

26 Mel'nik, *'Zhensovety-vazhnaia forma razvitiia*, pp. 59–63.

27 Z. Krylova, 'Problemy nazvany, pora perekhodit' k ikh resheniiu', *Rabotnitsa*, no. 12, December 1988, p. 12.

28 I. Pokrovskaia, 'Mnogo del u zhensoveta', *Golos Dzerzhintsa*, no. 3, (3073), 20 January 1989, p. 2.

29 Z. P. Pukhova, 'Nastupilo vremia energichnykh prakticheskikh deistvii', *Rabotnitsa*, no. 12, December, 1988, p. 11.

30 Lugovskaia and Galkina, 'Zhensovet: drug, pomoshchnik? Da!', p. 4.

31 Pukhova, 'Nastupilo vremia energichnykh prakticheskikh deistvii', p. 11.

32 A. Egorova, a member of the zhensovety and Head of the Altai Territory Clinical Hospital in Barnaul points out that 'the violation of women's rights is not protected by law'. 'The zhensovety united under the Soviet Women's Committee', *Current Digest of the Soviet Press*, vol. 22, no. 31, p. 18.

33 Meeting with Marina Moskvina, Soviet Women's Committee, Moscow, November 1989.

34 Nadezhda Os'minina, 'Pereput'e ili povorot?', p. 15.

35 Lugovskaia and Galkina, 'Zhensovet: drug, pomoshchnik? Da!', p. 5.

36 Ibid.

36 Larisa Kuznetsova, 'Razgovor pered zerkalom?', *Rabotnitsa*, no. 3, March 1990, p. 14.

37 Lugovskaia and Galkina, 'Zhensovet: drug, pomoshchnik? Da!', p. 5.

38 Os'minina, 'Pereput'e ili povorot?', p. 15.

39 Buckley, *Women and Ideology in the Soviet Union*, pp. 153–7.

40 Lugovskaia and Galkina, 'Zhensovet: drug, pomoshchnik? Da!', p. 5.

41 'V raionnom zhensovete', *Golos dzerzhintsa*, no. 4 (3074), 27 January 1989, p. 2.

42 Lugovskaia and Galkina, 'Zhensovet: drug, pomoshchnik? Da!', p. 5.

43 Ibid.

44 *Moscow News*, no. 3, 1989, p. 9.

45 Nina Belyaeva, 'Feminism in the USSR', *Soviet Women, Canadian Woman Studies, les cahiers de la femme*, vol. 10, no. 4, Winter 1989, p. 19.

46 Belyaeva, 'Feminism in the USSR', p. 19.

47 Konstantinova, Gender Relations Workshop, Brighton, 12 April 1991.

48 Ol'ga Bessolova, quoted in Belyaeva, 'Feminism in the USSR', p. 19.

49 Ibid.

50 *Iz praktiki raboty zhenskikh sovetov oblasti*, p. 3.

51 One woman had five children, the other seven. Both fostered a further five and six children.

52 Tat'iana Probrazhenskaia, Ivanovo, November 1989.

53 Zhensovet, Ivanovskoi fabriki Krasnaia Talka, '"Aist", "Lada" i drugie', *Iz praktiki raboty*, p. 31.

54 E. Tiurina, 'Dobraia "Khoziaiushka"', *Iz praktiki raboty*. p. 21.

55 Pokrovskaia, 'Mnogo del u zhensoveta', p. 2.

56 Egorova, 'Zhensovety united under the Soviet Women's Committee', p. 18.

57 Mikhail Gorbachev, 'Improvement of social class relations and relations among the peoples of the USSR', *Report to 27th Congress*, CPSU, translated, *Soviet News*, 26 February 1986.

58 'V raionnom zhensovete', p. 2.

59 *Iz praktiki raboty*, p. 3.

60 Pokrovskaia, 'Mnogo del u zhensoveta', p. 2.

61 V. Solov'eva, 'Schast'e-kazhdomu domu', *Iz praktiki raboty*, p. 17.
62 N. Sinitsyna, 'Krepka sem'ia-krepka derzhava', *Iz praktiki raboty*, p. 11.
63 V. Kustova, 'Vnimanie-sem'e', *Iz praktiki raboty*, p. 4.
64 Ibid.
65 I. Motygina, 'Avtoritet-v delakh', *Iz praktiki raboty*, p. 10.
66 T. Solov'eva, 'Pozitsiia zhensoveta', *Iz praktiki raboty*, p. 19.
67 '"Aist", "Lada" i drugie', p. 30.
68 'Na puti dobra i doveriia', *Iz praktiki raboty*, p. 32.
69 Pokrovskaia, 'Mnogo del u zhensoveta', p. 2.
70 Solov'eva, 'Schast'e-kazhdomu domu', p. 15.
71 Ibid.
72 Ibid.
73 'Na puti dobra i doveriia', p. 32.
74 V. Kiseleva, 'Zabota o podrastaiushchem pokolenii', *Iz praktiki raboty*, p. 18.
75 Ibid.
76 Solov'eva, 'Pozitsiia zhensoveta', p. 19.
77 Pokrovskaia, 'Mnogo del u zhensoveta', p. 2.
78 Solov'eva, 'Schast'e-kazhdomu domu', p. 17. In Minsk the zhensovety help with the fostering of children, 'Mothering Nine', *Moscow News*, no. 9, 1989, p. 14.
79 V. Odinitsova and N. Grechishkina, 'Operatsiia "zabota"', *Iz praktiki raboty*, pp. 22–3.
80 Tiurina, 'Dobraia "khoziaiushka"', p. 20.
81 Senicheva, 'Esli zhivesh' v sele ...', p. 14.
82 Mnogo del u zhensoveta, p. 2.
83 V. Kustova, 'Vnimanie-sem'e', *Iz praktiki raboty*, p. 5.
84 N. Pozorova, 'Ne zabyvat' i ob otdykhe', *Iz praktiki raboty*, p. 37.
85 Ibid., p. 38.
86 N. Sinitsyna, '"Krepka sem'ia-krepka derzhava"', *Iz praktiki raboty*, pp. 12–13.
87 Z. Kuftyreva, 'Delu vremia-potekhe chas', *Iz praktiki raboty*, p. 35.
88 Ibid.
89 Senicheva, 'Esliu zhivesh' v sele ...', p. 14.
90 Ibid.
91 T. Nechaeva, 'Klub "Sovremennitsa"', *Iz praktiki raboty*, p. 28.
92 Pozorova, 'Ne zabyvat' i ob otdykhe', p. 38.
93 Elvira Novikova, quoted in Belyaeva, 'Feminism in the USSR', p. 18.
94 '"Davaite zhit' interesno"', *Tsikl vstrech*, Oktiabr' RK KPSS, Raionnyi zhenskii sovet, 1988–9; 1989–90.
95 Tiurina, 'Dobraia "khoziaiushka"', p. 21.
96 Ibid.
97 Ibid.
98 Bessolova, quoted in Belyaeva, 'Feminism in the USSR', p. 19.
99 *Krest'ianka*, no. 9, September, 1980, p. 27.

100 Belyaeva, 'Feminism in the USSR', p. 19.
101 Solov'eva, 'Schast'e-kazhdomu domu', p. 17.
102 Skliar and Laputina, 'Vremia doveriia', p. 20.
103 Bessolova, quoted in Belyaeva, 'Feminism in the USSR', p. 19.
104 Skliar and Laputina, 'Vremia doveriia', p. 20.
105 Larisa Kuznetsova, 'Razgovor pered zerkalom?', p. 14.

Chapter 8

The new women's studies

Natal'ia Rimashevskaia

For a long time, the 'woman question' was thought to be resolved in the USSR and consequently was only discussed as a 'great achievement'. Women's social and economic problems were insignificant 'imperfections' in a context of general well-being or taboo topics which could not be analysed in print. Many aspects of women's lives could not, in any case, be discussed because statistical data were missing, such as wages broken down according to sex. For some issues, information is still missing today. However, the general situation began to change radically in the late 1980s. Women's status was among the first topics to be affected by democratisation and glasnost.

'Gender' comes onto the academic agenda

The acuteness of women's problems, which were perceived by members of society, attracted the attention of those working in social and governmental structures. As a result, a Committee on questions concerning women, the family and the protection of motherhood and children was set up in the Supreme Soviet. A similar department was established in the Council of Ministers. Corresponding structures appeared in some republics and in regional bodies.

Sensitive to the changes which were taking place, the academic community in 1986 put onto the agenda the need for a specialised scientific council on women's problems. Such a council was created within the Academy of Social Sciences under the Central Committee of the Communist Party. Its general rubric covered 'the social activities of women in the contemporary world'. The council included men and women and drew together researchers from various institutions. Initially, the topics scrutinised by the council were rather traditional ones, in keeping with a Marxist perspective. These included women and work, women and the family, women and socialism, the socio-political activity of women and nationality and the woman question. Nevertheless, an important setting for discussion was created. Moreover, some experts on the council held non-traditional views. This general development was indeed significant for the development of gender studies.

Some of the first research findings discussed by the council were in a report on 'Some problems of women's status' written by myself. It was based on results from an ongoing study of Taganrog.[1] The report examined women's social status, reproductive behaviour, careers, wages, health, free time, and post-retirement behaviour. For the first time, data on the unfavourable status of women were published. The sharpness of the findings somewhat embarrassed the audience who were accustomed to hearing about achievements.

The report concluded that, contrary to common belief, there was no contradiction between women's roles as workers and mothers. Rather, a contradiction existed between families' needs in normal reproduction, and the possibilities for their realisation. The major problem for women was that their lives were pre-determined by society and their choices were very limited. An egalitarian approach was needed. The report argued against the traditional approach which assumed a differentiation of role functions between the sexes. The egalitarian approach was unfamiliar and met with opposition. Yet it could not be refuted. The common opinion remained that the goal of society should be to improve the status of women in the family and outside.

The new egalitarian approach was further developed in the article 'How we solve the woman question', written by A. Posadskaia, N. Zakharova and myself, which was published in *Kommunist* in 1989.[2] The article held that patriarchal relations should be replaced by egalitarian ones, based on a mutual complementarity of the sexes, which can only be realised in a 'free choice environment'. Here there should be no *a priori* conceptions of personality. What reaction did the article receive? None. Only a very narrow circle responded to this radically new approach. One can be sure that the majority of readers did not accept the ideas, but they were not ready to refute them. Later it became known that the article had a wide response abroad, and was translated and commented upon in a number of countries.

There were several academic reactions to our adoption of the concept 'gender'. Economists from the Institute of Economics, the Institute of International Economic and Political Research, the Institute of Forecasting and the Institute of Labour argued that women who participate in the work force but who also have a family need special privileges, such as longer maternity leave and opportunities to work part-time. In addition, they stressed that women's working conditions should be improved.

Sociologists, mainly from the Institute of Sociology, criticised the concept with patriarchal concerns in mind. They were worried about depopulation processes and low fertility rates in most regions of Russia. They looked at women from a demographic point of view, seeing them, primarily as the means for reproducing the population. Historians from the Institute of the International Labour Movement criticised the egalitarian basis underpinning 'gender', preferring to advocate psycho-physiological differences between the sexes leading to different role functions.

Only two groups of academics supported the adoption of 'gender'. Tat'iana Klimenkova and Ol'ga Voronina from the Institute of Philosophy gave their backing. And Professor Igor' Kon sent a special letter in which he argued that the concept was 'progressive' and that it opened up for study contemporary and future problems, hitherto not recognised. Kon stood out among male academics for being the only one to give open support. The majority remained silent, not wishing to be seen to criticise 'gender', but not wishing to be seen to back it. Above all, they did not wish to show that they were retrograde. Since equal opportunities were involved, they could not easily argue against. Policy-makers, too, could not refute our research findings, but criticised the strategic implications of the concept. It looked ahead of current problems.

Discussion of 'gender' revealed that men realise the importance, in decision-making, of improving the status of women, the family, mothers and children, but preferred to do so on the surface without radically changing the situation. Evidently that was why the males in the audience were not eager to accept our ideas. It was not by chance that the concept of 'gender' had not previously been discussed at the top of the Academy of Sciences. Male academics did not take such ideas seriously. Public consciousness is still extremely patriarchal, especially among men. Moreover, the higher the level of decision-making, the stronger this is the case. It is expressed in various ways. For instance, it is common to announce formal equality of the sexes, and to stress it and, at the same time, demand that women be removed from the workforce and stay at home: they should be there to perform their natural functions of mother and housekeeper. As theoretical and conceptual analyses of the 'woman question' develop, the need for praxis is increasingly pressing.

The Centre for Gender Studies

A Centre for Gender Studies has been organised in the Institute of Socio-Economic Problems of the Population. It is a research, information and training centre, which focuses on the issues of sex, as socially constructed. The Centre embraces the principles of openness and democracy and strives to make the results of its studies intelligible to both men and women.

Attitudes towards the Centre are rather dubious. Some who become acquainted with it support new approaches to the 'woman question'. The majority, however, does not take it seriously; nor does it, therefore, bother to protest. What critics dislike most is the term 'gender'.

The academic interests of the Centre cover various areas of research: the 'woman question' and perestroika; the evolution of gender relations – from patriarchal protection to egalitarian relations; women and transition to a market economy; women and labour – from conflict to harmony; social, economic and demographic reasons for the feminisation of poverty; indicators of male and female social status; women and leadership; crisis in formal women's organisations and the problems of informal women's movements in the USSR and in Eastern Europe; images of women in the mass media; gender and power; forms of social discrimination against men and women.

The main result of organising this Centre within the Academy of Sciences is a theoretical and ideological one. Its creation forced all state and social structures, especially those at the apex of power, seriously to look at women's problems, not allowing them easily to brush them aside, as had frequently been the case. The authority of the Academy of Sciences played an important role here.

The Centre for Gender Studies provides an organisational base for theoretical reflection and elaboration which is an essential foundation for understanding and addressing the various positions in which women find themselves. Until recently, the classics of Marxism-Leninism were considered the essential theory and all that was needed was to realise them in practice.

Integral to the theoretical work of the Centre, its members organised an international seminar on 'the position of women working in main industrial enterprises' together with participation from representatives of UNESCO. The results of joint research on women's roles involving the Institute of Socio-Economic Problems of the Population and KAMAZ tractor factory were imparted, discussed and shared with scholars from other countries.

Finally, the Centre has, in a sense, become a reference point in the activities of the independent women's movement, quite distinct in many ways from the directions supported by the Soviet Women's Committee. For instance, the Centre for Gender Studies participated in the organisation of the First Independent Women's Forum with the goal of 'showing the strength' of women and of women's organisations which are active in society today.

Without doubt the Centre for Gender Studies could fulfil its functions more efficiently and take on more commitments. But this is impossible as long as financial and material resources are inadequate and room space remains limited. We also lack computers, a FAX machine and simple technology. The Centre started with very little. However, one real achievement is a collection of books, largely donated by foreign scholars, for our vast library on gender issues, unique in our country.

NOTES

1 N. M. Rimashevskaia, I. A. Gerasimova and V. G. Kopnina, *Sem'ia, Trud, dokhody, potrebleniye* (Moscow: Nauka, 1977); N. M. Rimashevskaia and L. A. Onikov, *Narodnye Blagosostoianiye: Tendentsii i Perspektivy* (Moscow: Nauka, 1990).
2 N. Zahkarova, A. Posadskaia and N. M. Rimashevskaia, 'Kak my reshaem zhenskii vopros', *Kommunist*, no. 4, April, 1989, pp. 56–65.

Chapter 9

'Cuckoo-mothers' and 'apparatchiks': glasnost and children's homes

Elizabeth Waters

Glasnost opened up for discussion a range of social problems previously considered to be peculiar to capitalism and found them closer to home. Soviet journalists approached this new material with an eye for detail and sensation: they described the luxurious lifestyles and calculated the annual income of young women who slept with foreigners for hard currency, and exposed the ready market that heroin found among some sections of the population. Children's homes were another subject of investigation; in a series of articles published in the press over 1987 and 1988 their buildings were revealed to be in a state of disrepair, their supplies of food and clothing inadequate, their inmates ill-treated. Attention was drawn to the size of the problem, to the hundreds of thousands of children in care, and to the large number who were not orphans, who had been placed in homes by parents or parent. This last circumstance was cited as evidence of the alarming decline of moral standards, a reflection of the disintegration of the social fabric.

Precisely because the right to a happy childhood had always been an important ingredient of Soviet propaganda,[1] these revelations were made with much bitterness. Initially this was directed, in part, against the staff of the children's homes who took such poor care of their charges, but principally against the parents – specifically the mothers – who abandoned their children. By 1989 and 1990, the target of censure had shifted: an understanding attitude was adopted towards single mothers whose poverty obliged them to give up their babies and the largest share of blame for the situation laid at the feet of the government and the 'system', for failing to provide the material and moral prerequisites of normal family life. This new approach to social problems was a reflection of wider changes: of the extension of glasnost

and perestroika and of the mounting disillusionment with the Soviet
social and political order.

Glasnost and children's homes

In 1987 a round table on children, their health and welfare, was
organised by the journal *Kommunist* in collaboration with the Central
Committee of the Komsomol, and the published proceedings of the
meeting made widely available information of unprecedented scope on
the state of the children's homes. The USSR, it was disclosed, had a
total of 284,000 children in care: 35,000 in 422 infants' homes, 84,000
in 745 children's homes, 71,000 in 237 boarding schools for orphans
and a further 94,000 children in regular boarding schools. A further
729,000 children lived not with parents but with relatives and guardians. The standard of care provided by these institutions came in for
criticism: the homes were poorly furnished, the children lacked proper
clothing and were ill-fed.[2]

The low quality of care was dramatically confirmed by S. Karkhanin
and S. Stepinina, two correspondents for *Sovetskaia Rossiia*, who the
same month broke the story of Special Boarding School No. 2 in the
Siberian town of Angarsk, where children who misbehaved were
locked in a tiny, empty room without heat or light or adequate
ventilation for up to two and three weeks. Twenty-five children were
said to have been punished in this manner and the same number
injected with magnesia to keep them docile. An enquiry set up by the
Irkutsk provincial soviet to investigate the running of the boarding
school ruled there was no basis for charges against its director, G. P.
Poroshina[3]; and local support for her pedagogical methods was
registered. This tale of inhuman treatment, and of complacency in the
face of suffering, elicited an immediate and overwhelming response
from the public, the paper receiving over 2,300 letters in the space of a
few weeks, demanding that the cruel regime in School No. 2 be brought
to an end. While the chairperson of the Irkutsk *obkom* was, by the
summer of 1987, admitting that *Sovetskaia Rossiia*'s coverage of the
situation had been accurate, this was not a view shared by all of those
involved; a good half of the teaching staff signed a letter protesting
their 'trial-by-the-press'; a group of night-nannies complained that all
discipline at the home had broken down since the controversy got into
the newspapers; seventeen parents publicly expressed approval for the
director and her punishment cell. A mixture of the carrot and the stick
eventually brought about reform: by the autumn, staff at the home

were reported to have been won over to civilised pedagogical methods;[4] the director and a number of others implicated in the affair lost their jobs.

Readers' letters in the wake of the Angarsk scandal made clear that Special School No. 2 was not an exceptional case.[5] The physical abuse to which inmates of children's homes were subjected was in subsequent months reported widely in the press. One in three children, in one survey, were beaten, some of them by the directors of the institutions caring for them:[6] a girl had elastoplast stuck across her mouth to stop her from talking too much;[7] in Home No. 10, in Rostov, the older children, left to look after the younger ones, stuck needles into them, forced them to curtsy 300 times before they went to bed, and hit them with skipping ropes.[8] Children's health was placed in jeopardy, also, it was revealed, through the misappropriation of food supplies. Cooks often had no training in catering, were former cashiers or photographers who had chosen to work in a home purely for the perks, which were considerable. Over 90 per cent of meals at the 14 children's homes in Frunze and its environs did not meet the required standards; in some cases dishes contained only 70 per cent of the regulation calorie content. At one institution the cooks were found by a Control Commission to have kept back 25 kilos of meat and 7 of fat; a second check of the same premises shortly afterwards revealed that the thefts were continuing; a third visit registered the disappearance of 12 kilos of chicken.[9] In the space of one month, children at boarding school No. 59 in Moscow 'failed to receive' 300 kilos of vegetables, 35 kilos of soft cheese and 45 kilos of vegetable oil.[10]

It was recognized that there were 'objective' reasons for the cruelty and the heartlessness. Earnings were low and work in the homes was exhausting, both physically and emotionally. For these reasons there was a high staff turn-over, and hiring committees had to take what candidates they were offered, who were very often without the relevant qualifications. *Komsomol'skaia pravda* received only thirty expressions of interest when, in 1985, it called on students at teacher training colleges to take up work in homes; by 1987 the number had dwindled to twelve.[11]

Not all the complaints about the children's homes were found to be justified.[12] The majority of employees was said to be doing a valiant job in very difficult circumstances – in circumstances that were made more difficult, it was suggested, by the inefficiency and penny-pinching of the central bureaucracy. The RSFSR Minister of Education had, for example, passed a directive prohibiting children's homes from buying

frankfurters and sausages; similarly, subscriptions to popular magazines like *Ogonek* and *Krokodil* were not permitted.[13] Budget allo-
cations for children's homes did not include money for outings to the
circus and other places of entertainment, nor were opportunities for
summer trips and holidays always provided. Supplies of basic foodstuffs such as beetroot and even potatoes were erratic;[14] urgent pleas to
stock bare cupboards went unheeded.[15] A range of government ministries had a part in the running of the homes but none the ultimate
authority.

The CPSU response

In the summer of 1987 the communist party responded to press and
public anxiety about conditions in the children's homes. In August,
Pravda published a Central Committee resolution 'on measures to
eliminate serious shortcomings in the work with orphaned children'. It
condemned the 'callous' attitude of some of the staff and noted that
many institutions had 'not overcome their indifference to the inner
world and spiritual development of the children'. The resolution placed
some of the blame for the poor conditions on society at large – 'the
defence of the rights and interests of orphaned children', it declared,
'has yet to become the vital concern of state and public organisations
and labour collectives'. There was, at least by implication, a measure
also of self-criticism, and a promise to increase the commitment of the
government, as well as the academic community, to the study of the
problems of family and childhood: the Ministries of Justice, Health,
Education, and Finance, and the USSR State Committee on Labour and
Social Questions, would proceed to examine family law with a view to
increasing the protection of children; and the USSR Academy of
Sciences and the USSR Academy of Pedagogy would research 'the
problems of the socialist family and its role in the development,
upbringing and education of the individual and the acceleration of the
country's socio-economic development'. Promises of 'improvements'
had been the common currency of political rhetoric in the pre-
perestroika era,[16] but the resolution also announced a substantial
increase in government expenditure on children's homes, from 600
million to 1,420 million roubles, and the setting up of a Children's
Fund, a charitable organisation to solicit and administer public donations.[17]

In the 1930s charity had been labelled a 'bourgeois' phenomenon,
unnecessary in a socialist society, which was by definition capable of

providing for all its citizens; the reforming impulses of perestroika had recast it as a legitimate, indeed a necessary, element in a society that desired to base itself upon morality, conscience and public duty. In October 1987 the V.I. Lenin Soviet Children's Fund (SCF) was officially inaugurated with wide media coverage and blessing,[18] its name suggesting a conscious attempt to seek legitimacy in the Bolshevik tradition, yet its very existence, more than seventy years after the revolution, hinted that the Bolshevik tradition was in some way flawed. The early pronouncements of the Fund espoused the critical and reforming spirit of the 'new thinking'. Collectivisation and the purges were condemned;[19] the sufferings of children under Stalinism as well as under Nazism were described;[20] 'industrial egotism', bureaucratic inefficiency and wastefulness were attacked.[21] The SCF would not be replicating the mode of operation of the old-style apparatus, the public was assured: donations, for instance, were to be spent entirely on helping children in need, and running costs met by the proceeds of publishing and other commercial ventures.[22] According to its Chairperson, Albert Likhanov, a writer and the editor of the journal *Smena* who had long made children's homes his particular concern, the Fund also intended to adopt a fresh approach to matters of principle. In the past, he told the Fund's Constituent Assembly, parents were taught that children ought to be raised primarily by the state, and their responsibilities were confined to working hard and enjoying themselves. 'To this day there has been no real rehabilitation of family responsibility for children, of parenting and of mutual obligations between family members . . . We must revive the only cult permissible in our country – the cult of the family.'[23]

This interpretation of the past is misleading. In the 1920s, the Bolsheviks were obliged to take into care over one million children whose parents were dead or missing, and in some cases they did so with enthusiasm, believing that the 'withering away' of the family was part of the transition to socialism. Theorists like Aleksandra Kollomtai predicted that the domestic economy would be superseded by communal services such as canteens, laundries, childcare centres; the family was widely criticised as a conservative institution incapable of bringing up children in a modern, progressive manner. But, in the 1930s, the socialisation of domestic life was denounced as petit bourgeois, anarchist, and unmarxist. Karl Marx himself was presented to the Soviet public as the friend of the younger generation, a father who played paper boats with his children in the parks of London. From that time on, officials, academics and journalists all argued tirelessly that the family was the basic cell of socialist society and must be defended and protected.

This traditional view on family matters was rarely challenged in the early stages of perestroika by advocates of reform. Radicals as well as conservatives were for the most part agreed that the 'basic cell' should be strengthened. The Central Committee advocated action to ensure that the family performed its 'crucial social functions'.[24] The reformers referred to the 'crisis in the family', and wanted women relieved from work in production so that they could spend more time with children. According to the demographer, Mark Tolts, 'the foundations of physical and mental health are laid in the family and nowhere else'; our history and sufferings have taught us, he said, the 'true role of the family'. He shared Albert Likhanov's view that society in the past had neglected the family because it believed public upbringing to be more healthy, effective and correct than private family care, a misconception which in his view had 'cost us dear'.[25]

Why, given the historical evidence, did such a picture of past Soviet policies as fundamentally 'anti-family' gain currency? Perhaps what was being remembered by both Albert Likhanov and Mark Tolts was the sharp controversy of the sixties that followed Khrushchev's promotion of boarding schools as the ideal educational institution, a debate that made a big impression on their generation. Perhaps it was the inconsistencies within Soviet ideology, rather than the shortcomings of past practice, that were the real object of attack. Tenets of Marxism-Leninism, such as the emancipation of women and the superiority of state-organised facilities did have a place in the 'rhetorical' creed of the party, alongside the celebration of the family, even if their impact on policy formulation had been minimal. Perestroika targeted inconsistencies of this kind and created a climate in which revisions of the classical canon were made respectable, and could inform the party's ideological pronouncements as well as daily decision-making.

'Cuckoo-mothers'

A further reason for the widespread reaffirmation of the importance of the family was the revelation that a large number of the inmates of the children's homes were not orphans. *Kommunist* in May 1987 admitted that many children in care had either one or both parents still living. Elsewhere it was reported that in the Russian republic about 70,000 children were in homes because parental care had been ruled unsatisfactory by the authorities, and that many more parents voluntarily gave up their children to the homes. According to A. A. Likhanov, only 4 or 5 per cent of the million children in institutions and foster homes were in fact orphans.[26] 'Orphanhood when parents are still living' was, in the view of the Central Committee, 'particularly intolerable and alien to the humane principles of socialism'.[27]

The plight of those children in the homes who had no prospect of being reunited with their parents and yet, because they had parents, could not be adopted was truly tragic, and a number of accounts touched on these problems in a serious and moving way.[28] But there was almost no discussion of the economic circumstances that made single parenthood difficult – the accommodation shortage, the shortcomings of child care, the poverty. 'We hate [the parents] of course for refusing [their children]', Marina Gurgenovna Kontareva, the head doctor at Moscow Home of the Child No. 12 and a Hero of Socialist Labour, was quoted as saying.[29] Almost all commentators placed all blame on parents.

And parents, it was usually assumed, were female; mothers had the major responsibility in the upbringing of children and by the same token must shoulder the major blame for the high number of children abandoned to the homes. Examples proliferated in the press of women who refused to renounce their parental rights because of the perks to which motherhood entitled them,[30] and whose children in consequence languished in the homes, ineligible for adoption. *Sovetskaia Rossiia* told the story of one woman who was in no hurry to take her baby out of Ivanovo's Home No. 1 (where only 6 of 76 children were true orphans) even though she lived just across the road.[31] There was another woman who had given birth to thirteen children, all subnormal, and all in homes; she, an alcoholic, said the lifestyle suited her because of the benefits, including the extra living space.[32] Moral opprobrium was encapsulated in the name by which these women who left the state to look after babies were constantly referred to in the press: 'cuckoo-mothers' (*materi-kukushki*).

The desire to punish the 'cuckoo mother' was almost universal. A frequent demand was that women be forced to pay towards the upkeep of the children. 'It is absolutely necessary', wrote *Pravda Ukrainy*, 'to search for the cruel strangers and force them to reimburse at least the material expenses which the state spends on the education of these tiny orphans.' V. Kiseleva, a 'labour veteran' from Kiev, agreed that women should be forced to work, or to pay a fine and alimony. Twelve doctors from Minsk in Belorussia suggested that alimony payments be kept in trust for the child; they were also of the opinion that the woman's decision to abandon a child should be made known and discussed at her place of work. According to a Moldavian actress, what was required was a law depriving these mothers 'of the very title of woman'.[33] Other suggested punishments included stamping internal passports,[34] and sending 'cuckoo-mothers' to camps along with prostitutes and alcoholics. When a reader wrote to *Sovetskaia Rossiia* recommending forced sterilization, the paper commented that while this proposal was obviously unacceptable, no one would reproach the letter writer for having made it.[35] Though official organisations did not go as far as to suggest medical intervention, proposals for punishment were not confined to readers' letters and newspaper columns. The *Kommunist*/Komsomol round table in early 1987 had discussed 'harsh legal measures' against those who gave up their children. 'These demands' commented the editors of *Kommunist* were 'well-founded'.[36] The Committee of Soviet Women drafted legislation setting out penalties for 'cuckoo-mothers' including the stamping of their passports.[37] The SCF took the view that the law giving mothers the right to hand over their babies to the state should be rescinded. Understandable as a war-time measure, the Fund argued – the law was passed in 1943 – it had no rationale in Soviet society of the late 1980s.[38]

The SCF and its critics

The main work of the Fund was directed, nevertheless, not at devising methods of dealing with the 'cuckoo-mothers', but at providing for the welfare of children, both those with 'living parents' and those without. The Fund spent several million roubles improving the staff–child ratio in homes for babies and toddlers, it purchased buses and funded trips to the sea and overseas. It successfully lobbied to strengthen the legal position of young people after they graduated from children's homes, winning them the right to jump the housing queue, to receive one-off payments for clothes and other essentials, and – in the case of those going on to higher education – a monthly allowance;[39] it made efforts to deal with the individual problems faced by the former inmates of children's homes as they adjusted to the wider world. In Albert Likhanov's estimation, the most important work of the Fund was its promotion of 'family-type' children's homes such as already existed in some East European countries, homes which sought to reduce the isolation characteristic of large institutions of the past and reproduce as far as possible the atmosphere and relationships of the family. In

August 1988 the Council of Ministers approved plans for the building
of thirty such homes in fourteen republics over a three-year period,
each designed as a cluster of houses offering accommodation for fifteen
to twenty families bringing up ten or more orphans and provided with
recreational facilities to be used also by other children from the
surrounding area.[40]

These successes were set out in the speech Albert Likhanov made to
the Fund's 2nd Plenum in the autumn of 1988. He also had less positive
matters to report. He complained of the lack of media interest in the
work of the Fund. If it were not for its own weekly newspaper, *Sem'ia*
(*The Family*), he said, the SCF would be at a loss to get its message
across.[41] He accused a section of the media of libel and slander: *Soviet
Sport* in September 1988 had announced that the SCF was preparing to
finance an All-Union beauty contest, an allegation that it had not
checked and was groundless; other papers and the National Radio
took up the story, precipitating a large number of angry letters to the
Fund. *Soviet Sport* later published the official protest lodged by the SCF
(though in abridged form) but, in Albert Likhanov's view, the harm
had already been done.[42]

The decline in media coverage of the Fund and the accusations of
funds misspent would appear to have been fuelled by unease at the
SCF's official status. In the second half of 1988 the political climate in
the Soviet Union had changed sharply as realisation of the gravity of the
country's economic problems took root and dissatisfaction with the
pace of reform grew among perestroika's radical supporters. To them
the Fund now appeared to share the shortcomings of all official
organisations. The reference in its title to the founder of the Soviet
state, in 1987 a pledge of loyalty to a nobler age, a symbol of renewal,
became if not a liability then certainly less of an advantage.

The increasing recognition of the deep-seated difficulties facing
Soviet society also affected the discussion of children's homes, prompt-
ing a questioning of the notion that individuals were to blame for social
problems. The idea that it was poverty and poor living conditions
rather than heartlessness and lack of spirituality that drove single
mothers to tip their young from the nest began to take hold. *Pravda*, in
the summer of 1990, found 'objective reasons' for the fact that 95 per
cent of orphans had 'living parents'. The social portrait painted in
Molodoi kommunist (*Young Communist*) by Mariia Rubinstein of
mothers who gave up their children to the homes suggested they were
the victims of misfortune, not moral monsters: they were aged 15–25
years, unmarried, with minimal education, or still in school. Until sex

education and access to contraception were improved, she said, the problem of abandoned children would not go away.[43] *Sem'ia i Shkola* (*Family and School*) was convinced that economic problems were the cause of the large number of 'orphans with parents alive' and that the tragedy of these children could be avoided if people were guaranteed the basic necessities of life; single mothers could not be expected to live on the tiny benefits they received.[44] A. Nechaeva, from the Institute of State and Law of the USSR Academy of Sciences and member of the group drafting new legislation on the rights of the child, was equally categorical that the present level of benefits was far too low.[45] A single mother, Irina Zagornova from Orenburg, pointed out the absurdity of a system which demanded that prospective adoptive parents produce every possible documentation of their status including proof of adequate earnings, but allocated single mothers only 20 roubles a month.

As the emphasis on the economic basis of the problem grew more insistent, so too did the criticism of the SCF. Why, it was asked, did the Fund have to adopt a centralised system mirroring the Soviet bureaucracy? Why should local and Republican branches of the Fund have to send money to Moscow?[46] And why was the RSFSR, alone among the fifteen republics, without its own Republican branch?[47] At the beginning of 1990 events in Leningrad furnished proof for those looking for it that, despite its early protestations to the contrary, the Fund had not rid itself of the vices of the old-style apparatus, was in the party's pocket, was itself flesh and blood of the 'administrative-command' system. Gross malpractices came to light in the city's children's homes and some of the staff who held high position in the local branch of the Fund were found to be among those accused of cruel pedagogical methods; one of them, B. Avlas, a member of the Regional Fund Administration, while under investigation by the procuracy for her treatment of the orphaned children in her charge, was awarded the honour of Merited Teacher of the RSFSR. The city's party organisation was accused of interfering in the Fund's administration, and Fund officials of having acted in a haughty manner and discouraged public initiative and participation. A commission from Moscow, headed by Albert Likhanov, which visited the city in March, pronounced B. Avlas an 'odious character' and reprimanded the Leningrad branch of the Fund for its style of work. However, it either would not or could not implement reforms in the face of local opposition, and eventually washed its hands of the affair and returned home.[48] But the debate about the operation of the Fund did not die away. In fact it came to the Fund's doorstep in Moscow in dramatic fashion when, in the autumn of that year, the two employees of the SCF directly responsible for children's homes, Nail' Shamsutdinov and Aleksei Golovan', went on hunger strike. In their view the SCF had become incorporated into the party machine and instead of doing good works carried out tasks that should have been shouldered by the government. They attacked the Fund's leadership for its authoritarian style and for its preference for grandiose projects which left no money for helping children in need.[49] Working in the Social Guardianship Bureau they received a constant stream of visitors, young people just out of the children's homes, with nowhere to live and no money, but were unable to offer assistance, so tight were the rules and regulations regarding the release of even the smallest sums from the kitty. The two young men were not alone in their discontent. In fact, some thirty members of staff had already left during the preceding months because of their dissatisfaction with the way the Fund was being run, and many of those who remained supported the hunger-strikers. Supporters of the hunger-strikers referred to the leadership as 'dyed-in-the-wool bureaucrats' and 'apparatchiks'. Those loyal to the leadership, in turn, called the protesters 'little Pavel Morozovs', a reference to a peasant boy who, during the collectivization of the early 1930s denounced his father to the authorities as an enemy of the people and a member of a kulak conspiracy. On 23 October 1990, People's Deputies of the RSFSR attended a meeting of the staff to hear grievances. The following month the Supreme Soviet committees on education, youth affairs and the protection of motherhood and infancy recommended a commission of inquiry.

As a result of these developments press interest in the SCF increased, though the coverage was hardly of the sort Albert Likhanov had been looking for. 'The V. I. Lenin Soviet Children's Fund has fully justified its name', declared the Mossovet journal, *Stolitsa*, in one of its first issues; '[c]reated according to the canons of the administrative system, it makes miserable those whom it should make happy.'[50] The Fund was criticised for the handling of its finances.[51] The perks enjoyed by the leadership were listed and condemned. The chairperson and his deputies (all five of them) were, it was disclosed, *nomenklatura* appointments, and therefore eligible for certain privileges, including special medical treatment. Albert Likhanov was alleged to have a personal cook, and a separate toilet, his secretary's daughter to have made several trips abroad.[52] This concern with privilege and personality was not shared by all commentators: if Albert Likhanov came to work on a bicycle instead of in a Volga, and brought a packed lunch from home, would that change anything?' asked one journalist. The essential point, in her view, was the Fund's lack of independence, its party orientation.[53]

This, in fact, was a constant theme. Criticisms of the CPSU and the government became increasingly voluble and direct. The Fund, it was said, set itself, in typical party fashion, over-ambitious goals which it duly failed to achieve. One example cited was an impressive residence on Moscow's Prospekt Mira, rented by the Fund soon after its foundation to serve as a Palace of Childhood, then left to stand, unrenovated and empty. Another was the plan for family-type children's homes, previously praised on all sides. In the new economic context this, the Fund's major project, was ridiculed as a piece of irresponsible Utopian dreaming, imported 'without consideration for our realities'.[54] Saving up for expensive projects, the Fund had no money for everyday acts of charity. The SCF, in mid-1989, it was pointed out, had invested 150 million roubles in Zhilsotsbank for a fixed three-year term; in contrast, over the first nine months of that year it spent a mere 5.3 million roubles on charitable works. Instead of promoting the spirit of charity, and a new moral climate, instead of offering specific help to specific individuals in need, it had, the critics alleged, become an off-shoot of the apparatus. If the V. I. Lenin Fund were to survive, it was said, a major overhaul must be carried out. Charities that were independent and community-oriented were held up by the critics as the model. The Leningrad komsomol paper *Smena* featured information on the recently formed Infancy Foundation which was keeping itself at a distance from party and soviet organisations;[55] the magazine, *Sotsial'naia zashchita* (*Social Defence*), gave space to E. V. Tolstaia and T. I. Iasharova, members of the independent group, 'Pedagogical Search', to discuss the problems of finding accommodation for young people leaving children's homes,[56] and also published an interview with Svetlana Vasil'kova, founder of 'Mama', an unofficial organisation which aimed to offer moral and material support to women who were bringing up children alone.

By the end of 1990 and beginning of 1991 the escalating economic problems and the seemingly intractable political gulf between radicals and conservatives, and between Moscow and the republics, were deepening the already widespread disillusionment with a social and political system that had after seventy years succeeded, it was gloomily observed, only in bringing the country to the brink of disaster. The difficulties faced by vulnerable social groups such as orphans were now perceived as symptoms of a much deeper malaise, their needs only marginally greater than those of children who had parents and lived in families. 'Let's show we care not only about the children in homes, but also about the children in families', wrote Vladimir Lipskii in *Komsomol'skaia pravda* in January 1991.[57] That same month *Megopolis-Express* carried an article entitled 'SOS: Children. Our "privileged class" has become the most oppressed class', while *Rossiiskaia Gazeta* discussed the poor state of child health under the heading 'Catastrophe is just one step away'.[58] Elsewhere the shocking state of childcare institutions – creches and kindergartens – received attention, and readers' letters described the grinding poverty in which many families lived.[59] Academician V. A. Tabolin warned that because of the food crisis 'low quality' children were being born, children were falling ill more often and were tiring more easily, and their learning ability was impaired.[60] Soviet children, according to S. Doletskii, corresponding member of the Academy of Sciences, were often the victims of child abuse, due to the instability of the family, and the prevalence of alcoholism.

For decades the system of authoritarian upbringing ravaged and lay waste the living souls of children on a national scale. It 'produced' most of the mothers and fathers of today. And brought up on slogans and a hobbled culture, these parents are now strangling and suppressing young peoples' personalities and trampling on their dignity.[61]

Conclusion

The discussion about children's homes has moved with the times, as reforms were tried and failed, as assessments of past, present and future grew more negative. In the early period, 1987–8, traditional Soviet policy towards children was viewed as basically humane and socialist, despite the deformations of the Stalinist period. Mikhail Gorbachev, addressing the delegates at the SCF's Constituent Assembly, identified state protection of motherhood and childhood as one of the gains of the October revolution.[62] At this stage it was confidently expected that society could reform the children's homes, just as it would overcome other social problems such as alcoholism and prostitution. The abuses that were uncovered in the homes were said to be the result of the failings of individual staff members or the unfortunate oversight of the authorities. Heartless women who lived anti-socialist, non-conformist life-styles and abandoned their offspring were blamed for the large numbers of non-orphans in the homes.

Glasnost opened a Pandora's box of new and uncomfortable

information about individuals whose lives had little in common with the New Soviet Man. But perestroika did not immediately provide a conceptual framework that would encourage a fresh analysis of social problems or comparison with the Western experience, and initially popular prejudices against non-conformist behaviour were given free rein, theoretically justified by the notion of personal responsibility for character flaws that had been influential in Soviet social sciences before the mid-eighties. Moral panic about the decline in the nation's spiritual health was then at its height. The finger was pointed in a selective fashion at small groups of the population who deviated from the norm – at the promiscuous, the drug addicts and the alcoholics. Children's homes were seen, in this context, as the product of anti-social life styles, the dumping ground for the offspring of those unfit or unwilling to provide a normal family environment.

Over 1988 this picture changed substantially. The critique of Soviet society, of its economic and political structures sharpened and the government pledged its commitment to universal human values. Human failings were thereafter more often ascribed to unfavourable circumstances, to the imperfections of the social system, and deviant behaviour no longer attracted the same thirst for vengeance. The campaign against alcoholism was brought to a close; prostitutes were no longer described in the press as unclean and treacherous, but rather as young women making a protest against the demagogy and falsehood of society. The hardships faced by single mothers bringing up a child on tiny benefits were recognized and the campaign against the 'cuckoo-mothers' subsided. Increasingly it was the state that was held responsible both for the poor conditions in the homes and for the large numbers of their non-orphan inmates. There was optimism, however, that social problems would prove responsive to a liberal treatment, that as society moved towards democratic modernity they could be tackled successfully.

Over 1990 and 1991 the country's political and economic situation deteriorated further and optimism faltered. The party had lost credibility yet continued to wield power, industrial and agricultural production was continuing to fall and the distribution system to fall apart. Pervasive despair at the country's current chaos and scepticism about its ability to forge a civilized future provided the backdrop for a third stage in the treatment of social problems. The line between the pathological and the normal, between social problems and the state of the nation began to blur. The poverty in which all children, and not just the inmates of children's homes, lived was now the focus of attention.

As Anatolii Lunacharskii, Commissar of Enlightenment in the 1920s once remarked, 'The puddles cease to be noticed when there's a flood.'

I am indebted to Nail' Shamsutdinov who in November 1989 talked to me about his work in the Soviet Children's Fund.

I am grateful to the Australian National University for a grant from the Faculties Research Fund and for a place on its exchange with Moscow State University in the winter of 1989 and 1990 when much of the work for this article was carried out.

I would also like to thank Andrei Bondarev, Zhanna Dolgopolova, Garrick Dombrovski and Alexander Trapeznik who located some of the material on which this article is based.

NOTES

 1 We 'hypnotized ourselves with the slogan that children in our country are the only privileged class', admitted Albert Likhanov, see 'Obernut'sya k detstvu', *Pravda*, 13 August 1987. Ironic references to 'the privileged class' have been frequent in recent commentary on the children's homes.
 2 'Obshchaia nasha otvetstvennost' i zabota. "Kruglyi stol" zhurnala "Kommunist" i TsK VLKSM', *Kommunist*, no. 8, 1987, p. 85.
 3 S. Karkhanin, S. Stepunina, 'Diktant strakha', *Sovetskaia Rossiia*, 6 May 1987.
 4 S. Karkhanin, S. Stepunina, 'Vsled za protestami nesoglasnykh. Piatero protiv strakha', *Sovetskaia Rossiia*, 6 October 1987.
 5 S. Stepunina, 'Sovest' protiv strakha', *Sovetskaia Rossiia*, 4 September 1987.
 6 T. Posysaeva, 'Rabota vo imia budushchego', *Uchitel'skaia gazeta*, 15 August 1987.
 7 S. Stepunina, 'Sovest' protiv strakha'.
 8 T. Posysaeva, 'Rabota vo imia budushchego'.
 9 M. Kuznev, A. Kurilov, N. Riabova, 'Sirotskii stol. Zametki s zasedaniia Komiteta narodnogo kontroliia Kirgizskoi SSR', *Sovetskaia Kirgiziia*, 25 March 1988.
10 N. Fedotov, 'Kogda "ekonomiat" na detiakh. Chto pokazala proverka shkola-internatov', *Moskovskaia pravda*, 3 February 1987.

11 In consequence, educational standards were low: in 1986 only 397 pupils in homes in the RSFSR graduated from the 10th class and a mere 50 went on to further study. See 'Po zovu serdtsa', *Izvestiia*, 15 October 1987.

12 L. Eberzenok, 'Ty – ne sirota', *Pravda vostoka*, 17 August 1987.

13 V. Novikov, 'Vrachuia sirotskie bedy', 24 April 1987.

14 'Pri zhivykh roditeliakh, *Pravda Ukrainy*, 3 September 1987.

15 M. Kuznev, 'Sirotskii stol'.

16 As the satirist Mikhail Zhvanetskii has remarked, the country progressed by means of continuous improvements from bad to worse!

17 'V tsentral'nom komitete KPSS', *Pravda*, 8 August 1987.

18 For reports of the setting up of the Fund and its first conference see 'Sozdan orgkomitet sovetskogo detskogo fonda imeni V. I. Lenina', *Uchitel'skaia gazeta*, 15 August 1987; 'Obshchaia zabota', *Sovetskaia Rossiia*, 14 August 1987. The Founding Conference was covered by the major central papers, see 'Vospitat' grazhdanina', *Pravda* 15 October 1987; 'Delegaty detstva', *Izvestiia*, 15 October 1987; 'Po zovu serdtsa. Uchreditel'naia konferentsiia sovetskogo detskogo fonda imeni V. I. Lenina', *Izvestiia* 15 October 1987.

19 'One of the bitterest pages of the history of children's homes was 1937', said the Fund's Chairperson. He spoke also of the impact on the lives of children of the civil war, of collectivization and dekulakization. See 'Po zovu serdtsa', *Izvestiia*.

20 The Fund gave publicity to the efforts of A. Mil'chakov, the son of a repressed Komsomol leader, to locate the graves of the victims of Stalin in Moscow. See A. Mil'chakov, 'Pepel' kaznennykh stuchit v nashi serdtsa', *Sem'ia*, no. 36, no. 40, 1988; no. 5, 1989; *My i nashi deti. Materialy 11 plenuma pravlenia sovetskogo detskogo fonda imeni V. I. Lenina. 14 oktiabriia 1988 g*, M. 1989, p. 37.

21 See 'Po zovu serdtsa', *Izvestiia*.

22 This clause, however, was not specifically included in the Fund's statute. To squash 'idle speculation and rumour', however, the Fund in 1988 set up a second bank account so that one of the two could be reserved for money earned by the Fund and used to finance its operation. *My i nashi deti*, p. 32.

23 A. Likhanov, 'Obernut'sia k detstvu', *Pravda* 13 August 1987. One of the major aims of the Fund listed in its Statute was 'strengthening the authority and role of the family', see *Statute of the Lenin Children's Fund*, Moscow, 1987, p. 3. This document also stated that members of the Fund 'must exemplify a caring attitude to children and *be a model family person*' (italics mine).

24 'V tsentral'nom komitete KPSS', *Pravda*.

25 M. Tolts, 'Sem'ia', *Pravda*, 20 March 1987.

26 T. Posysaeva, 'Rabota vo imia budushchego'.

27 'V Tsentral'nom Komitete KPSS', *Pravda*.

28 The difficulties faced by couples seeking to adopt were discussed by

M. Rubinshtein, 'Brosaiushchie mamy i broshennye deti', *Molodoi kommunist*, no. 1 1990.

29 N. Rad'ko, 'Kruto posolennyi khleb detstva', *Sovetskaia Rossiia*, 28 March 1987.

30 L. Eberzenok, 'Ty – ne sirota', *Pravda vostoka* 17 August 1987.

31 L. Gladysheva, 'Miloserdie po beznariadke', *Sovetskaia Rossiia*, 22 October 1987. Investigative-style reporting was very sparing with figures. Journalists left readers with the impression that the number of orphans 'with living parents' was far too high, rather than providing information on the exact dimension of the problem. Whether seventy 'orphans with living parents' out of seventy-six was typical for the children's homes in Ivanovo, or for the region, or for the country as a whole, was not disclosed. Ivanovo is a textile town with a preponderantly female population. The consequent social problems have been aired from time to time in the press both before and during perestroika, but were not mentioned here.

32 L. Belozerova, 'Polyn' s vershiny liubvi', *Pravda Ukrainy*, 27 October 1987.

33 N. Karanfil, 'Net chuzhikh detei', *Pravda*, 5 October 1987.

34 See the letter of O. Fomenko, from a village in Dnepropetrovsk region, published in 'Chitateli: za i protiv "Zhestokie neznakomki"', *Pravda Ukrainy*, 13 August 1987.

35 If readers condemned the proposer of sterilization, they should visit a children's home, the journalist added. See S. Stepunina, 'Sovest' protiv strakha'.

36 'Obshchaia nasha otvetstvennost' i zabota', *Kommunist*, p. 51.

37 I am grateful to Anastasiia Posadskaia of the Centre for Gender Studies in Moscow for this information.

38 T. Posysaeva, 'Rabota v imia budushchego'.

39 Interview with Nail' Shamsutdinov, Moscow, November, 1989.

40 'V Sovet ministrov SSSR', *Pravda*, 25 August 1988. The resolution also envisaged foster parents living in ordinary apartment blocks and bringing up smaller numbers of orphans. For discussion of 'family-type' homes see also, 'Semeinye detskie doma', *Godovoi otchet*, p. 10; 'Vremennoe tipovoe polozhenie o detskikh domakh semeinogo tipa', *Sem'ia*, no. 1, 1989; 'Dobroe nachalo', *Sem'ia*, no. 25, 1989; 'O vvedenii v deistvie vremennogo polozheniia o detskikh domakh semeinego tipa'; 'Prikaz gosudarstvennogo komiteta SSSR po narodnomu obrazovaniiu ot 23 X 1989 no. 800', *Biulleten' gosudarstvennogo komiteta SSSR po narodnomu obrazovaniie*, no. 2 1990, pp. 12–17

41 *My i nashi deti*, p. 36.

42 *Ibid.*, pp. 35–6. Indeed, several people I spoke to in Moscow in 1989 and 1990 were convinced that the SCF had financed a beauty contest.

43 M. Rubinshtein, 'Brosaiushchie mamy', pp. 51–2.

44 G. Belikova, 'My ne zhaleem detei (Reportazh iz doma rebenka)', *Sem'ia i shkola*, no. 4, 1990, p. 18.

45 M. Usanova, 'SOS: Deti. "Privilegirovannyi klass" stal u nas samym unizhennym', *Megapolis-Express*, 3 January 1991.

46 S. Maloi, 'Moskve – ni grosha', *Smena*, 29 April 1990.

47 G. Myl'nikova, 'Do katastrofy – vsego lish' shag', *Rossiiskaia gazeta*, 11 January 1991.

48 E. Seregina, '"Khoziaeva" i "gosti". Razmyshleniia posle odnogo meropriiatiia', *Vechernyi Leningrad*, 26 July 1990; T. Voloshina, 'Kuda bezhish' Serega?', *Sobesednik*, no. 50, 1990, p. 3.

49 For the full text of their statement see O. Boguslavskaia, 'Golodovka', *Moskovskii komsomolets*, 20 October 1990.

50 G. Myl'nikova, 'Skandal v blagorodnom fonde', *Stolitsa*, no. 1991, p. 50.

51 The USSR People's Control Committee had gone through the Fund's books and though it found nothing illegal, reported muddle, and noted improprieties in the activities of a number of cooperatives connected with the Fund. A. Golovenko, V. Emel'ianov, 'Komu kontrol' ne nuzhen?', *Pravda*, 1 July 1990.

52 See T. Voloshina, 'Kuda bezhish' Serega?'. For similar allegations of the misuse of public donations see the exposé of the Soviet Peace Committee in V. Tsekov, 'V bor'be za pozhivku', *Domostroi*, no. 3, 1991.

53 T. Voloshina, 'Kuda bezhish' Serega?'.

54 G. Myl'nikova, 'Skandal v blagorodnom fonde', p. 51.

55 'Fond "Mladenchestvo": rodit'sya i vyzhit'', *Smena*, 24 April 1990. See also E. Seregina, '"Khoziaeva" i "gosti"' for the mention of other independent organisations: the Association of Guardians and Parents, the Association of Parents of Hard-of-Hearing Children and the Union of Enlightenment.

56 E. V. Tolstaia and T. I. Iasharova, 'Vnimanie sud'ba!' *Sotsial'naia zashchita*, no. 1, 1991, p. 13. On 'Pedagogical Search' see also 'Eto nashi deti zhdut tepla, zaboty, laski', *Moskovskaia pravda*, 28 February 1988 and L. Maslennikova and B. Minaev, 'Diaden'ka, dai piat' rublei'.

57 V. Lipskii, ' .. I vyrashchu ego v svoego brata', *Komsomol'skaia pravda*, 5 January 1991.

58 M. Usanova, 'SOS: Deti'; G. Myl'nikova, 'Do katastrofy – vsego lish' odin shag'.

59 'Zashchitit' zdorov'e detei', *Miloserdiia*, no. 3, 1991.

Tanya Sandakova wrote to 'Mama', the single mothers' organisation, that she had nothing to live on. She could not work because she had no one to leave her younger daughter with. She was afraid she would be evicted from her flat because she had not paid her rent for twelve months and because of the arrears was ineligible for rationed items such as sugar, soap and sausage. See *Sotsial'naia zashchita*, no. 1, 1991, p. 25. See also the letter from M. Bondarenko of Zaporozh'e who had lived for fifteen years with two children in a hostel with drunks as neighbours; her family, she said, did not always have enough to eat. *Komsomol'skaia pravda* 27 May 1990.

60 Iu. Kozyreva, 'Deti po talonam', *Komsomol'skaia pravda*, 16 January 1991.
61 V. Shchepkin, 'Po isku detstva', *Pravda*, 1 March 1991.
62 M. Gorbachev, 'Uchreditel'noi konferentsii sovetskogo detskogo fonda imeni V. I. Lenina', *Izvestiia*, 15 October 1987.

Chapter 10

Going out in 'style': girls in youth cultural activity

Hilary Pilkington

Sergei: 'What's your main ambition in life?'
Vera: 'What?'
Sergei: 'Do you have any special goal?'
Vera: 'Of course I do! We all share a common goal Seriozha ... and that is Communism!'[1]

The character of *Little Vera* (who first appeared in the Soviet film of the same name in 1988) caused outrage among the older generation in the Soviet Union and provoked hundreds of letters of complaint. Ostensibly the cause of concern was the sex scene portrayed in the film, the explicit nature of which was unprecedented in Soviet cinema. In fact, however, it was not the bohemian extravagances of the character of Vera but her banality which was subversive. The moral anxiety felt by the Soviet public stemmed from the fact that Vera's provincial, teenage life was wholly believable, and that among the younger generation its portrayal evoked not outrage but empathy. It was a life characterised by the struggle of young people to create a meaningful existence for themselves away from the mundane reality of the adult world. Vera became a symbol of the times: times in which, as Vera's ironic reply to Sergei's question shows, not even a ritualistic acceptance of the prevailing ideology on youth could be adhered to. The baton of communism which had been passed from generation to generation – from fathers to sons – had stopped at Vera.

Glasnost: youth exposed

Although, since the 1960s, concern about youth cultural activity[2] has been voiced periodically, those involved have been characterised as imitators of Western consumerist culture or juvenile delinquents who could be cured of their infantilism by improved ideological training.[3] The vast majority of youth, in contrast, were portrayed by the

142

pre-glasnost press as joyfully participating in the task defined for them by Lenin – the 'construction of communism'.[4] Young people were seen to be building the new society both in a symbolic and a material way. They were the living embodiment of the new Soviet citizen who was patriotic, dedicated to work or study and socially and politically active (through membership of the Communist Party's youth branch, the Komsomol).[5] Young people were also portrayed as constructing communism with their own hands through their participation in large-scale construction projects such as the Baikal-Amur railway (BAM), the Dnepr hydropower station and the Moscow metro system, the reclamation of the virgin lands in Central Asia and the development of the non-black-earth zone of the RSFSR, and the Northern, Siberian and far Eastern regions.[6] Youth was both body and soul of the future Soviet society.

Glasnost shattered this picture. From early 1986 there was hardly a newspaper in the country which was not cashing in on the public's almost morbid fascination with the activities of the hippies, punks, bikers, football and rock fans, vigilante and criminal groups. The most radical television programmes of the early glasnost period such as *Vzgliad* (View), *Piatoe Koleso* (Fifth Wheel) and *Dvenadtsatii Etazh* (Twelfth Floor) were also essentially youth programmes and provided a forum not only for the discussion of youth issues but also for young people to speak out themselves.

The world of youth also took the cinema by storm. Young people were the heroes and anti-heroes of numerous box-office sensations, from Iuris Podnieks's classic documentary about youth cultures in Riga *Is it easy to be young?* (1986), via Vasilii Pichul's *Little Vera* (1988), to Iurii Shchekochikhin's *Puppy* (1989) which portrays a young man's struggle to defend the values of perestroika in the unrestructured depths of the Voronezh oblast.

The spotlight of glasnost, however, fell unevenly. Its full glare rested upon those groups who could be classified, along ideological lines, as either 'socially positive' (those who tried, in their own way, to further the aims of perestroika) or 'socially negative' (those who had sunk into empty materialism, or mindless violence).[7] The media created a vision of a youth world which had been carved up between groups of neo-fascists (whose very existence struck at the heart of Soviet patriotism), punks (who fought 'construction' with 'destruction'), bikers (whose night-riding and disregard for traffic regulations constituted a rejection of perestroika's call for civic responsibility) and various vigilante groups who fought these anti-Soviet elements. This vision was a product of the fact that journalists and academics alike were less interested in what young people were doing in their own world, than in why they were doing it. Glasnost, it seemed, was concerned with the political attitudes and value orientations of Soviet youth (in the abstract) not in the (concrete) concerns of young people about where they lived, where they went to school, their friends, where they could go at night, and what kind of future life they could look forward to. This is not surprising since, as an integral component of perestroika, glasnost was concerned with the big, public world not the little worlds inhabited by Little Vera and her like. This concern with the political implications of young people's 'informal activity', however, obscured the very essence of youth cultural activity. In their subcultural worlds, young people sought not a strategy for changing the world, but a strategy for survival – a means of imbuing their own small words with meaning.

Girls in youth cultural activity: the official version

The recognition of the orientation of glasnost towards the public rather than the private sphere helps explain a further crucial limitation of the 'restructured' approach to youth: the virtual invisibility of young women in youth cultural activity. Glasnost may have illuminated new worlds – in which the rules were made not by parents, teachers or Komsomol workers but by the young people who inhabited them – but the power of interpreting these worlds has remained with the adults. This means that, when trying to explore the experiences of young women in these youth cultural worlds, we are confronted with an extremely partial picture. Young women are virtually invisible and, where they do stray into the spotlight of glasnost, their activity is seen as primarily sexual. This sexualisation of girls' activity is articulated via two images of girls in youth groups: the girlfriend and the prostitute.

Girls as girlfriends

The macho image of most subcultural groups (bikers, punks, heavy-metal fans, vigilante groups) means that the activity of girls is either simply ignored, or seen as peripheral to the main activity of the group. In Fain's description of the biker subculture (*rokery*), for example, he recognises the existence of female bikers (*rokereshi*), but refers to them only as the girlfriends of male bikers who 'accompany' their men on the rear seat of the bike and soon end up in sexual relations with the men because of the night hours spent together.[8] This is a very literal example of how girls are seen only in the capacity of 'girlfriend'. The image of the girlfriend, however, is more generally associated with the portrayal of girls as the objects of the sexual desires and behaviour of male members of youth cultural groups rather than as members in their own right. This is apparent in Fain's discussion of another subcultural group, the punks. Punks, he claims, are 'disrespectful' of women whom they refer to as 'toads' (*zhaby*), and he makes no mention of female punks at all. In his discussion of the *Liuber* type of subculture (discussed in more detail below), moreover, he states that, 'No girls have been observed in these groups. There are sympathizers, but they do not take part in the activity of groups. Relations with persons of the opposite sex do not have any particular systematic features.'[9]

Young women have been more visible in the counter-cultural (and generally more middle-class) groups such as the hippy and peace movements, religious, bohemian and artistic groups. Their visibility, however, is confined to discussions of the hippy notion of 'free love' which, it is suggested, is exploitative of women. In the case of the hippies, though, women are portrayed as the victims not of sexual virility but sexual inadequacy. Rozin explains 'free love' thus: 'A hippy boy finds himself unable to live together with one girl; this means that he is following the principle of free love. Thus, hippyism is a special cultural niche where people condemned to be failures in society may acquire high self-esteem and the recognition of others.'[10] Despite this 'inadequacy', hippy women are portrayed, nonetheless, as being sub-servient to male members of the group. One ex-hippy woman, talking on a Leningrad television programme, said that she had left the hippy movement (*sistema*) because she had grown tired of spending her time feeding and looking after hippies to whom she opened her flat, receiving neither help nor gratitude. 'Those who came to stay with me,' she said, 'slept, ate and then left.'[11]

Girls have surfaced as an issue of concern most of all, however, in relation to a third form of youth cultural activity – street gangs. These groups are a separate phenomenon from the sub- and counter-cultural groups which make up the neformaly.[12] The street gangs are usually referred to as *gruppirovki* (little groups) or *bandy* (gangs) and are formed on a territorial basis most frequently around the courtyard (*dvor*) where they live. These groups are extremely territorial and engage in inter-group fighting, making their nearest equivalent the urban gangs of American cities. Male members of such groups say that girls not only participate in their gangs but have gangs of their own. Girls' gangs have names such as 'The Golden Girls', 'The Sisters of

Salem' and 'The Black Foxes' and, both in these gangs and in mixed gangs, girls are involved in exactly the same activities as the lads: fighting, having fun, drinking, taking drugs, extorting money and petty-thieving.[13]

In press discussion of the *dvor* groups, however, girls are discussed only as objects of sexual abuse by male members of the group. Within individual groups, girls are depicted as being used to negotiate power relations between the lads through the institution of 'girls for common sexual use' (*obshchie devushki*).' Such girls are used in the groups as 'a means of socialisation – a way of "registering" lads in the group'.[14] Public concern has been even greater over threats posed to 'innocent' girls, i.e. those not implicated in the groups at all. In Kazan (where warring youth gangs are said to have carved up the city into spheres of control), it was reported that, in order to display the extent of their control, the groups agreed a temporary truce between themselves and declared a 'month of love'. During this month the gangs resolved to make Kazan 'a city without virgins'.[15] Subsequently there were scares about 'love months' and 'love days' in the cities of Cheboksary, Ioshkar Ola, Izhevsk, and Naberezhnie Chelny.

Although it is these incidents which tend to cause 'moral panics', perhaps more disturbing is the fact that this type of social control of young women is not restricted to the 'extreme model' of Kazan, nor even to isolated, deviant subcultures. A male reader from Odessa writing to the weekly youth newspaper *Sobesednik* in 1988, described the common practice in schools of *pristavaniia* (pesterings) which involved groups of boys 'tricking' girls into accompanying them to secluded places where they were forced to undress or were undressed by force. In some cases, photographs were taken of the naked girls.[16] Moreover, this image of girls' experience of subcultural activity has been popularised and reinforced in a number of films about youth. In films such as *My Name Is Harlequin*, *Tragedy in the Style of Rock*, *Dear Elena Sergeevna*, and *Avariia – the Cop's Daughter*, pivotal scenes have centred on rape or attempted rape of girls in youth groups. The rape is portrayed not through the eyes of the girl concerned, however, but through the suffering of the male whose 'girl' is being raped (her boyfriend in *My Name is Harlequin* and in *Tragedy in the Style of Rock* and her father in *Avariia – the Cop's Daughter*). Just as in the press debate, therefore, the experience of girls is used primarily as a way of exploring relations between men. Furthermore, since neither the power relations involved in the rape, nor the consequences of the act for the girl are explored, rape is portrayed not as the violation of the right of women over their own bodies but as a violation of male sex-right over women, or as a purely symbolic act, revealing the depths to which society has sunk.

If we are to explain the experience of girls in youth cultural groups, therefore, we need to confront two facts: that those writing about the activity of youth groups are blind to the presence of girls except as sexual objects; yet that controlling the sexuality of girls is indeed an important means of negotiating hierarchies within or between male-dominated youth groups. One way of reconciling these facts is not to 'desexualise' the activity of girls but to sexualise that of boys. Boys' activity in youth cultural groups is generally seen as being ideologically motivated (as in the case of the punks, hippies and vigilante groups) or as arising from adolescent aggression or delinquency (as in the case of the *dvor* groups, the bikers, the punks and the heavy-metal fans). More socio-psychological interpretations of the behaviour of teenage boys, however, point to the need for 'self-assertion' which might lead them into the kinds of activities undertaken in youth cultural groups.[17] Such self-assertion is a process of constructing, and reconstructing, an image of self, and a crucial dimension of such an image is a sense of one's own masculine (or feminine) identity which sits comfortably with other aspects of 'self', and which can be carried off in the company of others. If we begin to look at what young people are doing in youth cultural groups with this in mind, we may come to very different conclusions, not only about the activity of boys but also about the centrality of girls to this activity. The example of the infamous youth cultural group known as the *Liubery* provides a useful example.

The term *Liubery* originally referred to groups of lads from the town of Liubertsy (a suburb of Moscow) who caused a 'moral panic' in Moscow between 1986 and 1988 when numerous incidents of attacks on Moscow youths were attributed to them. Ostensibly the targets of the *Liubery* were young people who could be openly identified as *neformaly* and it soon became widely publicised that the *Liubery* had a specific ideological mission to cleanse Russian society of Western imitators.[18] Before long, it became clear that the *Liubery* were not a phenomenon peculiar to Moscow but that there were similar groups in many provincial towns on the periphery of large cities,[19] and those who knew the *Liubery* best – the Moscow *neformaly* who were the targets of their action – started to refer not to the *Liubery* as such but to groups and individuals who were '*Liuber* types' (*tipa Liubera*). Within the youth cultural world, therefore, being a *Liuber* was associated first and foremost not with where one came from or one's political opinions, but with the adoption of a particular strategy of self-assertion: a cult of strength. This macho masculine identity was expressed in the *Liubery*'s unofficial body-building dens (*kachalki*), a penchant for beating up members of other subcultural groups (especially hippies and heavy-metal fans), and a habit of 'snatching' Moscow girls from discos and cafés and taking them back to Liubertsy.

The snatching of Moscow girls is rarely mentioned in discussions of *Liuber* activity. It is largely assumed that the *Liubery* engaged in body-building as a form of training for assaults on 'anti-Soviet' elements at central Moscow cafés, discos and bars. Bearing in mind the importance of masculinity to one's sense of self, we might come to a different interpretation. The cafés, discos and clubs visited by the *Liubery* are important locations for gaining access to women. By kidnapping, or otherwise 'persuading' Moscow girls to go back to Liubertsy with them, the *Liubery* are invading the territory of other groups and violating the norms regulating access to girls. This is more likely to provoke fight situations among teenagers than any ideological squabble. In order to explain the attacks by *Liubery* on the male members of other youth cultural groups, it is important to remember that the security of one's adopted masculine (or feminine) identity is dependent on the ability to assert it not only over girls, but also over boys who adopt alternative forms of masculine identity.[20] Such alternative masculine images are most visible among the capital's *neformaly* – the long hair and pacifism of the hippies being the most obvious example.

The connection between male youth cultural groups and the violation of peer-group control of sexual relations can be seen in Shcheko-chikhin's film *My Name is Harlequin*. The film is set in Minsk and shows how 'gang warfare' between a group of suburban 'toughs' and a group of 'city-slickers' is triggered by a dispute over with which of the groups' leaders the central female character is going out. The need to control girls' sexuality is also evident in the activities of a similar group to the *Liubery* which emerged in the city of Volzhskii. When local girls started going out with Italian workers from a factory in the city, a vigilante group called the *Striguny* emerged to protect rights over 'their' girls. Defining themselves as 'fighters for morality' the lads (as their name suggests) took to cutting off the hair of the girls in order to force them to stay at home and 'reflect upon their behaviour'.[21]

Girls as prostitutes

Girls may appear in discussions of youth cultural activity not only as the victims of sexual abuse by male members of groups but as perpetrators of sexual deviancy themselves. This image is associated with the figure of the young female prostitute who, in the glasnost era, is not only someone who earns her living from selling access to her body, but a whole cultural phenomenon.

Prostitution is often seen as integrally linked to women's participation in youth cultural activity. Discussing the roots of prostitution, Chernyshkova argues that the association of money and sex for young women begins with the common teenage games of 'spin the bottle' and 'daisy',[22] which often lead to more serious acts, such as taking money for rendering trivial favours like watching videos and going for car rides and, eventually, onto the street.[23] Sexual favours (with or without payment) may also be girls' ways into youth cultural groups. Fain notes that girls involved in the *mazhory*[24] turn to prostitution in order to afford the high-life followed by the group.[25] In other instances girls may be coerced into sexual relations with boys in one group in order to gain protection from boys in enemy groups.[26] In this case, there is a fine line between images of young women as sexual deviants (prostitutes) and of young women as victims of male sexual abuse. The problem this dual image presents even the most strident exponents of glasnost is reflected in an article by Elena Lesoto in which she reflects on the trial of ten young men accused of sexually coercing underage girls. Over an extended period of time, the girls took part in a sadistic ritual in which the boys played fascist officers and the girls local partisans. The girls were raped, beaten and forced to eat glass, yet, it was claimed, the older girls willingly sought out younger girls to join in the ritual. Lesoto is unsure as to whether the girls are victims or accomplices. 'Let us recall', she writes, 'that both morality and the law forbid the coercion of girls, regardless of whether their behaviour is good, dubious or the sort that leaves no room for doubt. In this instance, we are dealing with the third type.'[27]

Whether victims or villains, what is certain is that young women's participation in subcultural activity is portrayed as being diametrically opposed to femininity. Although boys' abuse of girls in youth cultural groups affirms their masculinity, girls' willing or unwilling participation is seen as destroying the very essence of femininity. According to a Moscow social-psychologist, the juvenile prostitute loses all feminine identity, becomes 'barely distinguishable from a boy' and has 'much which is masculine in her behaviour'.[28] In the same way, although prostitution may be the only means by which *mazhory* girls can gain the material pre-requisites for entrance into the group, it also ensures their ultimate exclusion. Fain notes that these girls are looked down upon by the male *mazhory*, who will seek 'steady relationships' outside the group in order to avoid sexually transmitted diseases.[29]

But the term 'prostitute' is more than a description of a specific form of sexual behaviour; it is a metaphor or label for any young woman who appears to be failing to conform to a feminine identity which society finds acceptable. This is illustrated in the portraits of women in Podnieks's otherwise excellent documentary film *Is it easy to be young?* One of the only two girls to speak in the film is seen being interviewed in the juvenile affairs department after a failed suicide attempt. The girl had been arrested for theft (she had taken a wedding dress from the opera house, had herself photographed in it, and then found she could not get back into the building to return it) and, after being verbally and physically abused by the police, she tried to commit suicide by jumping out of the window of the interrogation room. The film shows her being lectured on her irresponsibility and failure to understand the meaning of life. When, in tears, she expains that she had been called a 'prostitute' by the police, the reply ('don't forget you have not got such a sweet character') implies that that is precisely what she is. The wife/whore binary which shapes society's images of women is reinforced in the film by the figure of the only other young woman who speaks. She is photographed holding her baby and talking about her fears for the future of her child – this young woman clearly knows the value of life and death. The message of the images is clear: feminine identity is rooted in motherhood, where sexuality is firmly tied to marriage and reproduction, and those who fail to conform risk mental instability.

Girls in youth cultural activity: the case of the *Stiliagi*

Glasnost has revealed the youth cultural sphere as, at worst, a wholly male sphere and, at best, a space inhabited by both boys and girls, but controlled by boys. But can youth cultures and subcultures only be forms of exploration of masculinity?[30] In order to answer this question, we need to get inside the little worlds created by young people beyond the glare of the media, and find out more about what Soviet girls actually do in youth cultural groups. The world that will be explored here is that of one of the groups active in Moscow in 1988–89: the *Stiliagi*.[31]

Present-day *Stiliagi* define themselves as lovers of rock'n'roll music, and have revived the style of their namesakes of the 1950s.[32] Like many other subcultural groups the *Stiliagi* is a predominantly male subculture and its activity is mainly public – their *tusovki* (places they 'hang out') include concerts, cafés, parks, or even metro stations. Nevertheless young women are highly visible within the group and they appear to conform to none of the images of young women in youth groups with which the press has furnished us. The *Stiliagi* girls are neither the silent appendages of their male partners, nor are they sexual pawns in power struggles between the boys. In fact, the girls, just like the boys, become members of the group because it offers them a world in which they can create a positive identity for themselves.

The essence of the group's identity is style (*stil*) and its activity revolves around dressing 'in style' (*v stile*). 'Style' does not just mean any classy style, however, but is used very strictly to describe the dress-style adopted by the *Stiliagi* of the 1950s which is reproduced by contemporary followers. Since 'style' is both the purpose and the form of the group's activities, it is not surprising that authority within the group is determined by how well and for how long one has been dressing in 'style'. In the period 1988–9 the ultimate authority on 'style' was Zhanna Aguzarova, then lead singer of the Soviet rock group Bravo. Many of the *Stiliagi* had come to the group via the *Bravisty*, that is fans of Bravo. Aguzarova's 'style' was striking – black man's suit, white shirt, narrow tie and patent leather shoes – and was painstakingly followed by both male and female *Stiliagi*. Although, with Zhanna, many of the girls subsequently moved on to try to recreate more traditionally feminine styles of the 1950s, nevertheless, in the winter months (for practical reasons) they continued to dress in this highly masculine style. This dress-style is crucial to understanding the masculine and feminine identities adopted by both male and female members of the group, as is the fact that the *Stiliagi*'s 'teen-idol' is a woman, since this means that the activity of the girls cannot be equated with that of the 'teeny-boppers' of the Osmond and Cassidy era.[33] The status of the girls was also determined by the fact that authority within the group was accorded on the basis of how long one had dressed in 'style'. The male members of the group tended to be younger and less permanent members than the girls, since at 17 or 18 the boys would be called up for army service for two years and usually did not return to the group afterwards. Consequently, the girls oversaw the continuity of generations within the group and introduced new members to the rules of what should and should not be worn, what was and what was not correct 'style'.

This does not mean that the *Stiliagi* were some kind of Amazonian matriarchy, or even that there was any significant subversion of traditional gender roles: the *Stiliagi* remained a male-dominated subculture. It does mean, however, that the girls in the group were able to win themselves a good deal of space in which they could construct positive images of their own femininity. The girls prided themselves on how they had got hold of certain necessary items for their 'style', on how they sewed their own clothes, and on the way they looked when they went out 'in style'. An important part of feeling good about themselves was a conscious pride in the fact that their particular style meant they could avoid much of the constant search for Western, fashionable, and affordable, clothes and records which took up most of the time and money of their 'straight' friends. Belonging to 'the group' also gave the girls a certain freedom and independence. Central to group identity was the conviction that one's love of rock'n'roll should override all other concerns. This meant that conventions such as girls having to wait to be asked to dance were made redundant – as soon as the first note of any rock'n'roll tune was heard, the whole group would charge onto the dance floor. The same priorities were carried over into the way the girls talked about their lives. The girls' concerns were with what item of clothing was being 'obtained' or 'made' and what concerts were coming up, rather than with boyfriends, husbands or families. When pressed to speculate on a future life outside the group, they rather reluctantly admitted that pressures of work and family would eventually force them out of their present life-style, although remaining confident that this would not change their value-orientations.

Central to the ability of the girls to determine their own space within the group, was the fact that, unlike the *rokershi* of whom Fain talked, the *Stiliagi* girls had come to the group in their own right, not as the girlfriends of male members. The girls I talked to had entered the group either after chance encounters with the *Stiliagi* at concerts, or through female friends who were already members. When asked whether there were many romantic relationships within the group, the girls appeared to find themselves thinking about the question for the first time. They finally concluded that there were very few such relationships, but those that had developed – they recalled three cases – had all ended in marriage. This also belies any notion of the *obshchie devushki* syndrome within the *Stiliagi*. On the contrary, the girls talked of their pity for those girls who had left their group to join the *Rokabilly*, who, according to them, treated girls badly.

This apparent lack of concern with romance and willingness to brave the derision of adults for their masculine dress, however, is intriguingly mixed with seemingly stereotyped views on gender-roles. When asked how they felt about relations between the girls and boys in the group, one of the members stated,

They make me feel like a girl, a real girl . . . our lads always get out of the bus first and offer us their hand, so that the girls can get out and through the crowd . . . it shocks everybody. This is really nice for us – we walk with a look on our faces, as if to say, 'go ahead, laugh at us, at how we look, but look how we are treated, just look' . . .[34]

For the *Stiliagi* girls this was not an act of conformity but of resistance – a rejection of the general disrespect accorded to women in adult society. The reaction they imputed to the older generation on seeing this behaviour was one of shock. Unlike some of the more macho subcultural groups, 'rebellion' for the *Stiliagi* did not mean hooliganism, drink, drugs or crime. They preferred to shock adult society not with their anti-socialness, but with their super-sociability. The *Stiliagi* built their group identity (i.e., defined what set them apart from other groups) on being less egotistical and less disrespectful to the older generation, on being more polite, more 'cultured' and more 'normal'. Such behaviour, they claimed, shocked the older generation because it was not the type of behaviour which they had come to expect of today's youth. This image of themselves also tied in with the group's nostalgia for the fifties which they saw as being a period when society was simpler, more caring, and more honest. The group, therefore, expressed no desire to subvert adult authority in general, and relations with their own parents were good. A number of the girls said that their mothers helped them either to get hold of fifties' style dress or to sew their own, and there was general agreement that parents accepted their 'style' better than their peer-group acquaintances who often dissociated themselves from them when they joined the *Stiliagi*.

Obviously one cannot generalise from the specifics of the groups discussed – both boys and girls create different masculine and feminine images for themselves in the youth cultural sphere. The lads in the *Stiliagi* group, for example, adopt a very different masculine image than that of the *Liuber*-type groups. These images, or strategies, moreover, are likely to change over the life-course of each individual. Many of the *Stiliagi* lads had left to join the *Rokabilly*, who had a much more overtly hard image, while others had gone back into 'straight youth culture'. The important point here is not to define the spectrum of images adopted by different groups, but simply to acknowledge that both femininity and masculinity are important parts of individual and group identity and are not passively accepted by young people but are developed within each individual's notion of self.

Girls in youth cultural activity; glasnost's blind spot

If girls are active in youth groups such as the *Stiliagi* and even in the violent, semi-criminal gangs of the Volga cities, why are they largely absent from academic and press discussions? One reason is that there are more real constraints on their participation. Girls are required to be in the house more, either because they are expected to help with housework or with looking after younger children, or simply because this is where it is assumed they will spend their leisure time. Girls rarely spend time just 'hanging out' on the street (where the most visible forms of youth cultural activity take place) and when girls do go out, it is generally with a group of friends, or a 'boyfriend', and they are expected back afterwards. If a girl comes back late, she does more than break house rules, she casts doubt on her own virtue. When directed at girls, the question 'where have you been?' implies more than polite parental interest. This need to control girls' time and space in order to protect their maidenly honour (and therefore their social standing) was at the heart of an incident reported to have taken place in a village in Kazakhstan. When it became known that six pregnant girls were being allowed to sit their exams by a headteacher, the local police declared an 'emergency situation' in the school, and teachers were forced to go to the homes of the pupils and question their parents about the times at which their daughters came home at night.[35]

There are also less tangible reasons why girls appear invisible in youth cultural activity. One of these is that the images which shape what is considered to be 'youth activity' are masculine ones. This is true of both pre-and post-glasnost images of youth. In the pre-glasnost days, although the 'constructors of communism' were, in principle, ungendered, the images used to convey what young people were doing were not: young people built roads and railways, served in the armed forces, overfulfilled plans in steel factories and excelled at sport. In the era of glasnost the images of youth may have changed, but they remain masculine: young people vent their aggression in gang warfare, seek excitement and danger on the backs of motorbikes, are hedonistic and irresponsible, and rebel against the authority of the adult world. The importance of these images is that although irresponsibility, rebellion, aggression and search for adventure are not necessarily positive images of boys, they can be accepted by society as 'adolescent phases' which boys will grow out of. For boys the need for 'self-assertion' – often expressed in a rebellion against their subordinate status in the adult world – is seen as natural. Indeed, youth cultural activity in this sense might act as a useful pressure valve, providing a space for this necessary self-assertion.

In contrast, adolescent behaviour for girls is highly subversive. Displays of aggression or irresponsibility associated with adolescence not only disrupt public order, but subvert what is considered to be normal feminine identity.[36] Displays of adolescence by girls are treated much more seriously: girls are not just 'adolescent' but abnormal and deviant, and deviant in a way which is directly linked to their sexuality. This helps us explain why it is that when girls are seen in groups, they appear either as the victims or as the perpetrators of sexual deviancy. The sexualisation of young women's activity, however, is also related to the fact that girls often use their sexuality as a form of resistance. Unlike boys, who see their subordination as temporary – and are therefore likely to rebel against it in order to establish their position as fathers – for girls, womanhood offers only a partial release from subordination. The most obvious strategy for gaining adult status, therefore, is through the resistance of adult control of sexuality. As a result, girls often 'rebel' against subordination through overt expressions of sexuality which may involve pregnancy and motherhood,[37] and we can see this strategy being employed in a very conscious way by Little Vera. For Vera and many other girls, however, this strategy may free them from paternal control, but it ties them even more securely to their position within the patriarchal system.

Conclusion: the limits of glasnost

Glasnost has brought youth culture into our field of vision – but as yet we have gained only partial sight of the phenomenon. The policy of openness in the media has brought an end to the monotone image of youth as the obedient servant of the state in the construction of communism. Instead we see Soviet youth as constituted from a multitude of individuals who construct their own worlds, in which they live according to rules they themselves define. The potential of glasnost, however, was always a limited one, and with relation to youth it is already exhausted. As a social tool, glasnost could reveal and shock, it could publicise and mobilise, but it could not understand or explain. Even in the full glare of glasnost, the discussion of youth could not go beyond the symbolic level, but remained couched in the language of moral and social anxiety about 'the state of things',[38] or wistful yearnings for youth to employ their supposed natural tendency towards rebellion as the 'pioneers of change'.[39] Our images of youth, therefore, remain products of society's concern with securing its own future, and glasnost has made young people visible only to the extent to which they pose a threat to the stability of society, or offer a way out of the perceived malaise. In concrete terms this is manifested in images of extravagant, semi-criminal (and male) subcultural groups which openly display an ideological or anti-social position, and of young women whose overt sexuality makes them unfit to be the mothers of future generations. If we are to transcend such a symbolic understanding of young people's experience, we need to move from the big world of Gorbachev and perestroika to the little world of Vera and her like for, although 'meaning' may be imputed in the big world, it is in the little worlds that it is made.

NOTES

1 M. Khmelik, *Little Vera* (transl. by Cathy Porter) (London: Bloomsbury Publishing Ltd, 1990), pp. 64–5.

2 'Youth cultural activity' is employed here as a shorthand for the many different forms of involvement of young people in groups outside the family, school or work. Youth cultural activity offers a space in which a collective identity is formed, from which youth can develop an individual identity (M. Brake, *Comparative Youth Culture*, (London: Routledge and Kegan Paul, 1985), pp. 189–91.

3 This approach persisted even in the early 1980s when a multitude of different youth cultural groups could be seen in the larger cities of the Soviet Union. See, for example: B. Balkarei and G. Zhavoronkov, 'Adults, teenagers and the street', *Sovetskaia Rossiia*, 1 February 1984, p. 3, in *Current Digest of the Soviet Press*, vol. 36, no. 5, pp. 1–4, 23; V. Mishin, 'Learn communism in the Leninist way', *Pravda*, 12 July 1984, pp. 2–3, in *Current Digest of the Soviet Press*, vol. 36, no. 5, pp. 5–6, 20.

4 V. I. Lenin, *Zadachi Soiuzov Molodezhi* (Moscow: Molodaia Gvardiia, 1987).

5 N. M. Blinov, 'The sociology of youth: achievements and problems', *Soviet Sociology*, vol. 21, no. 4 (Spring 1983), pp. 3–19.

6 The mobilisation of young people into the physical construction of communism was not peculiar to Stalinism but has been a feature of the whole Soviet period. See: *Youth and the Party: Documents* (Moscow: Progress, 1976), especially pp. 23, 100, 116, 132–3.

7 This classification is typical of the work of sociologists and journalists closely associated with the Komsomol. See, for example: Iu. Bluvshtein, and V. Iustitskii, 'Neformal'naia gruppa: Chto eto takoe?', *Molodoi Kommunist*, 1987, no. 6, pp. 61–8; N. Rubanova, 'Samodeiatel'nie ob"edineniia kak forma realizatsii interesov molodezhi', Unpublished paper (Moscow, NITs, VKSh pri TsK VLKSM, 1988).

8 A. Fain, 'Specific features of informal youth associations in large cities', *Soviet Sociology*, vol. 29, no. 1 (1990), p. 38.

9 *Ibid.*, p. 28.

10 M. Rozin, 'The psychology of Moscow's hippies', *Soviet Sociology*, vol. 29, no. 1 (1990) p. 69.

11 A. Gromov and O. Kuzin, *Neformaly: Kto est' Kto?*, (Moscow: Mysl', 1990), p. 20.

12 '*Neformaly*' was the term adopted by the press to describe the myriad of groups (mainly of young people) which formed in the late 1970s and emerged into the public eye in the early 1980s. The press originally treated the *neformaly* as a single social and political phenomenon but, by 1988, it had begun to differentiate between the informal political groups (who were seen as either fighters for, or wreckers of, perestroika) and youth sub- and counter-cultural groups (who were seen as playing childish games). The street gangs were seen as a separate phenomenon which was largely discussed within the discourse of deviancy and social deprivation, and their existence was characterised as a problem of social control.

13 A. Gromov and O. Kuzin, *Neformaly: Kto est' Kto?* (Moscow: Mysl', 1990), p. 26.

14 V. Yeremin, 'Podval', *Ogonek*, no. 8, (February) 1989, p. 10; A. Pankratov, 'Kazan'-nostra', *Komsomol'skaia Pravda*, 17 January 1990, p. 3.

15 Iu. Shchekochikhin, 'Extremal'naia Model'', *Literaturnaia Gazeta*, no. 41, 12 October 1988, p. 13.

16 '"Foto" na pamiat'?', *Sobesednik*, no. 47, (November) 1988, p. 10.

17 D. Fel'dshtein, 'Psikhologo-pedagogicheskie aspekty izucheniia neformal'nikh molodezhnikh ob"edinenii', *Sovetskaia Pedagogika*, no. 6, 1987, pp. 42–7.

18 V. Iakovlev, 'Kontora "Liuberov', *Ogonek*, no. 5, (January) 1987, pp. 20–1. In this key article in the creation of the Liubery as a folk devil of Soviet society, Iakovlev described the members of the group in great detail, including their characteristic checked trousers, white shirts and narrow black ties, their typical gait, their developed muscles from weight-training and their abstinence from smoking, drinking and use of drugs. Above all,

the article claimed that the *Liubery* had a defined philosophy of cleansing the city of hippies, punks and heavy metal fans who, according to them, disgraced the Soviet way of life.

19 One article which was crucial in deflating the myth of the *Liubery* was that by Aleksandr Kupriianov – '*Liubery* – pri svete fonarei, ili pasynki stolitsy', *Sobesednik* no. 7, (February) 1987, pp. 10–15. Kupriianov argued that the *Liubery* were little more than uncoordinated groups of suburban teenagers whose trips to Moscow were inspired by boredom, because Liubertsy was poorly provided for in terms of leisure and entertainment facilities. Kupriianov also suggested that the *Liubery* united only in reaction to specific incidents such as not being allowed into city-centre cafés or discos.

20 R. W. Connell, *Gender and Power* (Cambridge: Polity Press, 1987), pp. 183–5.

21 F. Ratvanin, 'Vorota-degtem', *Sobesednik*, no. 50, 1987, p. 10.

22 Daisy (*romashka*) is often cited by Soviet writers as a typical 'sexual game' played by teenagers. It consists of the girls in the group lying in a circle – thus forming the shape of a daisy – while the boys work their way round the daisy, having sexual intercourse with each of the girls.

23 T. Chernyshkova, 'Khau du iu du, interdevochki!', *Sobesednik*, no. 35, (August) 1989, p. 6.

24 The 'mazhory' are generally young people from privileged backgrounds who dress in imported, high quality clothes and follow various Western trends in fashion and music.

25 A. Fain, 'Specific features of informal youth associations in large cities', *Soviet Sociology*, vol. 29, no. 1 (1990), p. 27.

26 V. Yeremin, 'Podval', *Ogonek*, no. 8, (February) 1989, p. 10.

27 E. Lesoto, 'Some thoughts about a trial', *Komosmol'skaia Pravda*, 17 September 1985, p. 2, in *Current Digest of the Soviet Press*, vol. 37, no. 38, pp. 13–14.

28 M. Borshchevskaia, 'Dzhuletty na "shchelchke"', *Moskovskii Komsomolets*, 21 October 1988, p. 2.

29 A. Fain, 'Specific features of informal youth associations in large cities', *Soviet Sociology*, vol. 29, no. 1 (1990), p. 27.

30 M. Brake, *Comparative Youth Culture*, p. ix.

31 References to youth cultural groups here are based on structured interviewing of young people in Moscow between September 1988 and June 1989 and follow-up interviews conducted in Spring 1990. The conclusions drawn, therefore, can only be said to apply to the experience of urban Russian youth, although some of those interviewed had moved to Moscow relatively recently or lived in the Moscow region rather than the city.

32 According to Soviet rock critic Artem Troitsky, the original *Stiliagi* were 'a scandalous, outrageous youth cult of the 1950s – the first hipsters, the first devotees of exotic music, the first advocates of an alternative style', A. Troitsky, *Back in the USSR. The True Story of Rock in Russia* (London, Omnibus Press, 1987), p. 2.

33 Feminist interventions into the debate on youth subculture in the 1970s suggested that girls were invisible in youth culture because the site of their activity was not the street, but the home. Girls, it was argued, were involved in 'teeny-bopper culture' or 'bedroom culture' which took the form of fantasising romantic relationships with male pop stars. The seminal article here is: A. McRobbie and J. Garber, 'Girls and subcultures', in S. Hall and T. Jefferson, *Resistance Through Rituals* (London, Hutchinson, 1976), pp. 209–22.

34 From an interview with members and ex-members of the *Stiliagi* conducted in Moscow in April 1990.

35 M. Makarova, 'Eto my ne prokhodili', *Sobesednik*, no. 35, (August), 1988, p. 11.

36 B. Hudson, 'Femininity and adolescence', in A. Mcrobbie and M. Nava, *Gender and Generation* (Basingstoke, Macmillan, 1984).

37 M. Nava, 'Youth service provision, social order and the question of girls', in A. McRobbie and M. Nava, *Gender and Generation*, p. 15.

38 What Stuart Hall et al. concluded about the moral panic concerning black street crime in Britain in the 1970s rings true for contemporary Soviet society. 'A generalised moral anxiety about the "state of things" becomes first precipitated with respect to "youth" which came to provide, for a time, a metaphor for social change and an index for social anxiety'. See, S. Hall, C. Critcher, T. Jefferson, and B. Roberts, *Policing and Crisis* (London: Macmillan, 1978), p. 235.

39 J. Riordan, 'Soviet youth: pioneers of change', *Soviet Studies*, vol. 40, no. 4 (1988), p. 568.

Chapter 11

Gynoglasnost: writing the feminine

Barbara Heldt

Has glasnost been good for women? Now let us put the question in a more sophisticated manner: does glasnost have a gendered aspect and, if so, what is its sexual symbolism and of what use or value is this symbolism to the society of disunity and debate that is the Soviet Union today? What continuities does its mythology, although appearing at first glance to be contemporary, provide with the ideologies of the past? To what extent are women themselves taking part in the new discussion? Are they merely being asked to raise their voices in different speaking parts scripted by the men who still control the media? What areas of real, woman-authored creativity have been opened up by glasnost? To try and answer these questions for the early years of glasnost we will have to examine a range of forms of expression: in the visual media, in written polemics and, finally, in the newest creative literature – areas currently far from discrete.

Iconisation of the feminine

The essence of glasnost is speaking out. But speaking out for women in a woman's voice has often been a more complicated and dangerous occupation in Russia and the rest of the Soviet Union than in Europe or North America. Women have most often been spoken and written for by men. The needs of humanity have been generalised to exclude women through the denial of any reality – and specifically female reality – not on an approved agenda for progress under communism. But there exists another strategy, one not unrelated to this strategy of exclusion, and this one definitely did not begin with the October revolution, nor has it ended with glasnost: it might be called the iconisation of the feminine. This phenomenon seems to be growing in the visual and print media at an even more rapid rate under glasnost

160

than before. Whether appearing on an agenda of sexploitation or one of religious nationalism, it consistently denies women the right to self-determination.

The patriarchal myth of the pure nature and abstract goodness of Woman has endured to this day, not least because it is also a symbol of nationhood – a symbol all the more potent in a nation divided into many different nationalities like the USSR. As one of the nation's few all-encompassing images, the icon of Woman as Motherland unites where the myth of Revolution has failed to do so. It does so even beyond Soviet borders. *Moscow News* recently published five letters from Afghanistan written by an army officer named Konstantin Panov. One of these contains a striking articulation of how the female as icon goes beyond socially and historically constructed gender, becoming an impulse which transcends even the particular nation for which it was originally conceived and transmitted:

During the day on TV they often show pictures of the Afghan landscape to the sounds of music and a woman's voice repeating 'beloved Afghanistan' or slowly chanting verses. Occasionally her face comes through on the screen against the backdrop of mountains and foliage. She is as it were the personification of the Motherland. It is an impressive experience.[1]

This abstracted disembodied use of the female as symbol of the Nation is apparently so potent that it has equal appeal to two quite different and warring cultures, the Russian and the Afghan.

Back on Soviet television women appear as grounds for debate and backgrounds for male-centred events. An early programme called 'Perestroika: Problems and Solutions' had learned specialists sitting in the centre in large leather chairs, while young females, surrounding them in booths, simultaneously answered phoned-in questions and typed them out. Periodically, they delivered the typed questions to the armchairs who would then speak to the viewers. This all-female contingent was referred to as 'our girls'. The specialists were all male, except the noted social scientist Tat'iana Zaslavskaia.[2] The format of this television show seemed not to strike any chord of protest. Typists are women; learned specialists are men. The former have to complete three physical tasks, one of which includes showing their bodies as they leave their booths and bend over the chairs. The latter sit comfortably and show their minds.

Zaslavskaia and other high-profile Soviet women have complained in print about the need for women like themselves to appear well-dressed and well-coiffed, wearing a sort of armour of respectability.

Soviet women are increasingly aware, as they begin to travel abroad, that especially in North America, dress is less complicated. In an article entitled 'Life in Canada' the journalist S. Timofeeva slips in the observation that 'well-off people in Canada dress very simply: plain slacks, sweaters, running shoes. They even go visiting dressed like this. The requisite Moscow attire turned out to be simply unnecessary for me in Canada.'[3]

If professional status requires dressing up, undress is increasingly the other side of the picture. The Icon Woman can protect herself from becoming the Nude (as in 'art') or the Naked (as in pornographic 'social' reportage). Examples of both of the latter can be found in the leading Soviet magazine *Ogonek*, which has a circulation of around three million. In various issues, paintings or photographs show a pointlessly graphic female body: male nudes so far have been excluded except for one full frontal sculpture at a German exhibition. All the photographers without exception seem to be male. The association of the female body with nature is frequently made, as women are made to pose ludicrously in a natural setting, usually one of exotic interest. One woman perches precariously on an ice floe in what appears to be a wet suit; but actually her naked body has been painted black: in spots the skin shows through. In a photo display entitled 'Beauty Saves the World'[4] the women models' faces display the vacuous look of our own pornography: one thin woman sprawls naked on desert sands, the nudity of another is tastefully almost covered by ferns in a grove, a third holds a sprig of berries in her teeth between parted lips.

Most of *Ogonek* is devoted to serious reportage. There are no women on its editorial board and its editor in chief, Vitali Korotich, has said that he does not allow women reporters to do journalism involving subjects that might be dangerous.[5] The absence of women in editorial decision-making jobs is felt throughout the Soviet media. The writer Elena Vorontsova sees this situation as one that continues under glasnost:

In the 1960s I worked on the most influential young people's newspaper in the country. Most of my male colleagues nurtured ambitions to become chief editors. I never even dreamt of it. That path, I knew, was closed to me. A woman can become the head of an educational publishing house. That is acceptable and it bolsters the figures proving that women bosses do exist. But a woman in charge of major journal or newspaper? I've never heard of a single case. The quota for women working in the prestigious establishments is strictly observed. The usual (unofficial) explanation goes like this: 'But we already have one Jew, two non-Party members, two women ...'[6]

This quota for women seems to be the one most long-lived in the liberal press, but these unofficial restrictions on women have more than their quota of results in one-sided journalism. Male clichés mar what could otherwise be good muckraking reportage – especially when the subject is women. For example, a detailed *Ogonek* article on a Moscow sobering-up station for women is accompanied by a sensationalistic photograph of a young woman clad only in underpants being dragged away by two fully uniformed men.[7] There was a critique of the photographer, V. Shapovalov, in the professional magazine *Zhurnalist*[8] as part of commentaries on the work of three beginning (male) photojournalists. In this article five other photos by Shapovalov accompany the only one selected by the editors of *Ogonek*: all are of old or old-looking women in the same detention facility. The only one selected to appear was a young woman's body spread over two pages, its value as a voyeuristic eye-catcher apparently superseding the 'humane' considerations voiced in the text, which would have been better illustrated by the poignant older women's faces.

The text itself contains such sententious phrases as: 'losing one's womanly dignity (*dostoinstvo*) is the beginning of the end'. The article condemns society: 'society is choking on a lack (*defitsit*) of mercy'. It alludes to the loneliness of women's lives. The writer, however, expresses gender difference with a confidence appearing throughout Soviet journalism. He states categorically: 'Woman is weak. Primordially weaker than man.' And it ends with a prayer for forgiveness which also forms the title of the piece: 'Drinking women, forgive us all!' The martyred female underclass is thus iconicised. This sexual/religious symbolism seems to be accepted by the Soviet reader, believer and atheist alike. In many rhetorical stances in the Soviet Union today the curse of communism is prayerfully exorcised by a sentimentalized discourse of religiosity.

Reality and the discourse of dignity

There is, of course, a gaping dichotomy between the rhetoric of reverence for women prevailing in the Soviet Union and the actual use of their bodies in truly dangerous work, whether outside the home or in domestic drudgery. The high abortion rate, 6.5 million performed annually, is also part of this disregard; contraceptive devices are in *defitsit* or not used by men. The casual visitor can see women laying track for a new trolleybus line or sweeping the streets. One of my students was taken to a Swedish dairy project in the Beskudnikovo district of Moscow, where she saw young women assigned the task of insulating a new building with a product containing asbestos; they wore no protective materials.

Prostitution is also dangerous work and difficult to ignore in all major tourist hotels. Given the alternatives of women's work, and the fact that black-market operations in general seem to be controlled by men, this area of not-so-free enterprise might be regarded as one of the few available to women. Yet press coverage of prostitution is utterly censorious of the prostitute, not the client: punitive measures are called for and the moral failure of the women is condemned. This is a far cry from the ethic of the revolution which viewed prostitution as a social evil of capitalism in general.

In this context, and not in a feminist one, the word *dostoinstvo* occurs again. It appears as the leitmotif of a twenty-minute short film on prostitution in Tashkent. Directed by Razika Merganbaiba, the film is called *Dignity, or the Secret of the Smile*. The word *dostoinstvo* means 'dignity' in the sense both of virtue and of self-respect. Whereas feminists stress the latter, most of the current usage of the word in the Soviet Union emphasizes the former. In the Uzbek film, images of Botticelli alternate with interviews and shots of young women prostitutes, never their clients. One calls herself 'almost fallen, but not completely': the pre-revolutionary concept of the 'fallen woman' remains alive and well. Another says, 'they never arrest the men'.

These two comments echo other female voices speaking on the fringes of the male-dominated political and cultural outpourings that characterise glasnost. One voice provides a moral view that measures women's worth in terms of a high place from which she has been cast down, and to which she had better return. The other voice says, 'What about the men? – but with less of the anger which, over two decades ago, touched off the women's movement in the West.

The protests over Moscow's first beauty contest seem to have come largely from the West. A British TV documentary chronicled the misgivings of a family in Central Asia over having their daughter pose in a swimsuit (who would then marry her?) and the hopes of the contestants for a way out of assembly-line life. The organisers of the contest, moonlighting Mosfilm men, and their deals with Western contest organisers, were themselves less than beautiful. But the idea of 'Russian beauties' has been seized upon as a money-maker both in the USSR and in the snide headlines of Western checkout counters. When copies of *Playboy* with Soviet models were held up at US customs who thought that, under their agreement with the Soviet Ministry of

Communications, these would be considered pornographic, Soviet customs officials hastened to assure them it was not so.

As we turn from media images to written polemics, the pornographic seems to be used as an issue chiefly by two groups of intellectuals: those liberals who favour unbridled 'creativity', especially if it is offensive to previous 'prudish' norms, and those conservatives who see the new freedom as costing women their dignity (as would many feminists) but relate such loss of dignity not to selfhood but to the desecration of the Nation. The growing ills of society are seen increasingly to arise from a break-up of the family, whose last resort and greatest resource has been the woman on whom all caring depends. Since Russian women and those of other nationalities affected by the Second World War have been everything – wage-earners, household workers and continuous caregivers – for so many decades, the spectre of their being less than that strikes fear and outrage in the hearts of men, resulting in a media debate whose parameters seem to define Woman's significance more often than women's choice.

From sex to the saving of the nation

The polemicists who have access to major journals and newspapers use gender to explore another agenda. The 'avant-garde' who favour non-authoritarian expression and the nationalists on the other end of the patriarchal spectrum are both, I would argue, interested primarily in a new morality that supersedes social reform. The avant-garde stands for renewal of culture through means 'new' to the Soviet Union since its own early twentieth-century modernism was suppressed. The term avant-garde has itself become one of (often anti-semitic) abuse by conservatives. Its less tasteful aspect includes a sort of *épatage* which denigrates women in the spirit of bold innovatory freedom, as illustrated, for example, by erotic art exhibits containing live female objects.[9] A 1990 film, *Taxi Blues*, epitomizes the pleasures of the working man in a working-class 'girlfriend' who donates meat from a plant where she works as willingly as her own body for consumption and contrasts these pleasures with the more arcane ones of the artistic intelligentsia, epitomized by an inflatable doll imported from the West. The doll is presented to the taxi-driver as a mockery of what real feeling he has for his girlfriend: it is the emotional turning-point of the film's varied expressions of male anger and male bonding.

Most women polemicists use a rhetoric of seriousness and wit, rather than *épatage*; they sound moderate even when their ideas are potentially far-reaching. Larisa Vasil'eva writes eloquently about how men erect barriers between themselves and women to avoid hearing what women are saying.[10] It sounds oddly like early consciousness-raising but *with* a belief in the feminine mystique. Vasil'eva continues to take a stance that incorporates the traditional Russian view that there actually is a great difference between the 'female principle',[11] an instinct for preserving life, and men who (she does not quite say) have no such instinct. She professes wonderment that Western women who have much better food and clothing incomprehensibly struggle for power in the male world, power which only subordinates their femininity to a masculinised bureaucracy, one with which Soviet women are all too familiar.

Vasil'eva is the first President of the New Federation of Women Writers – a group which began as a walk-out from a typically male-dominated meeting of the Writers' Union. Other scholars, writers and professionals from Petrozavodsk to Irkutsk have formed women's groups and clubs, spontaneously and unofficially. The Soviet experience of official women representatives has, perhaps unjustly, given affirmative action a bad name. Official women did speak for women within limits set by men, making it unnecessary for men to do so. Thus, writers like Evgeniia Al'bats in an article entitled 'According to gender' (Po polovomu priznaku),[12] voices the general resentment towards tokenism, saying that these women and men who speak of women's problems while standing outside them are not true representatives.

At the conservative end of the spectrum, all of the foregoing positions are attacked, in a fusion of gender and nationalism. When a woman writes on the pages of a conservative journal, she uses the woman question to proclaim a disaster scenario for Russia if it follows the West and fails to become itself. In an article entitled 'We need good wives and good mothers' by Tat'iana Okulova[13] the author begins with a chronicle of the new eroticism in the Soviet Union, and then proceeds to denounce the horrors of the West, especially her view of homoeroticism and child pornography. Okulova sees a sense of shame (*styd*) as lacking in contemporary men and women. The theme that Woman is Mother runs throughout. The wish of some young families to return to the age-old traditions of the *narod* is lauded in the image of the Virgin Mother, the icon protecting the household. The question of nationalism thus conjoins that of family: 'Isn't it time for what is Russian to be called Russian, what is Latvian Latvian, and what is Jewish Jewish?' The final lines of the article best express this conflation: 'Will we become ourselves? There is the main woman question.'

When male writers advance their arguments about women, all genres from journalism to belles-lettres are available to them in Russian journals. A sub-genre of poetry with a middle-aged male persona full of guilt towards his aged mother persists.[14] Much of village prose is about the squandering of a female ecology, and concomitant male guilt. Although the Soviet system stands accused, it has a gender – a largely male bureaucracy set against female Nature. In other works the Good Mother is Russia, but she is either dead or threatened with imminent destruction. The Wicked Stepmother is the Soviet Union who has taken her place and is destroying her children. Traces of the Good Mother can be found in very old women or a younger one who dies or is victimized; but, generally speaking, ordinary wives and girlfriends are Stepmothers who do not measure up to the male narrator's guilty memory of the Real Mother. Politics/ideology and gender are so closely bound as to be inextricable in works from *Dr Zhivago* to village prose to urban writing.

Since in these fictions only inarticulate women are capable of incarnating the truth, these mothers' silence is broken by the male narrator who may understand too late to save them but who can subsequently articulate their larger significance. It is one short step from this sort of fiction or poetry to the poet Yevgeny Yevtushenko proclaiming in prose: 'Woman has not been raised, but lowered to equality with men', and 'With women the nation (*narod*) begins.'[15] Or to the prose writer Valentin Rasputin invoking woman's very selfless-ness as her true being:

In bringing forth her fruit, loving her man, bringing up her children, that is, being mother, woman, and teacher, it is as if she did all this not only for herself, but in accordance with a precept acting through her. These echoes and reflections of her god-bearing quality, though, must sometimes appear to be for a woman an unexpected and passionate longing for her own self.[16]

These two writers are opposed politically, but so much of their discourse on Woman overlaps because it is a rhetorical trope of great power for their discourse on the Nation.

Gynoglasnost?

Under glasnost some women are beginning to make small counterpro-nouncements. One sees glimpses of both independent female creativity and a feminist point of view. Although creative artists seem to feel it is bad for business to say that they are feminists (in spite of their being feted in the West by women who feel they are), they certainly seem to be creating believable women in recognisable settings rather than icons in encrusted frames. The writers Tat'iana Tolstaia and Liudmila Petrushevskaia tear at the cliché of the female victim; their males are equally manipulative, but somewhat more passive in demeanor. Women film directors, in particular, have put female subjectivity on screen.[17] Kira Muratova's *A Long Farewell* deals with a mother anticipating her son's going away, the premonition of a separation being subtler than its realization. Muratova's 1990 film *Asthenic Syndrome* is the best glasnost film to date. It uses human nakedness (as opposed to nudity) anti-erotically. It mocks the idea of women as the keepers of culture ('I thought if everyone read Tolstoi, society would become better', three deaf old ladies scream) and of the hearth. It jars the senses, depicting recognisable situations with a surreal realism. Another director, Lana Gogoberidze, jokes that out of ten Georgian film directors, eleven are women. Her movies show the connections between lives, especially coincidental meetings between women, as the tissue of life itself. She said, 'I know women who have nothing, and yet, they make their lives beautiful.'[18]

There is such a range of women's writing in Russia alone today that any list one makes of promising poets and prosaists will be obsolete in months.[19] Many works written before glasnost have been published or produced, like Petrushevskaia's plays, only since, giving them a resonance of glasnost that echoes their reception rather than their genesis. The question of where these writers are published and who introduces them often tells us something about how they (rather than others) have emerged into print. From small collections to major journals, final publishing decisions are generally made by men. Artistic considerations are often subordinated to ideological ones, so that a not-so-hidden polemic of use to men can suddenly make a woman's name big. It is worth discussing one such example in particular: a story written by a woman, with a male physician as narrator (although in reality 68 per cent of Soviet doctors are female). Its subject is birth, but its subtext is abortion. It was published in the premier 'liberal' journal, *Novyi mir*.[20]

Natal'ia Sukhanova's 'Delos' is a story with a point: women are foetal vessels and gynaecology determines being. It is introduced briefly by the conservative writer Victor Astaf'ev who characterizes this story as having a 'chaste quality which is not at all coarsely womanish' (*'tselomudrennosti kakoi-to, vovse ne bab'ei'*). It is as difficult to translate this phrase with its mixture of old Church Slavonic and colloquial patriarchal ring, as it is to imagine any major publication of a Western industrialized nation actually using it. The mystery of life with the authority of the physician combine in this story to determine the use of women's bodies. Women who have abortions cry bitterly; those who give birth (although actual birth itself is not shown in the story) triumph, even when putting their own lives in danger. There is a cult of the 'natural' in the story. Caesarian sections are cautioned against: 'You have to be careful for three years afterwards. No pregnancy. No abortions.' Another 'medical' myth of the story is that 'an abortion rarely happens without consequences. Most often bleeding during labour.' Do the failures of Soviet medicine produce these anomalies or are they part of the personal, punitive myths of the society and of the author, who also misuses 'Delos' as a welcoming rather than an austere exiled place of birth. The story may be a plea for humane conditions of childbirth, but its rhetoric results in a guilt-inducing warning to future mothers who will dream of their dead children if they abort. The male doctor-narrator is a sort of surrogate husband (the real ones are characteristically missing) who combines sympathy and prestige: hence the peculiar choice of a man to express what is closest to a woman in a story by a woman.

If glasnost has provided some venues for writing by women, a second line of attack on their writing comes from what might be called gendered criticism – i.e., attempts to marginalize women authors by assigning gender to their writing, calling it 'lady-like' (i.e., not concerned with big issues). *Damskii* is a damning word, used to denigrate women's writing about women and men. Tat'iana Tolstaia, whose outspokenness kept her banned from the Writers Union well after her works made her famous, counterattacks that 'feminine prose today is mostly written by men.'[21] She means a flaccid, conformist sort of writing. I prefer to apply the gendered dichotomy to both sexes as Tolstaia does, but in a slightly different way. Feminine writing, in my view, is about how all the little things in life go wrong. It began with the 'young prose' of the late fifties as a reaction to socialist realism, which is about how all the big things go right. It continues today largely among urban writers, both male and female. Trifonov brought it to the level of very good writing; Petrushevskaia and Tolstaia have renewed it with their ironic linguistic narrative strategies. What I call 'masculine' writing is a kind of third stage, only now publishable under glasnost but not necessarily an improvement. While it may be politically daring, this sort of writing tends to be conservative on gender issues. Masculine writing is about how all the big things go wrong. Big things include history, ecology and patriarchal values, such as religion and family.

'Masculine' writing often rings with accusatory rhetoric, as in the works of Solzhenitsyn or Belov. We have also seen it in 'Delos'.

Tolstaia herself is really a satiric/lyrical writer: her writing has an unusual tone which often lyricises and deflates simultaneously. The tone and theme resemble that of Fay Weldon among Western writers: a sort of self-help feminism is darkly implied. The cherished women's themes of the fifties' anglophone world had a long after-life as they passed into the sixties in the form of advertising slogans. Sacrificing for one's man's career and keeping a spotless house are ideals even more of a mockery in terms of Soviet reality where one-earner families and separate houses are a rarity; nevertheless the fifties' ethic of triumphant possessiveness prevails in Soviet society. In Tolstaia's stories it literally attacks the very body of men, who shrink to passivity or infantilism. Women who choose the path of personal happiness through a man are mocked, often cruelly. But the implied criticism of Soviet society which makes even small comforts for women unattainable is never lost from sight.

A writer who wavers between validating the caring ideal in her heroines and showing that for ordinary women it creates superhuman obstacles is Victoriia Tokareva, whose novella *A Long Day*[22] shows a successful journalist mother doing battle with an inefficient male world to save a sick daughter. A dull husband, an unconcerned boss and an arrogant surgeon all have to be manipulated or managed. Their professional skills have little use, finally, as the child is cured by natural women's remedies. The heroine will pretend to love a man in order to save a child: this sort of conflict is just beginning to appear in American fiction. In Soviet fiction there is no contest: men are secondary.

A third prose writer who has emerged post-glasnost began writing in 1968, but published almost nothing from the seventies to the early eighties. The plays and short stories of Liudmila Petrushevskaia seem to be a truly innovative departure from women's and men's fiction both in language and in theme. Close to actual contemporary speech, they have broken down the barriers between the literary and spoken languages more surely than the regional dialect used (in the context of literary language) by village prose writers. In Petrushevskaia's world there is no other language, and there is no way at all for the protagonist through the harshness of life. What is really revolutionary about her writing is that neither family nor friends (not only men) can be relied upon in time of crisis.[23]

In a story called 'A girl like that' (*'Takaia devochka'*)[24] Petrushevskaia has one woman narrate another's existence as if speaking conversationally to the reader, implicating us. The 'girl', Raisa, is given a sordid childhood: from the age of five she glued pill-packets, her invalid father's livelihood. When she ran away from home, she was imprisoned for months in an empty flat by a gang of youths. Then she spent time in a penal colony. She fears crowds, does not work, cries all day. But the narrator has problems of her own: her husband is chronically unfaithful but she always wants him to come back to her. He gives her the details of his affairs and invites the women to their home, so wife and mistress will interact. The narrator cries less frequently and keeps an orderly household. At the story's end the narrator realizes that her friend Raisa is her husband's last affair, and that he has returned home only at Raisa's behest. 'That's how Raisa betrayed me.' The moral levels of this tale are quite complex. Raisa is a victim who gives herself to anyone – becoming an object of sex for men, of gossip for women. 'Something was ruined in her, an instinct of self-preservation.' The latter is precisely what the narrator possesses. But neither woman 'wins' because the men use them against each other. In the narrow world of Soviet flats and offices those closest betray most surely. This bleakly masterful story was submitted to *Novyi Mir* in 1968 and rejected, but the editor-in-chief (Aleksandr Tvardovsky) commented: 'withhold from publication, but do not lose contact with the author'.

Petrushevskaia's work becomes increasingly interesting the more she publishes. A story called 'The new Robinsons' ('*Novye Robinzony*')[25] is a futuristic anti-utopian *Swiss Family Robinson* set in the countryside. The daughter of the family narrates a tale of temporary refuge from a police state in which even the grandparents participate prominently. A countryside of old women and abandoned children yields few kernels for a new life: it may also turn out to be the place from which they are hunted down and taken. This 'chronicle of the end of the twentieth century' is neither end nor beginning.

Aside from these three prominent women writers, whole clusters of new writers' names now appear. In the late 1980s splinter groups began to form in what had been official circles – within the Moscow branch of the Writers' Union, for example. Some independent groups seem to be working within established frameworks and state presses – for example the almanacs *Moskovskii vestnik* and *Aprel'* which began in 1989. The latter features works by Tat'iana Bek, Elena Aksel'rod, Olesia Nikolaeva and the well-known writer Iunna Morits in its first issue. Other new groups seem joined by a common ideology and purpose. One called 'Laterna Magica' (in Roman letters) hopes to rejoin itself to Russian culture of the early twentieth century and effect a spiritual renewal in today's society. Its first almanac, published in early 1990, actually has a majority of women among its authors, the most prominent being the poet Ol'ga Sedakova, who is also an editor. The other women authors in the almanac are Anna Bernshtein, Marianna Vekhova, Elena Ogneva, Lilit Kozlova, Mira Pliushch, Liia Vladimirova, Vera Khalizeva and Margarita Sabashnikova.

Among poets, Elena Shvarts, who has been writing in Leningrad for twenty years, has finally achieved the 'open' prominence she has deserved for so long. Shvarts is a completely original poetic voice. Whether speaking in the persona of Cynthia, a Roman poet of legend, or of Lavinia, nun of the 'Order of Circumcision of the Heart', the poetry combines intensity with simplicity, religious feeling with humour and linguistic virtuosity with a sophisticated awareness of form. It is poetry that has a vision of other worlds without being tepid or vaguely mystical.[26]

New prose writers also enter areas previously forbidden. Valeriia Narbikova writes what has been called eroticism, a confusion of pronouns in an experimental style of plotless fancifulness and sly references to literary predecessors (from a woman's point of view). Bella Ulanovskaia brings the Russian village into the orbit of the female narrator who no longer mythologises but narrates what she calls *dokumental'nye povesti* (documentary novellas) of life in the Kalinin and Pskov *oblast*. The narrator herself is an unobtrusive but honest presence in 'The Autumn March of Frogs' (*Osennii pokhod lia-gushek*).[27] She carries a gun and hunts with it, repaying the hospitality of old women from literally forgotten villages from or to which people were resettled under a policy that judged these places either *perspektiv-nye* or *neperspektivnye*, having or not having prospects. Her women speak to the reader in their own voices. Their boots cannot be repaired, one has no bread, all wish to stay and live, regardless of decisions from on high.

Conclusion

The Soviet Union has just completed a seventy-year history of obedience to questionable authority. There is little doubt that that authority has been 'masculine' in its leadership (even when its repre-sentatives have been female), in the rituals used to reinforce its authority (e.g., the military parade) and in the categories and 'perspec-tives' imposed on its people. No 'feminine' principle has ever determined the social order. Yet, persistently, the more powerless women have been in actuality, the more powerful the myth that has arisen of their redemptive, caregiving, nation-identified essence. Is this myth a pallid reflection of presumed matri-focal societies of the past? Is it a cynical manipulation of rulers to keep the unpaid labour of women on course? Will women re-define themselves post-glasnost? Anti-Western sentiment is so much a matter of pride with so many nationalities of the Soviet Union that a mythical Western feminism may inevitably be rejected in favour of other myths seen as more indigenous.

It becomes clearer all the time that neither the older political discourse of the social good nor the increasing legitimacy given to sexual difference can provide any sweeping solution to the largely man-made ills of Soviet women. Contemporary official policy is still reluctant to involve men fully in the definition of family. Instead it sees the family unit in terms of a contract between mother and child and the state. A new more conservative discourse involves men only slightly more, as benign patriarchs who extol the virtuous wife and mother in theory and castigate other women by implication. The legitimacy that might be given to sexual difference thus becomes another moral object lesson. Both rhetorics trade all too often in a politics of exclusion – the 'moral' excluding the 'immoral,' domestic work excluding the work-place, the family as a mother-and-child unit excluding the other caregivers, the village with prospects excluding the ones without. Neither the discourses nor the politics they reflect have much chance of radically improving the lives of women.

Glasnost has made a difference primarily in artistic expression. The closer a film or a written work to the truly empathetic creative imagination, the greater the gains of glasnost. The opportunities for women's creativity, while endless in themselves, are still constricted by limited venues and an often reactionary critical atmosphere. Finally, the tradition of subsuming debate on art to a general debate on society has particular implications for writing by or about women. As the feminine takes up greater space in the general polemic, it becomes a myth of regeneration for a society in flux. Fiction and polemics thus find a common vocabulary. Many writers use Woman as the central metaphor for the wasting of the Nation, a part of nature eroded by Soviet culture, a final resource and a last preserve. But, as glasnost speaks of the feminine, we must listen carefully before actually hearing a woman's voice.

NOTES

1 *Moscow News*, No.51, 1988, p. 12.
2 For more on the important role of television see Ellen Propper Mickiewicz, *Split Signals: Television and Politics in the Soviet Union* (New York: Oxford University Press, 1988).
3 *Argumenty i fakty*, No.4, 1990, p. 4.
4 *Ogonek*, No.48, 1989, pp. 26–7.
5 In conversation with Dr Catriona Kelly. *Literaturnaia gazeta* apparently does not have this restrictive policy, as evidenced by an excellent article on the murders of women in Smolensk, written by a woman journalist in a dispassionate tone which separates fact from opinion. See Ol'ga Chaikovskaia, 'Na dne kolodtsa', *Literaturnaia gazeta*, 16 May 1990, p. 12.
6 Yelena Vorontsova, 'Women Writers in Russia', *Index on Censorship*, No.3, 1989, p. 26.
7 *Ogonek*, No.29, 1989, pp. 32–3.
8 *Zhurnalist*, July, 1989, pp. 62–5.
9 See Victor Erofeev, 'Sex and perestroika', *Liber*, No.1, 1989, p. 17. This commentary on the new Moscow scene positively revels in the overcoming of Party prudery and conservative qualms by 'the erotic self-expressiveness of the younger generation'.
10 *Leninskoe znamia*, 8 March 1988, p. 3.
11 *Literaturnaia gazeta*, 20 December 1989, p. 7.
12 *Ogonek*, No.10, 1990, p. 9.
13 *Nash sovremennik*, No.3, 1990, pp. 173–87.
14 See the anthology *Mat': Stikhotvoreniia russkikh i sovetskikh poetov o materi*, ed. V. Korotaev (Moscow: Sovetskii pisatel', 1979). Gerald Stanton Smith in *Songs to Seven Strings* (Bloomington: Indiana University Press, 1984), pp. 23–5, gives us the definitive discussion of what he calls the 'mommy song' as part of the image of the mother in Soviet official art: 'the dominant convention is to deal with the subject from the point of view of the erring son, whose mother never forgets, always forgives, is patient, not very well dressed and, above all, *tired*.'
15 *Literaturnaia gazeta*, 3 May 1989, p. 11.
16 *Nash sovremennik*, No.3, 1990, p. 169.
17 A recent (May 1989) Festival of Soviet Women Filmmakers held in Dortmund, Germany, was attended by directors Lana Gogoberidze, Inna Tumanyan, Leila Safarova, Marina Kurkumiya, Nana Janelidze and Nina Lapiashvili and documentalists Marina Goldovskaya, Yevgenia Golovnya and Tatiana Chirikova, as well as female film technicians. There has been no such festival inside the USSR.
18 In conversation with the author. The intelligentsia of all republics articulates the lives of most women to varying degrees. Soviet sociology has often overestimated the degree of secularism in Central Asia and underestimated

the influence of latent Islamic traditions on women's lives, according to M. A. Tolmacheva ('The Muslim woman in contemporary Central Asia', unpublished paper).

19 The noted critic Alla Latynina has compared the works of three beginning writers to 'visiting cards of the new generation, negating the conformism of their successful predecessors who bowed down before the ideological and aesthetic imperative. But a visiting card is only an application for a position in literature. It doesn't secure the position.' (*Moskovskii vestnik*, No. 1, 1989, p. 286).

20 *Novyi mir*, No.3, 1988, pp. 69–84.

21 *Moscow News*, No.8, 1987, p. 10.

22 *Novyi mir*, No.2, 1986, pp. 79–114.

23 See Adele Barker, 'Women without men in the writings of contemporary Soviet women writers', in D. Rancour-Laferriere (ed.), *Russian Literature and psychoanalysis* (Amsterdam: John Benjamins Publishing Co., 1989), p. 443: 'her heroines ... are rejected by the very group they wish to align themselves with, be it family, friends, or cohorts at work.'

24 *Ogonek*, No.40, 1988, pp. 9–11.

25 *Novyi mir*, No.8, 1989, pp. 166–72.

26 Barbara Heldt, 'The Poetry of Elena Shvarts', *World Literature Today*, Vol. 63, No.3 (Summer, 1989), pp. 381–84.

27 *Neva*, No.12, 1987, pp. 129–36.

Since this chapter was written, two anthologies of women writers have appeared. Their titles are curiously similar in their endorsement of female perfection: *Ne pomniashchaia zla* (*A Woman Without Malice*), Larisa Vaneeva, ed. (Moscow: Moskovskii rabochii, 1990); and *Chisten'kaia zhizn'* (*A Very Pure Life*), Anatolii Shavkuta, ed. (Moscow: Molodaia Gvardiia, 1990). Larisa Vaneeva is one of the best newly appearing authors and she has stories in both anthologies.

Index

176